NAVAHO INDIAN MYTHS

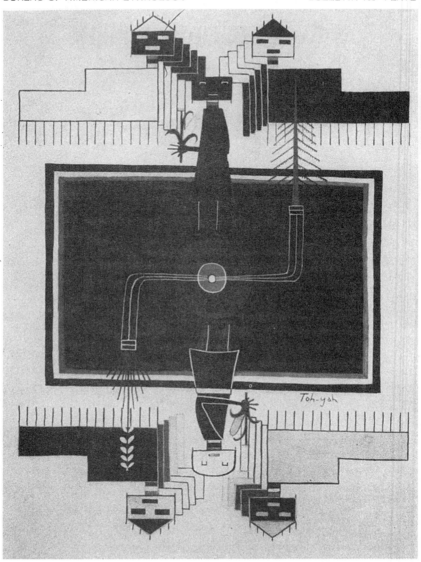

First Man, pine tree and white corn; First Woman, yucca and yellow corn. (From painting by Gerald Nailor, Mesa Verde National Park, under direction of Medicine Man.)

NAVAHO INDIAN MYTHS

Aileen O'Bryan

DOVER PUBLICATIONS, INC.
NEW YORK

Navaho Indian Myths, first published by Dover Publications, Inc., in 1993, is an unabridged, retitled republication of *The Dîné: Origin Myths of the Navaho Indians*, originally published by the United States Government Printing Office, Washington, D.C., in 1956 as Bulletin 163 of the Bureau of American Ethnology of the Smithsonian Institution.

Manufactured in the United States of America
Dover Publications, Inc., 31 East 2nd Street, Mineola, N.Y. 11501

Library of Congress Cataloging-in-Publication Data

Dîné.
    Navaho Indian myths / [transcribed by] Aileen O'Bryan.
        p.   cm.
    Myths told by Sandoval, Hastin Tlo'tsi hee (Old Man Buffalo Grass) to Aileen O'Bryan in late Nov. 1928.
    Originally published: The Dîné. Washington : U.S. G.P.O., 1956, in series: Smithsonian Institution, Bureau of American Ethnology, Bulletin ; 163.
    Includes bibliographical references.
    ISBN 0-486-27592-2 (pbk.)
    1. Navaho Indians—Legends.   2. Navaho Indians—Religion and mythology.   3. Legends—Southwest, New.   I. O'Bryan, Aileen.   II. Sandoval, Hastin Tlo'tsi hee, d. 1929.   III Title.
E99.N3D43   1993
398.2'089972—dc20   93–9688
                                                                          CIP

LETTER OF TRANSMITTAL

SMITHSONIAN INSTITUTION,
BUREAU OF AMERICAN ETHNOLOGY,
Washington, D. C., June 27, 1955.

SIR: I have the honor to transmit herewith a manuscript entitled "The Dîné: Origin Myths of the Navaho Indians," by Aileen O'Bryan, and to recommend that it be published as a bulletin of the Bureau of American Ethnology.

Very respectfully yours,

M. W. STIRLING, *Director.*

Dr. LEONARD CARMICHAEL,
Secretary, Smithsonian Institution.

CONTENTS

ILLUSTRATIONS

PLATE

Frontispiece. First Man and First Woman.

TEXT FIGURES

PREFACE

Sandoval, Hastin Tlo'tsi hee (Old Man Buffalo Grass), was the first of the four chiefs of the Navaho People. I had known him for years. In late November 1928, he came to the Mesa Verde National Park, where I was then living, for the purpose of having me record all that he knew about his people.

"You look at me," he said, "and you see only an ugly old man, but within I am filled with great beauty. I sit as on a mountaintop and I look into the future. I see my people and your people living together. In time to come my people will have forgotten their early way of life unless they learn it from white men's books. So you must write down all that I will tell you; and you must have it made into a book that coming generations may know this truth."

This I promised to do. I have recorded it without interpolation, and presented it, in so far as is possible, in the old man's words.

Sam Ahkeah, Sandoval's nephew, now head of the Navaho Council at Window Rock, as well as First Chief of his people, was the interpreter, as Sandoval spoke only the Athapascan tongue.

Sandoval told us that medicine men know the chants and the ceremonies in detail, but these stories are the origins from which the ceremonies were developed; also, that some medicine men divide the different periods into 12 worlds, whereas the older version holds to 4 dark worlds and the present or changeable world.

During the 17 days of his stay with us on this occasion, he spent the greater part of each day narrating the legends and checking them for correction. He would often stop and chant a short prayer, and sprinkle the manuscript, Sam, and myself with corn pollen.

He believed the Mesa Verde to be the center of the old cultures, and he said that it was fitting that the stories should be reborn, written down, in "the Place of the Ancients."

Sandoval died the following January.

AILEEN O'BRYAN,
Santa Fe, N. Mex., December 1953.

THE DÎNÉ: ORIGIN MYTHS OF THE NAVAHO INDIANS

By AILEEN O'BRYAN

THE CREATION OR AGE OF BEGINNING

THE FIRST WORLD

These stories were told to Sandoval, Hastin Tlo'tsi hee, by his grandmother, Esdzan Hosh kige. Her ancestor was Esdzan at a', the medicine woman who had the Calendar Stone in her keeping. Here are the stories of the Four Worlds that had no sun, and of the Fifth, the world we live in, which some call the Changeable World.

The First World, Ni'hodilqil,[1] was black as black wool. It had four corners, and over these appeared four clouds. These four clouds contained within themselves the elements of the First World. They were in color, black, white, blue, and yellow.

The Black Cloud represented the Female Being or Substance. For as a child sleeps when being nursed, so life slept in the darkness of the Female Being. The White Cloud represented the Male Being or Substance. He was the Dawn, the Light-Which-Awakens, of the First World.

In the East, at the place where the Black Cloud and the White Cloud met, First Man, Atse'hastqin,[2] was formed; and with him was formed the white corn, perfect in shape, with kernels covering the whole ear. Dohonot i'ni is the name of this first seed corn,[3] and it is also the name of the place where the Black Cloud and the White Cloud met.

---

[1] Informant's note: Five names were given to this First World in its relation to First Man. It was called Dark Earth, Ni'hodilqil; Red Earth, Ni'halchi; One Speech, Sada hat lai; Floating Land, Ni'ta na elth; and One Tree, De east'da eith.

Matthews (1897, p. 65): The First World was red. Franciscan Fathers (1912, p. 140): ni, the world or earth; ni' hodilqil, the dark or lowest of the underworlds; (p. 111) lai, one, or first. Franciscan Fathers (1910, p. 81): sad, a word, a language; Sad lai, First Speech.

[2] Franciscan Fathers (1912, p. 93): Aste'hastqin, First Man.

[3] Informant's note: Where much corn is raised one or two ears are found perfect. These are always kept for seed corn.

Franciscan Fathers (1912, p. 85): do honot'i ni, the name of a full ear, or seed corn.

1

The First World was small in size, a floating island in mist or water. On it there grew one tree, a pine tree, which was later brought to the present world for firewood.

Man was not, however, in his present form. The conception was of a male and a female being who were to become man and woman. The creatures of the First World are thought of as the Mist People; they had no definite form, but were to change to men, beasts, birds, and reptiles of this world.[4]

Now on the western side of the First World, in a place that later was to become the Land of Sunset, there appeared the Blue Cloud, and opposite it there appeared the Yellow Cloud. Where they came together First Woman was formed, and with her the yellow corn. This ear of corn was also perfect. With First Woman there came the white shell and the turquoise and the yucca.[5]

First Man stood on the eastern side of the First World. He represented the Dawn and was the Life Giver. First Woman stood opposite in the West. She represented Darkness and Death.

First Man burned a crystal for a fire. The crystal belonged to the male and was the symbol of the mind and of clear seeing. When First Man burned it, it was the mind's awakening. First Woman burned her turquoise for a fire. They saw each other's lights in the distance. When the Black Cloud and the White Cloud rose higher in the sky First Man set out to find the turquoise light. He went twice without success, and again a third time; then he broke a forked branch from his tree, and, looking through the fork, he marked the place where the light burned. And the fourth time he walked to it and found smoke coming from a home.

"Here is the home I could not find," First Man said.

First Woman answered: "Oh, it is you. I saw you walking around and I wondered why you did not come."

Again the same thing happened when the Blue Cloud and the Yellow Cloud rose higher in the sky. First Woman saw a light and she went out to find it. Three times she was unsuccessful, but the fourth time she saw the smoke and she found the home of First Man.

"I wondered what this thing could be," she said.

"I saw you walking and I wondered why you did not come to me," First Man answered.

---

[4] Informant's note: The Navaho people have always believed in evolution.

[5] Informant's note: Five names were given also to the First World in its relation to First Woman: White Bead Standing, Yolgaí'na ziha; Turquoise Standing, Dolt í'zhi na ziha; White Bead Floating Place, Yolgaí'dana elth gaí; Turquoise Floating Place, Dolt í'zhi na elth gaí; and Yucca Standing, Tasas y ah gaí. Yucca represents cleanliness and things ceremonial.

Franciscan Fathers (1912, p. 181): Tsa'zi ntqe'li, *Yucca baccata,* wide leaf yucca or Spanish bayonet. The roots of this species furnish a rich lather; the plant is frequently referred to as tqalawhush, soap.

First Woman saw that First Man had a crystal for a fire, and she saw that it was stronger than her turquoise fire. And as she was thinking, First Man spoke to her. "Why do you not come with your fire and we will live together." The woman agreed to this. So instead of the man going to the woman, as is the custom now, the woman went to the man.

About this time there came another person, the Great-Coyote-Who-Was-Formed-in-the-Water,[6] and he was in the form of a male being. He told the two that he had been hatched from an egg. He knew all that was under the water and all that was in the skies. First Man placed this person ahead of himself in all things. The three began to plan what was to come to pass; and while they were thus occupied another being came to them. He also had the form of a man, but he wore a hairy coat, lined with white fur, that fell to his knees and was belted in at the waist. His name was Atse'hashke', First Angry or Coyote.[7] He said to the three: "You believe that you were the first persons. You are mistaken. I was living when you were formed."

Then four beings came together. They were yellow in color and were called the tsts'na or wasp people. They knew the secret of shooting evil and could harm others. They were very powerful.

This made eight people.

Four more beings came. They were small in size and wore red shirts and had little black eyes. They were the naazo'zi or spider ants. They knew how to sting, and were a great people.

After these came a whole crowd of beings. Dark colored they were, with thick lips and dark, protruding eyes. They were the wolazhi'ni, the black ants. They also knew the secret of shooting evil and were powerful; but they killed each other steadily.

By this time there were many people. Then came a multitude of little creatures. They were peaceful and harmless, but the odor from them was unpleasant. They were called the wolazhi'ni nlchu nigi, meaning that which emits an odor.[8]

And after the wasps and the different ant people there came the beetles, dragonflies, bat people, the Spider Man and Woman, and the Salt Man and Woman,[9] and others that rightfully had no definite

---

[6] Informant's note: The Great Coyote who was formed in the water, Mai tqo y elth chili. Franciscan Fathers (1912, p. 117): ma'itso, wolf (big roamer); and ma'ists o'si, coyote (slender roamer).

[7] Informant's note: Some medicine men claim that witchcraft came with First Man and First Woman, others insist that devil conception or witchcraft originated with the Coyote called First Angry.

Franciscan Fathers (1912, pp. 140, 175, 351).

[8] Informant's note: No English name given this insect. Ants cause trouble, as also do wasps and other insects, if their homes are harmed.

Franciscan Fathers (1910 p. 346): Much evil, disease and bodily injury is due also to secret agents of evil, in consequence of which the belief . . . . shooting of evil (sting) is widely spread.

[9] Informant's note: Beetle, ntlsa'go; Dragonfly, tqanil al'; Bat people, ja aba'ni; Spider Man, nashjei hastqin; Spider Woman, nashjei esdza; Salt Man, ashi hastqin; Salt Woman, ashi esdza.

form but were among those people who peopled the First World.[10]
And this world, being small in size, became crowded, and the people
quarreled and fought among themselves, and in all ways made living
very unhappy.

THE SECOND WORLD

Because of the strife in the First World, First Man, First Woman,
the Great-Coyote-Who-Was-Formed-in-the-Water, and the Coyote
called First Angry, followed by all the others, climbed up from the
World of Darkness and Dampness to the Second or Blue World.[11]

They found a number of people already living there: blue birds,
blue hawks, blue jays, blue herons, and all the blue-feathered beings.[12]
The powerful swallow people [13] lived there also, and these people made
the Second World [14] unpleasant for those who had come from the First
World. There was fighting and killing.

The First Four found an opening in the World of Blue Haze; and
they climbed through this and led the people up into the Third or
Yellow world.

THE THIRD WORLD

The bluebird was the first to reach the Third or Yellow World.
After him came the First Four and all the others.

A great river crossed this land from north to south. It was the
Female River. There was another river crossing it from east to
west, it was the Male River. This Male River flowed through the
Female River and on; [15] and the name of this place is tqo alna'osdli,
the Crossing of the waters.[16]

There were six mountains in the Third World.[17] In the East was
Sis na' jin, the Standing Black Sash. Its ceremonial name is Yol

---

[10] Matthews (1897, p. 65); Stevenson (1891, pp. 275–285); Alexander (1916, vol. 10,
ch. 8, p. 159); Franciscan Fathers (1910, pp. 346–349); Klah-Wheelwright (1942, pp.
39–41); Haile and Wheelwright (1949, pp. 3–5).

[11] Informant's note: The Second World was the Blue World, Ni'hodotl'ish.
Alexander (1916, vol. 10, ch. 8, pp. 159–160).

[12] Informant's note: The names of the blue birds are: bluebird, do'le; blue hawk, gi'ni
tso dolt ish; blue jay, jozh ghae'gi; and blue heron, tqualtl a'gaale.

[13] Informant's note: The swallow is called tqash ji'zhi.
Matthews (1897, pp. 65–66): the swallow people, hast sosidine. Franciscan Fathers
(1910, p. 349): The Blue World. Klah-Wheelwright (1942, pp. 41–43).

[14] Haile and Wheelwright (1949, pp. 3–5).

[15] Informant's note: The introduction of generation.

[16] Matthews (1897, p. 63): To'bil haski'di, Place Where the Waters Crossed.

[17] Informant's note: Sis na' jin, Mount Baldy near Alamos, Colo.; Tso'dzil, Mount
Taylor, N. Mex.; Dook'oslid, San Francisco Mountain, Ariz.; Debe'ntsa, San Juan
Mountains, Colo.; Dzil na'odili, El Huerfano Peak, N. Mex.; and Choli, also given as
El Huerfano or El Huerfanito Peak, N. Mex. These mountains of the Third World
were not in their true form, but rather the substance of the mountains.
Matthews (1897, p. 71): The Third World, the mountains. The four mountains
named by the First Man: Tsisnadzi'ne, East; Tso'tsil, South; Do koslid, West; Debe'ntsa,
North. Also, note 51, pp. 220–221, version A and version B; notes 52, 53, 54, 56,
p. 221; and notes 58, 60, 62, 65, p. 222.
Franciscan Fathers (1910, pp. 56, 136), Sisnajiń, Pelado Peak; p. 137); Amsden
(1934, p. 123).
Recorders note: Although both Matthews and the Fransiccan Fathers give Sisnajin as

gai'dzil, the Dawn or White Shell Mountain. In the South stood Tso'dzil, the Great Mountain, also called Mountain Tongue. Its ceremonial name is Yodolt i'zhi dzil, the Blue Bead or Turquoise Mountain. In the West stood Dook'oslid, and the meaning of this name is forgotten. Its ceremonial name is Dichi'li dzil, the Abalone Shell Mountain. In the North stood Debe'ntsa, Many Sheep Mountain. Its ceremonial name is Bash'zhini dzil, Obsidian Mountain. Then there was Dzil na'odili, the Upper Mountain. It was very sacred; and its name means also the Center Place, and the people moved around it. Its ceremonial name is Ntl'is dzil, Precious Stone or Banded Rock Mountain. There was still another mountain called Chol'i'i or Dzil na'odili choli, and it was also a sacred mountain.

There was no sun in this land, only the two rivers and the six mountains. And these rivers and mountains were not in their present form, but rather the substance of mountains and rivers as were First Man, First Woman, and the others.

Now beyond Sis na' jin, in the east, there lived the Turquoise Hermaphrodite, Ashton nutli.[18] He was also known as the Turquoise Boy. And near this person grew the male reed. Beyond, still farther in the east, there lived a people called the Hadahuneya'nigi,[19] the Mirage or Agate People. Still farther in the east there lived twelve beings called the Naaskiddi.[20] And beyond the home of these beings there lived four others—the Holy Man, the Holy Woman, the Holy Boy, and the Holy Girl.

In the West there lived the White Shell Hermaphrodite [21] or Girl, and with her was the big female reed which grew at the water's edge. It had no tassel. Beyond her in the West there lived another stone people called the Hadahunes'tqin, the Ground Heat People. Still

---

Pelado Peak, Sam Ahkeah, the interpreter, after checking, identified it as Mount Baldy near Alamosa, Colo. Also, although the Franciscan Fathers give Dzil na odili choli as Huerfanito Peak, Sam Ahkeah says that it is the Mother Mountain near Taos.

[18] Informant's note: Ashon nutli', the Turquoise Hermaphrodite, later became masculine and was known as the Sun Bearer, Jo hona'ai.

[19] Informant's note: The Hadahuneya'nigi are the Stone people who live where there is a mirage on the desert.

Interpreter's note: These Stone People came from the East.

Morris (1921), p. 115): p. 127, this bulletin; Stevenson (1891, p. 275). Matthews (1897, p. 63): To the East there was a place called Tau (corn), to the South, a place called Nahodoo'la, and to the West a place called Lokatsos akad (Standing Reed). Again to the East there was a place called Essal'ai (One Pot), to the South a place called To'hadzitil (They came often for water), and to the West a place called Dsilitsibe hogan (House made of Red Mountain). Then again to the East there was a place called Ley a hogan (Underground house), and to the South a place called Tsil si'ntha (Among aromatic sumac), and to the West a place called Tse'lits ibe hogan (House made of red rock).

[20] Informant's note: The Naaskiddi or Gha'askidi are the hunchback figures connected with seeds, fertility, and phallus worship. They are said to have come from the mountain called Chol'i'i.

[21] Informant's note: The White Shell Hermaphrodite or Girl later entered the Moon and became the Moon Bearer. She is connected with Esdzanadle, the Woman-Who Changes, or Yolgai esdzan, the White Shell Woman.

farther on there lived another twelve beings, but these were all females.[22] And again, in the Far West, there lived four Holy Ones.

Within this land there lived the Kisa'ni, the ancients of the Pueblo People. On the six mountains there lived the Cave Dwellers or Great Swallow People.[23] On the mountains lived also the light and dark squirrels, chipmunks, mice, rats, the turkey people, the deer and cat people, the spider people, and the lizards and snakes. The beaver people lived along the rivers, and the frogs and turtles and all the underwater people in the water. So far all the people were similar. They had no definite form, but they had been given different names because of different characteristics.

Now the plan was to plant.

First Man called the people together. He brought forth the white corn which had been formed with him. First Woman brought the yellow corn. They laid the perfect ears side by side; then they asked one person from among the many to come and help them. The Turkey stepped forward. They asked him where he had come from, and he said that he had come from the Gray Mountain.[24] He danced back and forth four times, then he shook his feather coat and there dropped from his clothing four kernels of corn, one gray, one blue, one black, and one red. Another person was asked to help in the plan of the planting. The Big Snake came forward. He likewise brought forth four seeds, the pumpkin, the watermelon, the cantaloup, and the muskmelon. His plants all crawl on the ground.

They planted the seeds, and their harvest was great.

After the harvest the Turquoise Boy from the East came and visited First Woman. When First Man returned to his home he found his wife with this boy. First Woman told her husband that Ashon nutli' was of her flesh and not of his flesh.[25] She said that she had used her own fire, the turquoise, and had ground her own yellow corn into meal. This corn she had planted and cared for herself.

Now at that time there were four chiefs: Big Snake, Mountain Lion, Otter, and Bear.[26] And it was the custom when the black cloud rose

---

[22] Informant's note: The Corn Maidens are deities of fertility.

[23] Informant's note: The Great Swallow People, Tqashji'zhi ndilk'si, lived in rough houses of mud and sticks. They entered them from holes in the roof.

[24] Informant's note: The Gray Mountain is the home of the Gray Yei, Hasch el'ba'i, whose other name is Water Sprinkler. The turkey is connected with water and rain.
Interpreter's note: Gray Mountain is San Francisco Mountain, Ariz. Tqo'neinili, the Water Sprinkler, whose color is gray, lives there. He is also called the Gray God, Hasch e'lbai, and the Clown whose call is "do do," and whose name is Hasch e'dodi.

[25] Informant's note: First Woman and the Turquoise Hermaphrodite represented the female principle. Later he said: There is confusion among medicine men regarding this. Some say that the Turquoise Boy was Ashon nutli'; some say the Mirage Man, some contend that "it" was another "Turquoise Boy."

[26] Informant's note: Some medicine men call them the chiefs of the Four Directions.

in the morning [27] for First Man to come out of his dwelling and speak to the people. After First Man had spoken the four chiefs told them what they should do that day. They also spoke of the past and of the future. But after First Man found his wife with another he would not come out to speak to the people. The black cloud rose higher, but First Man would not leave his dwelling; neither would he eat or drink. No one spoke to the people for 4 days. All during this time First Man remained silent, and would not touch food or water. Four times the white cloud rose. Then the four chiefs went to First Man and demanded to know why he would not speak to the people. The chiefs asked this question three times, and a fourth, before First Man would answer them.

He told them to bring him an emetic.[28] This he took and purified himself. First Man then asked them to send the hermaphrodite to him. When he came First Man asked him if the metate and brush [29] were his. He said that they were. First Man asked him if he could cook and prepare food like a woman, if he could weave, and brush the hair. And when he had assured First Man that he could do all manner of woman's work, First Man said: "Go and prepare food and bring it to me." After he had eaten, First Man told the four chiefs what he had seen, and what his wife had said.

At this time the Great-Coyote-Who-Was-Formed-in-the-Water came to First Man and told him to cross the river. They made a big raft and crossed at the place where the Male River followed through the Female River. And all the male beings left the female beings on the river bank; and as they rowed across the river they looked back and saw that First Woman and the female beings were laughing. They were also behaving very wickedly.

In the beginning the women did not mind being alone. They cleared and planted a small field. On the other side of the river First Man and the chiefs hunted and planted their seeds. They had a good harvest. Nadle [30] ground the corn and cooked the food. Four seasons passed. The men continued to have plenty and were happy; but the women became lazy, and only weeds grew on their land. The women wanted fresh meat. Some of them tried to join the men and were drowned in the river.

---

[27] Informant's note: These are not the Black and White Clouds of the First World. As there was no sun, and no true division of night and day, time was counted by the black cloud rising and the white cloud rising.

Stevenson (1891, pp. 284–285) ; Matthews (1897, p. 67) ; Whitman (1925, p. 13) ; Alexander (1916, pp. 160–161).

[28] Informant's note (with recorder's) : The emetic was believed to be either *Babia woodhousei* Gray, of the thistle family, or the root of the wild cherry. In either case, after a hot brew is drunk, copious vomiting ensues.

[29] Informant's note : The metata and brush are symbolic of woman's implements.

[30] Informant's note: Nadle means that which changes. Ashon nutli', or nadle, the Turquoise Hermaphrodite, was the first man to change, or become, as a woman.

First Woman made a plan. As the women had no way to satisfy their passions, some fashioned long narrow rocks, some used the feathers of the turkey, and some used strange plants (cactus). First Woman told them to use these things. One woman brought forth a big stone. This stone-child was later the Great Stone that rolled over the earth killing men. Another woman brought forth the Big Birds of Tsa bida'hi; and others gave birth to the giants and monsters who later destroyed many people.

On the opposite side of the river the same condition existed. The men, wishing to satisfy their passions, killed the females of mountain sheep, lion, and antelope. Lightning struck these men. When First Man learned of this he warned his men that they would all be killed. He told them that they were indulging in a dangerous practice. Then the second chief spoke: he said that life was hard and that it was a pity to see women drowned. He asked why they should not bring the women across the river and all live together again.

"Now we can see for ourselves what comes from our wrong doing," he said. "We will know how to act in the future." The three other chiefs of the animals agreed with him, so First Man told them to go and bring the women.

After the women had been brought over the river First Man spoke: "We must be purified," he said. "Everyone must bathe. The men must dry themselves with white corn meal, and the women, with yellow."

This they did, living apart for 4 days. After the fourth day First Woman came and threw her right arm around her husband. She spoke to the others and said that she could see her mistakes, but with her husband's help she would henceforth lead a good life. Then all the male and female beings came and lived with each other again.

The people moved to different parts of the land. Some time passed; then First Woman became troubled by the monotony of life. She made a plan. She went to Atse'hashke, the Coyote called First Angry, and giving him the rainbow she said: "I have suffered greatly in the past. I have suffered from want of meat and corn and clothing. Many of my maidens have died. I have suffered many things. Take the rainbow and go to the place where the rivers cross. Bring me the two pretty children of Tqo holt sodi, the Water Buffalo,[31] a boy and a girl.

The Coyote agreed to do this. He walked over the rainbow. He entered the home of the Water Buffalo and stole the two children; and these he hid in his big skin coat with the white fur lining. And when he returned he refused to take off his coat, but pulled it around himself and looked very wise.

---

[31] Franciscan Fathers (1910, p. 157) : Tqo holt sodi, water buffalo, water ox, or water monster. Alexander (1916, p. 161, and note 9, p. 274).

After this happened the people saw white light in the East and in the South and West and North. One of the deer people ran to the East, and returning, said that the white light was a great sheet of water. The sparrow hawk flew to the South, the great hawk to the West, and the kingfisher to the North. They returned and said that a flood was coming. The kingfisher said that the water was greater in the North, and that it was near.

The flood was coming and the Earth was sinking. And all this happened because the Coyote had stolen the two children of the Water Buffalo, and only First Woman and the Coyote knew the truth.

When First Man learned of the coming of the water he sent word to all the people, and he told them to come to the mountain called Sis na'jin. He told them to bring with them all of the seeds of the plants used for food. All living beings were to gather on the top of Sis na'jin. First Man traveled to the six sacred mountains, and, gathering earth from them, he put it in his medicine bag.[32]

The water rose steadily.

When all the people were halfway up Sis na' jin, First Man discovered that he had forgotten his medicine bag. Now this bag contained not only the earth from the six sacred mountains, but his magic, the medicine he used to call the rain down upon the earth and to make things grow. He could not live without his medicine bag, and he wished to jump into the rising water; but the others begged him not to do this. They went to the kingfisher and asked him to dive into the water and recover the bag. This the bird did. When First Man had his medicine bag again in his possession he breathed on it four times and thanked his people.

When they had all arrived it was found that the Turquoise Boy had brought with him the big Male Reed;[33] and the White Shell Girl had brought with her the big Female Reed.[34] Another person brought poison ivy; and another, cotton, which was later used for cloth. This person was the spider. First Man had with him his spruce tree [35] which he planted on the top of Sis na'jin. He used his fox medicine [36] to make it grow; but the spruce tree began to send out branches and to taper at the top, so First Man planted the big Male Reed. All the people blew on it, and it grew and grew until it reached

---

[32] Informant's note: Here, and following, magic is associated with First Man.
Recorder's note: The magic of First Man was considered white magic, reason, logos.
[33] Informant's note: The big male reed is called luka'tso. It grows near Santo Domingo Pueblo, not far from the home of the Turquoise Boy, the little turquoise mountain south of Santa Fe, N. Mex.
[34] Informant's note: The big female reed is thought to be the joint cane which grows along the Colorado River. This was near the home of the White Shell Girl.
[35] Recorder's note: That the tree is here called a spruce and on page 2 a pine is not explained.
[36] First Man's name, Aste'hastqin, corresponds to the sacred name of the kit fox.

the canopy of the sky. They tried to blow inside the reed, but it was solid. They asked the woodpecker to drill out the hard heart. Soon they were able to peek through the opening, but they had to blow and blow before it was large enough to climb through. They climbed up inside the big male reed, and after them the water continued to rise.[37]

THE FOURTH WORLD

When the people reached the Fourth World they saw that it was not a very large place. Some say that it was called the White World; but not all medicine men agree that this is so.

The last person to crawl through the reed was the turkey from Gray Mountain. His feather coat was flecked with foam, for after him came the water. And with the water came the female Water Buffalo who pushed her head through the opening in the reed. She had a great quantity of curly hair which floated on the water, and she had two horns, half black and half yellow. From the tips of the horns the lightning flashed.

First Man asked the Water Buffalo why she had come and why she had sent the flood. She said nothing. Then the Coyote drew the two babies from his coat and said that it was, perhaps, because of them.

The Turquoise Boy took a basket and filled it with turquoise. On top of the turquoise he placed the blue pollen, tha'di'thee do tlij, from the blue flowers,[38] and the yellow pollen from the corn; and on top of these he placed the pollen from the water flags, tquel aqa'di din; and again on top of these he placed the crystal, which is river pollen. This basket he gave to the Coyote who put it between the horns of the Water Buffalo. The Coyote said that with this sacred offering he would give back the male child. He said that the male child would be known as the Black Cloud or Male Rain, and that he would bring the thunder and lightning. The female child he would keep. She would be known as the Blue, Yellow, and White Clouds or Female Rain. She would be the gentle rain that would moisten the earth and help them to live. So he kept the female child, and he placed the male child on the sacred basket between the horns of the Water Buffalo. And the Water Buffalo disappeared, and the waters with her.

After the water sank there appeared another person. They did not know him, and they asked him where he had come from. He told them that he was the badger, nahashch'id, and that he had been formed

---

[37] The Third or Yellow World: Matthews (1897, p. 66); Whitman (1925, pp. 7–9); Alexander (1916, p. 161); Parsons (1923, p. 161); Cushing (1923, p. 166).

[38] Recorder's note: This blue pollen, tha'di'thee do tlij, is thought to be *Delphinium scaposum* Green.

where the Yellow Cloud had touched the Earth.   Afterward this Yellow Cloud turned out to be a sunbeam.[39]

THE FIFTH WORLD

First Man was not satisfied with the Fourth World.   It was a small, barren land; and the great water had soaked the earth and made the sowing of seeds impossible.   He planted the big Female Reed and it grew up to the vaulted roof of this Fourth World.   First Man sent the newcomer, the badger, up inside the reed, but before he reached the upper world water began to drip, so he returned and said that he was frightened.

At this time there came another strange being.   First Man asked him where he had been formed, and he told him that he had come from the Earth itself.   This was the locust.[40]   He said that it was now his turn to do something, and he offered to climb up the reed.

The locust made a headband of a little reed, and on his forehead he crossed two arrows.   These arrows were dressed with yellow tail feathers.   With this sacred headdress and the help of all the Holy Beings the locust climbed up to the Fifth World.   He dug his way through the reed as he digs in the earth now.   He then pushed through mud until he came to water.   When he emerged he saw a black water bird [41] swimming toward him.   He had arrows [42] crossed on the back of his head and big eyes.

The bird said: "What are you doing here?   This is not your country."   And continuing, he told the locust that unless he could make magic he would not allow him to remain.

The black water bird drew an arrow from back of his head, and shoving it into his mouth drew it out his nether extremity.   He inserted it underneath his body and drew it out of his mouth.

"That is nothing," said the locust.   He took the arrows from his headband and pulled them both ways through his body, between his shell and his heart.   The bird believed that the locust possessed great medicine, and he swam away to the East, taking the water with him.

Then came the blue water bird from the South, and the yellow water bird from the West, and the white water bird from the North, and everything happened as before.   The locust performed the magic with

---

[39] Informant's and interpreter's note: The Four Worlds were really 12 worlds, or stages of development; but different medicine men divide them differently according to the ceremony held.   For the narrative they call them the Four Dark Worlds, and the Fifth World, the one we live in.   An old medicine man explained that the Sixth World would be that of the spirit; and that the one above that would be "cosmic," melting into one.

[40] Informant's note: The name of the locust was not given.
Franciscan Fathers (1912, p. 123): locust, nahacha'gi.   This also means grasshopper, cicada.

[41] Informant's note: The water birds were grebes.

[42] Recorder's note: The arrows crossed on the back of the bird's head.   See both Navaho and Zuni Arrow Ceremony.

his arrows; and when the last water bird had gone he found himself sitting on land.

The locust returned to the lower world and told the people that the beings above had strong medicine, and that he had had great difficulty getting the best of them.

Now two dark clouds and two white clouds rose, and this meant that two nights and two days had passed, for there was still no sun. First Man again sent the badger to the upper world, and he returned covered with mud, terrible mud. First Man gathered chips of turquoise which he offered to the five Chiefs of the Winds who [43] lived in the uppermost world of all. They were pleased with the gift, and they sent down the winds and dried the Fifth World.

First Man and his people saw four dark clouds and four white clouds pass, and then they sent the badger up the reed. This time when the badger returned he said that he had come out on solid earth. So First Man and First Woman led the people to the Fifth World, which some call the Many Colored Earth and some the Changeable Earth. They emerged through a lake surrounded by four mountains. The water bubbles in this lake when anyone goes near.[44]

Now after all the people had emerged from the lower worlds First Man and First Woman dressed the Mountain Lion with yellow, black, white, and grayish corn and placed him on one side. They dressed the Wolf with white tail feathers and placed him on the other side. They divided the people into two groups. The first group was told to choose whichever chief they wished. They made their choice, and, although they thought they had chosen the Mountain Lion, they found that they had taken the Wolf for their chief. The Mountain Lion was the chief for the other side. And these people who had the Mountain Lion for their chief turned out to be the people of the Earth. They were to plant seeds and harvest corn. The followers of the Wolf chief became the animals and birds; they turned into all the creatures that fly and crawl and run and swim.

And after all the beings were divided, and each had his own form, they went their ways.

[43] The First Chief, Nlchi ntla'ie, the Left Course Wind: the Second Chief, Nlchi lichi, the Red Wind; the Third Chief, Nlchi shada ji na'laghali, the Wind Turning from the Sun; the Fourth Chief, Nlchi qa'hashchi, the Wind with Many Points; the Fifth Chief, Nlchi che do et siedee, the Wind with the Fiery Temper.

[44] Informant's note: The place of emergence is said to be near Pagosa Springs, Colo. The white people have put a wire fence around our Sacred Lake.

Matthews (1897, p. 135): place of emergence. Franciscan Fathers (1910, pp. 347–354): The First or Dark World: ants, beetles, dragonflies, locusts, bats, frogs. The Second or Blue World: blue heron, swallow people. They lived in rough, lumpy houses with the entrance in a hole in the top of the roof or in caves. The Third or Yellow World: grasshoppers, etc. The Fourth or Larger World was of All Colors: four snow-covered mountains; the Pueblo People; corn, pumpkins.

Parsons (1933, pp. 611–631); Cushing (1923, p. 164).

This is the story of the Four Dark Worlds and the Fifth, the World we live in. Some medicine men tell us that there are two worlds above us, the first is the World of the Spirits of Living Things, the second is the Place of Melting into One.

THE ORDER OF THINGS, OR THE AGE OF ANIMAL HEROES

THE FIRST HOGAN [45]

Hash'ke ba'jilte, a powerful medicine man of the Blue Bird Clan, gave many of the origin myths to Sandoval.

First Man planned to build a home.

He dug a shallow pit in the earth and raised the poles. For the main poles First Man used the Black Bow, which is called Altqin dilqil.[46] There were two parts of this Black Bow, and two other parts, one cut from the Male Reed and one from the Female Reed.[47] The other poles were those at hand. Then the whole structure was covered with earth and grass, and the first dwelling was built. First Woman ground white corn into meal, and they powdered the poles with the meal, and they sprinkled it inside the dwelling from East to West.

First Man said as he sprinkled the cornmeal: "May my home be sacred and beautiful, and may the days be beautiful and plenty."

Today there is a hogan ceremony, and a song is sung as the poles are raised.

Now after the first hogan was built and they had seen four dark and four light clouds rising First Man said that they were tired and that they must rest. He asked if anyone had brought the river stones. The badger said that he had five. First Man said that he would heat four and leave one. He had a plan to build two sweat houses out of the remaining poles.[48]

There are four parts of a chant sung at this time. It is the Sweat House Chant. One part is like this:

> He made it. He made it. He made it.
> At the place where the people emerged from the underworld,
> Near the Lake of Emergence, he made it.
> He made it with the female wood and the male wood.
> He made it with the Black Mesa rock.
> He made it with the hard river rock.
> He made it with the help of The-Most-High-Power-Whose-Ways-Are-Fearful.

[45] Informant's note: The first hogan was not like the hogans of today. Franciscan Fathers (1910, p. 327); Nusbaum (1922.)

[46] Informant's note: The Dark or Black Bow is symbolic of the Slayers of the Enemies. It is a symbol of the overthrow of evil.

[47] Informant's note: The Male and the Female Reeds are the symbols of the male and the female principles.

[48] Informant's note: The building of the sweat house is very special, details will be given later.

Many chants are sung during this ceremony—the Horned Toad Chant, the Twin Brothers Chant, the Bear Chant, and the Mirage Stone Chant.[49]

THE CREATION OF THE SUN AND MOON [50]

After the hogan was finished everyone rested.

The dwelling was occupied by Atse'hastqin, First Man, and Atse'-esdza, First Woman. All their belongings were piled inside. The woman lay with her feet to the West, and the man lay with his feet to the East. Their heads crossed and their thoughts mingled, and these thoughts were sacred.

Now in the hogan there were also two other persons: Atse'ashki, First boy, and Atse'ataed, First Girl. They were not the children of First Man and First Woman, but the Turquoise Boy and the White Shell Girl who had come with the others from the underworld. Now First Boy lay to the south side of the hogan, and First Girl to the north. They lay down when they saw the period of darkness descending, and they listened. First Man and First Woman whispered together, but First Boy could not distinguish the words one from another. Each time the Dark Cloud covered them the four lay down, and First Man and First Woman whispered.

This happened four times, then First Boy stood and said: "What is this secret thing that you plan? We have lost our sleep through four dark spaces."

"It is not an unwise thing that we plan," said First Man. "We plan for the time which is to come, how we shall live, and how the people will live upon this earth. It is nothing but that, my child." And First Woman repeated what her husband had said. When First Boy heard this he agreed that it was better that the two should continue their planning.

First Man and First Woman whispered together during many nights. They planned with the help of the All-Wise-Coyote-Who-Was-Formed-in-the-Water. The three devised a scheme that would meet the problems that would later come to pass. They planned that there should be a sun, and day and night.[51] They said that the Coyote, called First Angry, had brought unhappiness and spoiled their life

---

[49] Mindeleff (1898, pt. 2, pp. 475–517) ; Stevenson (1891, pp. 239–242, 273–275) ; Cushing (1923, p. 163).

Recorder's note: The hogan faces the East. Hebrews of antiquity fronted their edifices to the East.

[50] Informant's note: Some medicine men say that the Turquoise Boy was without sex, or a hermaphrodite.

Stevenson (1891, p. 275) ; Alexander (1916, pp. 166–169, and note 31, p. 286) ; Matthews (1897, p. 80).

[51] Alexander (1916, p. 155) ; Matthews (1897, pp. 80–81) ; Franciscan Fathers (1912, p. 36) : The Black Yei or Fire God, Hashch'esh'zhini ; Parsons (1923, pp. 135–162).

down below, and that he was not the proper person to have with them at this time. He should be kept away.

They spread a beautiful buckskin on the ground. This was the skin of a deer not killed by a weapon.[52] On the buckskin they placed a perfect turquoise, round like the sun. It was as large as the height of an average man if he stretched his arm upward. They stood 12 tail feathers from the eagle around it, and also 12 tail feathers from the flicker. On the great turquoise they marked a mouth and nose and eyes. They made a yellow streak below the mouth on top of the chin.

Now, although they had stationed four guards to be on the lookout for the Coyote, Atse'hashke', he came and asked them what they were doing. They told him: "Nothing whatsoever". He said: "So I see," and went away.

After that they visited the different places where there was fire under the earth. In one of these places they found Hashche'zhini, the Black Yei, who is also called the Fire God. He was asked to use his fire to heat the great turquoise which they had planned to use as their sun.

They placed a perfect white shell on the buckskin below the turquoise that was to become the sun. This great, perfect, white shell was to become the moon. First Man planned to heat it with the first crystal that he had used for his fire.

By this time they had posted two circles of guards around the place where they were planning; but even with this precaution the Coyote came to them. He appeared in their midst and said: "This must be something that you are planning." But they assured him that he saw nothing; they said that they were just sitting there. And again the Coyote left them. First Man called the guards together and asked them why they had let the one whose name was Atse'hashke' pass. They said that they had not seen the Coyote. First Man then placed three circles of guards around the sacred buckskin.

The Holy Ones asked the Turquoise Boy to enter the great, perfect turquoise that was to become the sun; and they asked the White Shell Girl to enter the great, perfect, white shell that was to become the moon. The Turquoise Boy was to carry a whistle made from the Male Reed. This whistle had 12 holes in it, and each time that the Turquoise Boy would blow on his whistle the earth would move one month in time. The White Shell Girl was also to carry a whistle. It was made from the Female Reed, and with it she should move the tides of the sea.

---

[52] Interpreter's note: Medicine men prize highly the skin of a deer not killed by a weapon. A deer struck by a car in the winter of 1935 brought the Navaho who found it two cows in exchange.

Just as this was planned the Coyote came among them and said: "Well, my cousins, there is something that you are planning. What is it?"

First Man answered: "We are planning nothing at all. We are just sitting here."

"Very well," said the Coyote, "I wanted to know, that was all." And he went away.

After he had gone they planned the 12 months of the year.[53]

THE TWELVE MONTHS OF THE YEAR

(Fig. 1)

October is the first month of the year and of winter, which is called qai. October's name is Gah'ji, meaning Back-to-Back, or the Parting-of-the-Seasons. It is the time when the deer come, the time to hunt. Nalashi, the tarantula, is its feather or headdress. Nlchi achi, little cold, is its heart. The blue hanging haze is over this month. Women

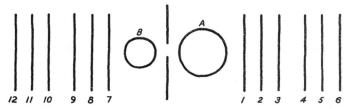

FIGURE 1.—The Calendar Stone: The plan of the twelve months of the year. A, Sun; B, Moon. 1, January; 2, February; 3, March; 4, April; 5, May; 6, June; 7, July; 8, August; 9, September; 10, October; 11, November; 12, December. (The drawing of the Calendar Stone was given by Sandoval.)

shell corn, thrash, and store food for the winter. It is the month when mountain sheep breed.

November is the second month. It is called Nlchi'tso'si, the month or Time of Slender Winds. Its heart is Nlchi'tso'si, Slender Wind. Its feather is Hastin sakai (Orion), the Old Man with Legs Spread. It is also a month for hunting. The women gather certain grass and plant seeds on warm days,[54] which later they dry and grind into flour for the different bread cakes eaten in winter. The antelope breed.

The third month of the year is December. It is called Nlchi'tso', the Great Wind. Its heart is also the Great Wind. Its feather is

[53] Recorder's note: The drawing of the Calendar Stone was checked by Sam Ahkeah and Gerald Nailor.

Informant's and interpreter's note: First Man made the marks on the buckskin. Later the people of Blue House had the Calendar Stone in their keeping. A medicine woman guarded it. The story of the sun and the moon and the 12 months were upon it. Hastin Tlo'tsi hee's (Sandoval's) ancestress, Ezdzan at'a', the Hopi woman, was the guardian of this stone. Later it was hidden near the Carriso Mountains.

[54] Recorder's note: Edible seeds known to the Navaho. (Any of the genus *Chenopodium*.)

Atse'etso, the Big First One.[55] Digging sticks are prepared in this month. They are made with the stone ax; and the wood is dried in the dwellings so that when the planting time comes the sticks will be smooth and well seasoned. The women make moccasins, and they tan the hides from the hunting season. It is the time to begin to tell the sacred stories. The deer breed.

January is the fourth month. Its name is Zas'ntl'tis, Crusted Snow. Its heart is Tqin, Ice. Akaisda'hi, Which-Awaits-the-Dawn, is its feather. This is the Milky Way. The young men hear the sacred stories and learn to become hatqa'li, singers or shamen. This is the time when preparations are made for the coming growing season. There are many ceremonies. The women cook the food and take part in certain rituals. The coyotes breed.

February, the fifth month, is called Atsa'biyazh, Baby Eagle. Nol'i, the Hail, is its heart. Its feather is Gahat'ei, the Rabbit Tracks (star cluster in Canis Major). It is the month of the changeable winds. The First Chief of the Winds shakes the earth and awakens the sleeping plants, the bear, the lizards and the snakes. The first plants start to come up. After this month the sacred stories must not be told to the young people. The rabbits breed.

The sixth month, March, is called Wozhchid.[56] It is the month when eaglets chirp in the shell and the antlers of the deer drop. Its heart is Becha na'chil,[57] Sudden Spring Storms. Its feather is Dede'-nii, the mountain sheep bird.[58] When you see these birds in the canyons it is spring. The mountain sheep drop their young. Nlchi'dotlish, the Blue Wind, moves over the earth and the first leaves come forth. Ceremonies are held to bless the fields before the seeds are planted.

April, the seventh month and the beginning of Shiji, summer, is called Da'chil, the month of little leaves. Its heart is Niyol, Wind-in-Action. Bit'aa, meaning little leaves, is its feather. Rabbits have their young. Nlchi'dilqil, the Black Wind, shakes the earth and it thunders. The leaves grow bigger and darker in color; and the people make ready for the planting.

May is the eighth month. It is called Dotso after the All-Wise Fly in the sacred legends. Its heart is Ayei'ne'denaiyote, meaning a mixture of rain and spring snow. Nlchi'dilqil, the Black Wind, is its feather. The grass becomes a darkish green. The antelope drop their young. Nlchi'litsui, the Yellow Wind, shakes the earth and it thunders. The flowers come forth and plants open their leaves. It is

---

[55] Recorder's note: Atse etso, the Big First One; part of Scorpio.
[56] Informant's note: The meaning is not known.
[57] Recorder's note: The spelling of this word is not certain.
[58] Informant's note: Dede'nii, the mountain sheep bird is the phoebe.

the time to plant.   The early part of this month is called the planting time.

The ninth month, June, is called Yaish jash'chili, When-Few Seeds-Ripen.   Its heart is Hado'yazhe, Little Heat.   Jadi'yazhe, Little Antelope, is its feather.   The women gather the first edible seeds, and they are used as the first fruits of the season.   They gather the cactus fruit.   This is the month of the first rain ceremonies.

July, the tenth month, is called Jas'tso, the great seed ripening. Big Heat, Hado'tso, is its heart.   Nltsa'najin, Dark Streaks of Rain, is its feather.   It is the time when people gather many seeds and guard their fields.   The deer drop their young.   Dilye'he, the Pleiades, are seen in the early morning; and the fawns have their pattern on their rumps.

The eleventh month, August, is called Binint A'tso'si, Little Ripening.   Its heart is A'tso'si, Light Ripening.   Nltsa'bakha', the Male Rain, is its feather.   The ears form on the corn and everything ripens. It is the time when wild fruits are gathered—the sourberry, the chokecherry, and yucca fruit.

The last month of the year and of summer is September. (See fig. 1.) [59]   It is called Binint a'tso, the Harvest Time.   Binint a'tso, Great Ripening, is its heart.   Nltsa'baad, the Female Rain, is its feather. Nuts are gathered.   The corn is harvested and taken to the dwellings. The first foodstuffs are stored for the winter.   And the Ceremony of All Blessings is held in thanksgiving.

When everything was in readiness they called Hashche'zhini from Heavy Rock where he lived.   He came to heat the turquoise that was to become the sun.   The Turquoise Boy stepped into the sun with his whistle, which was made from the male reed.   This whistle had 12 holes in it; and each time he blew on it the earth would move one space or month.   First Man heated with his crystal the Great White Shell that was to become the moon.   The White Shell Girl stepped into the moon.   She carried her whistle, made from the female reed, which also had 12 holes in it.   And whenever she blew upon it she would help move the earth and the tides.   These two Holy Beings were to form the seasons and the months and the days.

The Turquoise Boy asked to have 102 trails; and the White Shell Girl asked to have 100 trails.   They were to cross in the months of March and September.   The Sun was to turn back in June, and again in December.

The Turquoise Boy said: "Everything is right so far, but I will not travel for nothing.   I will travel if I am paid with the lives of the people of the earth, all the human beings, the animals which have four legs, the birds and insects of the air, the fishes and all the people

[59] Informant's note: Some medicine men believe the original plan was for 13 months.

of the under-water." And then the White Shell Girl repeated the
same thing. She also wanted to be paid with the lives of the living.[60]

After everything was finished and four circles made around the
whole, the Coyote, Atse'hashke', went to the great yei, Hasjelti, and
demanded to know why he had not been allowed to have a part in the
planning. He said that the others had tried to keep it a secret, but
that he had known all that had happened. This made Hasjelti very
angry, and seeing this, the Coyote ran away. He ran straight to the
place where the others were planning and appeared in their midst.
He asked First Man why he had kept everything a secret. He turned
to First Woman and asked her why she had kept this thing from him.
Then he told them everything that they had planned. He said that
they had even set the month when he should visit his woman. He
warned them that he had come for the purpose of spoiling their plan.

Atse'haske' drew five lines over other marks he had made in the
sand. He told the people that unless they could guess their proper
meanings they would suffer greatly. Now the little Breeze whispered
in First Man's ear and told him what to say. The first line was made
of turquoise and it represented the green leaves. The second line
drawn was of white shell. First Man said that he thought of ripe
leaves and falling leaves. The third mark was made of jet; and he
said that it stood for the dark, black mountains after the leaves had
fallen. The fourth line was made of white bead. First Man said
that it was the snow on the mountains. The fifth mark was of crystal,
and its meaning was of snow and ice on the frozen rivers and lakes.
(See fig. 2.)

The Coyote spoke, "All right, everything you have guessed correctly.
I thought of all those things as I made the five marks. By your

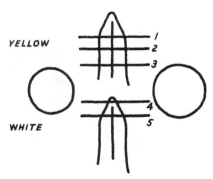

FIGURE 2.—Atse'hashke' the Coyote's five marks: 1, The turquoise mark; 2, the white
shell mark; 3, the jet mark; 4, the white bead mark; 5, the crystal mark. (Gerald
Nailor obtained this diagram from a medicine man at Shiprock.)

---

[60] Recorder's note: The Arctic Highlanders say: "Will ye have eternal darkness and
eternal life, or light and death?"

guessing you have made the summer months six, and the winter months six; and you expect to count by the changes of the moon. But I will put in some extra days so that the months will not be even. Sometimes frost will come early, and sometimes it will remain late. First plants will sometimes freeze, and so also will animals. Sometimes the full moon will come before the end of the month; and at the end of the year you will find that you have 13 moon periods instead of 12." The Coyote continued. "You have in your minds that it was I who spoiled your way of living down in the underworlds. It was not my plan."

Then he addressed First Woman. "Why did you keep this sacred thing from me? When you asked me to steal the Water Buffalo's babies you said that you had suffered many things because of your husband's plan. Everything was well when I did as you wished. I have kept the female Water Buffalo baby; and by keeping her I am able to call the male rain and the female rain and all the different clouds and vapors. It is well. I followed your desires so that the people might have the seasons and the flowers and all that grows from the earth during the different times of the year. Your plan was for the benefit of those to come. But now I will place the female child back into the River. Whenever you wish rain you will have to go for the Water Buffalo's girl baby; and after you have used her power you will have to return her to the River again." He told them where they would find her; and he said that they would know when they should use her. "Now go ahead with your plans, Brothers," [61] he said, and with that he left them.

After the Coyote had departed the others spread the blue sky above the earth. In the East they placed a black pole to hold up the eastern end of the sky. A blue one was planted in the South, a yellow one in the West, and a white one in the North. A hole was placed in the sky and sealed with water. Around the outer edge of the sky was placed a white ring, a yellow ring, a blue ring, and a black ring. They formed the border. They were placed there for the purpose of protecting the sky so that it would remain solid forever. No power on the earth or above the earth should harm it. And around the four posts they placed the same colors.

After all was finished they placed the sun in the sky, and also, they placed the moon there. And they placed Dilye'he, the Pleiades there; and Atse'etso, the Big First One; and the Coyote's Feather, Atse'etso'si, which is also called the Slender One; and Baalchini, the children of Dilye'ha and Atse'etso'si; and Hastin sakai, The-Old-Man-with-Feet-Apart; and the Rabbit Tracks, Gahat'ei; and

---

[61] Informant's note: The Coyote used the word "brother" first and last in all speeches after this.

Akaisda'hi, Moving-toward-the-Dawn; and Nahokhos bokho, The-Main-Pole-which-Holds-All; and Nahokhos bakhai, The-Revolving-Male-Warrior-with-his-Bow-and-Arrows; and his wife, Nahokhos baadi, Who-Carries the-Fire-in-her-Basket.[62]

THE SUN'S PATH

Above the mountain called Tso dzil [63] there is a square hole in the sky. And this hole in the sky is mirrored in a lake which lies between the two highest peaks of the mountain. There were three names given to the hole in the sky: the first is called Tse'an an hi'habetine, the Place Where the Most High Power Came Up; the second is Sash yota'betine, the Bear's Upper Sky Path; and the third name is Hojon yota'betine, Whose Ways Are Beautiful's Path. It is said that the Sun stops at this place at midday and eats his lunch; and the place where he stops and eats is called Nitsi ya'hatsis, The Place Where the Sun Man Has His Lunch and His Horse Eats Out of a Basket.

THE SKY AND THE EARTH

Then came the Earth Woman, Nahosdzan'esdza'. First Man told her that she was to be the wife of the Sky. She would face the East, and her husband over her, would face the West. And whenever the Fog covered the Earth they would know that the Sky had visited Nahosdzan'esdza'.

After that they set the corner posts and stretched the Sky in the four directions.

About twenty chants were sung at this time, and after the first ten sections of the first chant, the Sun Chant, the Sun began to move

---

[62] Informant's note (checked with interpreter) : Yaya ni'sin is the name of the corner or sky posts. Dilye'he, the pleiades. Atse'etso, the forepart of Scorpio. Atse'etso'si, the belt and sword of Orion. Baalchini, the central double stars in the lower part of the Hyades, Hastin sakai, Orion. The left foot is Rigel and the right foot is Betelgeuse. Gahat'ei, the star cluster under Canis Major, Akaisda'hi, the Milky Way. Nahokhos bokho, the North Star. Nahokos bakhai, Ursa Major, the Big Dipper. Nahokos baadi, Cassiopea, but some medicine men say Ursa Minor.

Lowie (1908): "According to the naturalistic theory, constellations are apperceived by primitive man as objects or persons according to the characteristics that appear to him, and an explantory tale is added" (p. 123) ; e. g., The Pleiades—"the Shoshone tale of Coyote and his daughters"; the "Plains' legend of the girl who turns into a bear, and, after killing the tribesmen, pursues her brothers, who ascend to become a constellation" (the Dipper) (p. 126).

Tozzer (1908, p. 28) ; Matthews (1897, p. 80, notes 67–70, pp. 223–224).

Interpreter's notes: 1. The Coyote added his own star, Mai'bizo, which is sometimes called So dondizidi, the No-Month Star. This is identified as Canopus. 2. The Coyote Man was thrown into the sky, and is known as Atse'etso'si. The Baalchini are his children by the woman Dilye'he, the Pleiades. Those who know of the Coyote cult and its weird rites understand incestuous relationship. 3. Dilye'he, the Pleiades, is sometime represented as the mother-in-law who must not meet her son-in-law, Aste'etso'si, but must continually run from him. The myth of the Coyote Man is the origin of the mother-in-law taboo.

[63] Informant's note : Tso dzil is Mount Taylor.

away.   The next chant was for the Moon, and after a little time, it also began to move away.

Today different medicine men use different chants and prayers for this ceremony; but the chants of the Sun and Moon and Earth are always sung.   Some say that black magic and evil entered the plan at this time, but others hold that it was not until later.

Now after the Sun rose in the sky the Dark Cloud that covered the earlier worlds during half periods became the night.   The White Cloud was the dawn, and the sun's light became our day.   And along the far horizons where the first ones used to see the blue and yellow clouds, there appeared the twilight and the false dawn.

The first day-period that the sun was raised in the sky the heat was unbearable.   So the Holy Ones stretched out the four corners of the sky and this raised the sun still higher in the heavens.   After they had done this four times it was like it is today.   There was room on the earth for everyone, and the sun's warmth was right for the growing plants and the animals and the people.

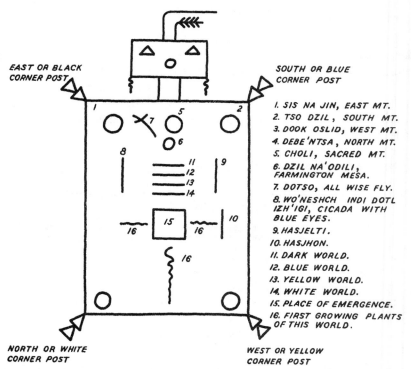

EAST OR BLACK CORNER POST

SOUTH OR BLUE CORNER POST

NORTH OR WHITE CORNER POST

WEST OR YELLOW CORNER POST

1. SIS NA JIN, EAST MT.
2. TSO DZIL, SOUTH MT.
3. DOOK OSLID, WEST MT.
4. DEBE'NTSA, NORTH MT.
5. CHOLI, SACRED MT.
6. DZIL NA'ODILI, FARMINGTON MESA.
7. DOTSO, ALL WISE FLY.
8. WO'NESHCH INDI DOTL IZH'IGI, CICADA WITH BLUE EYES.
9. HASJELTI.
10. HASJHON.
11. DARK WORLD.
12. BLUE WORLD.
13. YELLOW WORLD.
14. WHITE WORLD.
15. PLACE OF EMERGENCE.
16. FIRST GROWING PLANTS OF THIS WORLD.

FIGURE 3.—Sand Painting of the Earth.   (The plan of the earth.)   From the top of the mask projects a breath feather, tied with a white cotton string, the spider's gift.   Coral and turquoise ear pendants are indicated.   The body is dark gray.   Borders, mask, neck, etc.   The two arms and two legs are kos ischin, triangles set upon one another and symbolizing forming clouds or cloud terraces.   (Sam Ahkeak and Gerald Nailor got this from medicine men at Shiprock.)

Now it was the same with the earth as it was with the sky. They planned just how the earth should be.[64] (Fig. 3.) They made the face of the earth white, with eyes and nose and mouth. They made earrings of turquoise for the ears; and for a border they placed a black ring, a blue ring, a yellow ring, and a white ring, which is the earth's edge. These rings are for the earth's protection; no power shall harm her.

THE MOUNTAINS SACRED TO THE DÎNÈ

First Man and First Woman formed six sacred mountains from the soil that First Man had gathered from the mountains in the Third World and kept in his medicine bag.[65] As before they placed Sis na' jin in the East, Tso dzil in the South, Dook oslid in the West, and Debe'-ntsa in the North. They placed a sacred mountain, which they called Chol'i'i, on the earth; and they made the mountain, Dzil na'odili, around which the people were to travel.

There were four Holy Boys. These beings First Man called to him. He told the White Bead Boy [66] to enter the mountain of the East, Sis na' jin. The Turquoise Boy [67] he told to go into the mountain of the South, Tso dzil. The Abalone Shell Boy [68] entered the mountain of the West, Dook oslid. And into the mountain of the North, Debe'ntsa, went the Jet Boy.[69]

Now the mountains to the East and South were dissatisfied. The East wanted the Turquoise Boy and the South wanted the White Bead Boy for their bodies. There was quite a lot of trouble; the mountains would tremble as though they would fall to pieces, and it was a good time before they were satisfied. The other mountains were happy in their bodies and there was no trouble between them.

First Man and First Woman called other Holy Beings to them.

They put the Beautiful Mixed Stones Boy and Girl into the sacred mountain called Chol'i'. They put the Pollen Boy and Grasshopper Girl [70] into Dzil na'odili. They asked the Rock Crystal Girl to go into Sis na' jin. They put the White Corn Girl into Tso dzil; the Yellow Corn Girl into Dook Oslid; and the Darkness Girl into Debe'ntsa.[71]

After the Holy Beings had entered the Sacred Mountains First Man and First Woman dressed them according to their positions on the earth.

---

[64] Informant's note: The Sand Painting of the Earth and the description.

[65] Recorder's note: See page 9, ftn. 32, this bulletin.

[66] Informant's and interpreter's notes: The White Bead Boy is also called the Dawn Boy and the Rock Crystal Boy.

[67] Informant's note: The Turquoise Bead Boy is called the Daylight Boy.

[68] Informant's note: The Abalone Shell Boy is called the Twilight Boy.

[69] Informant's note: the Jet Boy is called the Darkness Boy and the Obsidian Boy.

[70] Informant's note: The Pollen Boy and the Grasshopper Girl are also called the Beautiful Goods Boy and Girl.

[71] Interpreter's note: Early remains near San Francisco Peak not mentioned by the informant, but spoken of by others.

They fastened Sis na' jin to the earth with a bolt of white lightning. They covered the mountain with a blanket of daylight, and they decorated it with white shells, white lightning, black clouds, and male rain. They placed the white shell basket on the summit; and in this basket two eggs of the hasbi'delgai, the pigeon. They said that the pigeons were to be the mountain's feather; and that is why there are many wild pigeons in this mountain today. And lastly they sent the bear to guard the doorway of the White Bead Boy in the East.

Tso dzil they fastened to the earth with a stone knife. They covered this mountain of the South with a blue cloud blanket; and they decorated it with turquoise, white corn, dark mists, and the female rain. They placed a turquoise basket on the highest peak, and in it they put two eggs of the blue bird, doli. Blue birds are Tso dzil's feather. They sent the big snake to guard the doorway of the Turquoise Boy in the South.

Dook oslid was fastened to the earth with a sunbeam. They covered the mountain of the West with a yellow cloud. They adorned it with haliotis shell, yellow corn, black clouds, and the male rain, and they called many animals to dwell upon it. They placed the abalone shell basket on the summit; and in it they placed the two eggs of the tsidiltsoi, the yellow warbler. These birds were to become its feather. The Black Wind was told to go to the West and guard the doorway of the Abalone Shell Boy.

They fastened the mountain of the North, Debe'ntsa, to the earth with a rainbow. Over it they spread a blanket of darkness. They decorated it with bash'zhini', obsidian, black vapors, and different plants and animals. The basket they placed on its highest peak was of obsidian; and in it they put the two eggs of the chagi, the blackbird. The blackbirds are the mountain's feather. The lightning was sent to guard the Jet Boy's doorway in the North.

First Man and First Woman fastened the Sacred Mountain Chol'i'i to the earth with a streak of rain. They decorated it with the pollens, mixed chips of stone precious to them, the dark mists, and the female rain. And they fastened Dzil na'odili to the earth with the sun's rays; and they decorated it with the beautiful goods of all kinds, the dark clouds, and the male rain. They left the summits of these mountains free. But some say that Dzil na'odili was fastened to the earth with Tse'hadahonige, the mirage stone; and those people associate the Mirage Boy and the Carnelian Girl with this mountain.[72]

All the mountains have their prayers and chants which are called Dressing the Mountains. All the corner posts have their prayers and chants, as have the stars and markings in the sky and on the earth. It is their custom to keep the sky and the earth and the day and the night beautiful. The belief is that if this is done, living among the people of the earth will be good.

---

[72] Matthews, 1897, pp. 78–79, similar legend.

One of the Mountain Chants: [73]

For ages and ages the plans have been made.
For ages and ages the plans of the Holy Mountains have been made.

For Sis na' jin, the mountain of the East, the plan was made.
The plan was made in the home of the First Man.
The planning took place on top of the Beautiful Goods.
They planned how a strong White Bead Boy should be formed;
How the White Bead Boy should be formed, and
How the Chief of the Mountain should be made.
How he should be made like the Most-High-Power-Whose-Ways-Are-Beautiful.

For Tso'dzil, the mountain of the South, the plan was made.
The plan was made in the home of the First Man.
The planning took place on the top of the Beautiful Goods.
They planned how a strong Turquoise Boy should be formed;
How the Turquoise Boy should be formed, and
How the Chief of the Mountain should be made.
How he should be made like the Most-High-Power-Whose-Ways-Are-Beautiful.

For Dook oslid, the mountain of the West, the plan was made.
The plan was made in the home of the First Man.
The planning took place on the top of the Beautiful Goods.
They planned how a strong Abalone Shell Boy should be formed;
How the Abalone Shell Boy should be formed, and
How the Chief of the Mountain should be made.
How he should be made like the Most-High-Power-Whose-Ways-Are-Beautiful.

For Debe'ntsa, the mountain of the North, the plan was made.
The plan was made in the home of the First Man.
The planning took place on the top of the Beautiful Goods.
They planned how a strong Jet Boy should be formed;
How the Jet Boy should be formed, and
How the Chief of the Mountain should be made.
How he should be made like the Most-High-Power-Whose-Ways-Are-Beautiful.

For Dzil na'odili, the Center Mountain, the plan was made.
The plan was made in the home of the First Man.
The planning took place on the top of the Beautiful Goods.
They planned how a strong Earth's Breath should be formed;
How the Banded Rock should be used, and
How the Chief of the Mountain should be made.
How he should be made like the Most-High-Power-Whose-Ways-Are-Beautiful.

For Chol'i'i, the Sacred Mountain, the plan was made.
The plan was made in the home of the First Man.
The planning took place on the top of the Beautiful Goods.
They planned how the strong Earth's Heart should be formed;
How the Mixed Chips should be used, and
How the Sacred Mountain should be made.
How she should be made like the Most-High-Power-Whose-Ways-Are-Beautiful.

---

[73] Informant's note: Matthews recorded the Mountain Top Chant; also another Mountain Chant, Dzil ki'ji jikae'shash na'dle, relates the metamorphoses of the bear and the horned rattlesnake (Matthews, 1887, pp. 385–467).

The Ceremony that has come down to us from this story is called the Mountain Chant.[74] There are about a hundred sections to this one great chant. There are many songs, and they are all beautiful. The words of the songs tell of the mountain people: the bear, the deer, the squirrel, and of all the others.

These persons were asked how many plants they brought with them from the first worlds, and how many seeds were collected and planted in the mountains. And after the mountain people came the people of the Plains. They were asked to bring forth the seeds of their plants. All that is seen growing on the Plains they brought with them. Next came the river people. They were asked about the willows, and the otter said that he had brought them with him. The beaver brought the cottonwoods, and also a stone which he chipped and scattered along the rivers and over the mesas, and they became the river boulders found today. First Man asked who had brought the cliff rocks. The little gray birds that live in those rocks, tse na'olch oshilchi', the rock wren, said that they had brought them. They said that they had ground it into powder and sprinkled it here and there and that the cliffs had sprung into being.

After First Man and First Woman had made and dressed the six mountains they found that there was still a little earth left in the medicine bag, so Tseya kan', the Hog Back Mountains, and the mesa south of them were formed. They were to be the lungs of the earth and the big diaphragm muscle separating the heart from the stomach.

The last of the earth was used to form Nltsa dzil, Strong Rain Mountain, the Carrizos. They made this great mountain with its legs to the South and its head to the North. It has for its dress Strong Goods, meaning many rocks for its clothing. This mountain has three other names: it is called Yolgai dzil, Bead Mountain; Nil tliz dzil, Mixed Chips Mountain; and Ta di din dzil, Strong Pollen Mountain. It holds the pollen of all the plants. And it was planned by First Man that the people should use this mountain, so he made it a strong mountain. First Man and First Woman set arrows around it to guard it. These are the rock formations such as Shiprock.

And after this was done and all was finished, the earth and all that was on it was stretched in the four directions so that there would be room for all. The people were told that they were to use the six sacred mountains indicated as their chief mountains. The place of emergence from the lower worlds was where it is now. The people could always see their great mountains above the lower mesa lands. When everything was finished a smoke was prepared for the mountains and the chants were sung.

---

[74] Matthews (1887, pp. 455–464).

MOUNTAIN CHANTS [75] [76] [77]

Chant I—It Stands Out

The mountain to the East is Sis na' jin.
It is standing out.
The strong White Bead is standing out,
A living mountain is standing out,
The Chief of the Mountain is standing out.
Like the Most-High-Power he is standing out,
Like the Most-High-Power-Whose-Ways-Are-Beautiful he is standing out.

It stands out,
It stands out,
It stands out.

The mountain to the South is Tso dzil.
It is standing out.
The strong Turquoise is standing out,
A living mountain is standing out,
The Chief of the Mountain is standing out,
Like the Most-High-Power he is standing out,
Like the Most-High-Power-Whose-Ways-Are-Beautiful he is standing out.

It stands out [repeated three times],

The mountain to the West is Dook oslid.
It is standing out.
The strong White Shell is standing out,
A living mountain is standing out,
The Chief of the Mountain is standing out.
Like the Most-High-Power he is standing out,
Like the Most-High-Power-Whose-Ways-Are-Beautiful he is standing out,

It stands out, . . .

The mountain to the North is Debe'ntsa.
It is standing out.
The strong Jet is standing out,
A living mountain is standing out,
The Chief of the Mountain is standing out.
Like the Most-High-Power he is standing out,
Like the Most-High-Power-Whose-Ways-Are-Beautiful he is standing out.

It stands out, . . .

The mountain in the Center is Dzil na'odili.
It is standing out.
The strong Beautiful Goods is standing out,
A living mountain is standing out,
The Chief of the Mountain is standing out.
Like the Most-High-Power he is standing out,
Like the Most-High-Power-Whose-Ways-Are-Beautiful he is standing out.

It stands out, . . .

[75] Matthews (1887, pp. 385–467) ; Songs of Sequence (pp. 455–464).
[76] Matthews (1885, pp. 271–274).
[77] Recorder's note: Matthews gives it as "It Looms Up." **Informant's note: The** Mountain Chant "It Stands Out" is Chant No. 1.

The Sacred Mountain is Chol'i'i.
It is standing out.
The strong Mixed Chips are standing out,
A living mountain is standing out,
The Chief of the Mountain is standing out.
Like the Most-High-Power he is standing out,
Like the Most-High-Power-Whose-Ways-Are-Beautiful he is standing out.

It stands out, . . .

Chant II—You See It [78]

Looking at the far distant horizon
You see it.
The strong White Bead rises,
You see it on the far distant horizon.
The Chief of the Mountain rises,
You see him.
Like the Most-High-Power you see him,
Like the Most-High-Power-Whose-Ways-Are-Beautiful you see him.
It stands out in the far distance,

You see it,
You see it,
You see it.

(In the six verses the names of the different mountains' trimmings
are changed as in the former chant.)

Chant III—It Rises Above the Earth

Now it rises in the far distance,
It rises above the earth.
The strong White Bead rises,
You can see it on the far distant horizon.
The Chief of the Mountain rises,
He rises above the earth.
Like the Most-High-Power he rises above the earth,
Like the Most-High-Power-Whose-Ways-Are-Beautiful he rises above the earth.

It rises above the earth,
You see it, you see it, you see it.

(As in Chant II the mountain's trimmings are changed in the
verses.)

Chant IV—The Chant of the Beautiful Mountains of the East and West [79]

1—Hasjelti's Song

Mountains of the East,
The Dawn Mountain,
The White Corn Mountain,
The Beautiful Goods Mountain,
The All-Water Mountain,
The Pollen Mountain.

---

[78] Informant gave Chants II and III later.
[79] Interpreter gave Chant IV, parts 1 and 2, later.

The people walk over me.
The old men all say to me, I am beautiful.
The people walk over me.
The old women all say to me, I am beautiful.
The people walk over me.
The young men all say to me, I am beautiful.
The people walk over me.
The young women all say to me, I am beautiful.
The people walk over me.
The children all say to me, I am beautiful.
The people walk over me.
The chiefs all say to me, I am beautiful.

2—Hasjohon's Song

Mountains of the West,
The Twilight Mountain,
The Yellow Corn Mountain,
The Mixed Chips Mountain,
The Little Water Mountain,
The Pollen Mountain.
Etc.

Chant V—The Chant of Hasjelti Boy and Hasjohon Boy [80]

1—The Dawn or Morning Chant

Starting out towards the Dawn Mountain,
Starting out towards the **White Corn Mountain,**
Starting out towards the Mixed Water Mountain,
Starting out towards the Pollen Mountain,
Like the Most-High-Power-Whose-Ways-Are-Beautiful Boy,
He starts out.
All is beautiful before him as he starts out.

Going out to the Dawn Mountain,
Going out to the White Corn Mountain,
Going out to the Mixed Water Mountain,
Going out to the Pollen Mountain,
Like the Most-High-Power-Whose-Ways-Are-Beautiful Boy,
He goes forth.
All is beautiful behind him.
All is beautiful before him.

He went to the Dawn Mountain,
He went to the White Corn Mountain,
He went to the Mixed Water Mountain,
He went to the Pollen Mountain,
Like the Most-High-Power-Whose-Ways-Are-Beautiful Boy,

---

[80] Interpreter's rendition of Chant V, both (1) the Dawn or Morning Chant, and (2) the Twilight or Evening Chant.

He went to them.
All was beautiful before him,
All was beautiful behind him,
All was beautiful above him,
All was beautiful below him,
All was beautiful around him,
As he went to them.

2—*The Twilight or Evening Chant*

[This is the same except for the names of the mountains:]

Starting out towards the Twilight Mountain,
Starting out towards the Yellow Corn Mountain,
Starting out towards the Mixed Chips Mountain,
Starting out towards the Pollen Mountain. . . .

Chant VI—The Chant Sung when Hasjelti Had a Bad Dream [81]

All is beautiful where I dream.
All is beautiful where I dream.
I dream amid the Dawn and all is beautiful.
I dream amid the White Corn and all is beautiful.
I dream amid the Beautiful Goods and all is beautiful.
I dream amid the Mixed Waters and all is beautiful.
I dream amid all the Pollens and all is beautiful.
I am the Most-High-Power-Whose-Ways-Are-Beautiful
And I dream that all is beautiful.

[The same chant is used for Hasjohon, but Twilight, Yellow Corn, Mixed Chips, Little Water and the Pollens are used.]

Chant VII—The Chant of the Plants

[This is used with the Third Sand Painting]

Now it is planned, in the East is the Corn.
Now it is planned, in the South is the Bean.
Now it is planned, in the West is the Pumpkin.
Now it is planned, in the North is the Tobacco.

2d. verse begins: Now it is made . . .
3d. verse begins: Now they dress it . . .
4th. verse begins: Now it is dressed.

THE COMING OF DEATH AND LIFE

Now the earth, which had been stretched, became solid, and the rivers flowed. Trees grew along the banks of the rivers, and flowers grew at the foot of the mountains with the rocks and the cliffs and other trees above them. The Mother Earth was very beautiful.

---

[81] Interpreter gave Chants VI and VII.

But just when everything on the earth was good and beautiful the people saw the first death. They remembered what the Sun had said. He had claimed the lives of all the living in payment for his light. The people wondered where the dead would go. "Is there another country?" they asked among themselves.

Now there came two beings called Alke'na ashi, Made Again, who looked like the Yei.[82] They were sent to the East to look for the dead body. They returned and said that they had not seen it. They were sent to the South and they brought back the same report. They were sent to the West and the North without success. They were asked to look into the Yellow World where they had come from. As they were about to start they felt the flesh around their knees pinched; but they went on. They had a strange feeling of sound, like a rale, in their throats. They felt rather than heard this sound, but they went on. Then there was a sensation in their noses, like an odor, but they went on to the place of emergence, and they looked down. Way below them there was someone combing his hair. He looked up and gave a little whistle, and they both experienced a strange feeling.

When the Alke'na ashi returned from the lower world they said that they had seen the spirit of the one who had died. They told just what they had felt and seen.

They warned the others saying that they must not try to return to the Country of the Past for it was not well to experience such sensations nor to see such things; and if in the future someone were to hear a whistle when no one was about that whistle came from an evil source, and a prayer should be said at once. If anyone should be so unfortunate as to see their double, or the form of a near relative in a vision, it would be a sign that dangerous things were about to befall them. Should this happen a chant must be held and prayers said in order to ward off the trouble.

The First People thought a great deal about this person's dying.

It had been First Man's and First Woman's plan to have everyone live forever. There was to have been no death. They could not understand this thing; and they were not satisfied.

First Man and First Woman got a piece of hard, black wood.[83] They made a smooth pole of it, and pointed it, as an arrow is pointed.

---

[82] Interpreter's note: The Alke'na ashi were originally the White Corn Girl and the Yellow Corn Girl, children of the White Shell Girl and the Wolf. They had been killed; but after twelve years the Holy Ones revived them, hence their name meaning Made Again. But they were revived as a boy and a girl. It is said that the Sun has their masks; and that their faces are never represented. This story is one of black magic; and these two are connected with death and evil.

Matthews (1897, p. 76): "To behold the dead is dangerous." Franciscan Fathers (1910, pp. 453-456).

[83] Interpreter's note: The petrified log is the fetish of the Goddess of Death.

Its length was the distance from a tall man's fingertip to his heart. After this pole was fashioned they dressed it; and they carried it on their shoulders to a lake. It was their plan to cast it into the water, and if the pole floated to the shore there would be no death; but if it sank down into the water, then death would remain. Now just as they raised it to cast it into the water the Coyote came to them. They saw that he carried a big stone ax. As they cast the pole into the water he threw the stone ax, saying: "Unless this stone ax returns to the surface there will be death." Now the stone ax remained in the lake, but the pole which First Man and First Woman had shaped and dressed returned to the shore. So it was decided that, although there would be death among the people of the earth, sometimes the very ill would recover because the log had floated back to the shore.

OLD AGE AND ILLNESS

First Man and First Woman had planned what was best for the sky and the earth and the people. And in the beginning whatever they planned became a fact; but after the Coyote interfered there were others who wished to have a part in the scheme of how the people should live.

The people's hair was to remain black. No one thought that the beings were to grow old. But there came a bird with a white head who said: "My grandchildren, look here, I am turning gray; I am growing old." This person was tsish'gai, the nut hatch; and after he had spoken old age descended upon many and their hair turned gray.

The people of the earth had been given strong white corn for teeth. They were made strong, solid and clean; and the plan was that they should remain so forever. But there came Old Man Gopher, Hastin Naazisi, with his face badly swollen for he was in great pain. "Oh, my grandchildren," he groaned, "I have a toothache. Pull my bad teeth for me." So they pulled the bad teeth, and only two remained that were really good. After that time it became a fact that people suffered from toothache, that teeth became old and worn.

So far there had been no babies born as they are now born. This was the plan. But a small bird with a red breast came and said: "My grandchildren, look at the blood that comes from me." It was a monthly occurrence after that, and it came to all female beings. The bird was chishgahi, the robin.

THE PLAN, OR ORDER OF THINGS

There was a plan from the stars down. The woman's strength was not to be as great as the man's strength. They could not attend to the planting and harvesting as the men could, therefore men would be worth more than women. And the plan was that women would propose marriage to men; but the Coyote came and said: "Brothers, listen, I have just married a woman." Again he spoiled their plan. Men propose marriage to women; but because of the older plan there are still cases where women go after men. Then not long after that, that which the bird, chishgahi, said came true; but they still thought it unwise to have babies born in the new way. Just then the Coyote came and said: "Brothers, I have a little baby."

Then they planned how a husband and a wife should feel toward each other, and how jealousy should affect both sexes. They got the yucca and the yucca fruit, and water from the sacred springs, and dew from all the plants, corn, trees, and flowers. These they gathered, and they called them tqo alchin, sacred waters. They rubbed the yucca and the sacred waters over the woman's heart and over the man's heart. This was done so they would love each other; but at the same time there arose jealousy between the man and the woman, his wife.

After that they planned how each sex would have its feeling of passion. A medicine was made and it was given to the man and to the woman. This medicine was for the organs of sex. The organ of the man would whistle; and then the organ of the woman would whistle. When they heard this each organ gave a long, clear whistle. After that they came together and the sound of the whistle was different. That is why the voices of the young boy and maiden are different; and it is why their voices change.

They planned that the rainbow should be used for a path whenever there was a deep canyon to cross; and it was to be thrown over a river and used as a bridge.

The gopher was told to remain hidden from the sun because he had caused toothache. That is why he stays down in the earth and seldom ventures out during the daytime.

First Man called the birds to him and said: "You who have wings, go to the mountains for your food and good living." So they went to the mountains. To each bird was given a name, and to each was given the directions of his way of living.

Then all the different types of lizards came. They were sent to the cliffs and told to make their homes among the rocks; and to every type of lizard was given a name.

First Man called the beavers and the otters and the underwater animals; and they were given their names and sent to the rivers and waters that would become their homes.

First Man and First Woman called the chiefs. First they called the wolf. They told him that, although he was a chief, he had done wrong, he had stolen. They told him that he should be called ma'itso, the big wanderer. "You shall travel far and wide over the face of the earth," they said.

The snake was called. They told him that because he could not travel the year round he would be given a bag of medicine, and, as he had no place to which he could tie it, they put it in his mouth. First Man gave this to him and told him that should the snake wish to harm someone he should swell this poison and cast it out. But for its possession he must pay by traveling but 6 months of the year.

Then First Man called another chief. "Come here, old man," he said. When this being came, First Man said that he should be named ma'i, the coyote.[84] But the coyote got angry and said: "Such a name!" And he declared that he would not have it; and that he would leave; but First Man called him back and told him that he would also be known as Atse'hashke', First Angry. After that the coyote felt better. He thought that he had a great name given him, and he went happily away, for he was told that he would know all the happenings on the face of the earth.

The bear was the next chief to be called. He was given a name but he was not satisfied. He became so angry that First Man used the word "shash" to quiet him. The bear repeated it four times, and he said that it had a strange sound, and when one said it aloud one had an awesome feeling. So he went off well content that "shash" should be his name.

Up to this time all beings were people and could remove their coat forms at will; [85] but because of wrongdoing they were made to keep their coats; and they were made to keep to their kind and to live among themselves in different parts of the earth.

When all the birds and animals had started out on their way, First Man called one little, gray bird back. It was tse na'olch'oshi, the little canyon wren, who had carried the cliff rock up from the Yellow World. First Man told him that, since he had been responsible for the cliffs he should make his home among the cliff rocks. And should anyone ever harm him he would have the power of getting even with him. That is why falling rocks sometimes harm people or animals.

All the people that First Man and First Woman named and sent forth now live on the earth. This is the way they planned the order of things.

---

[84] Recorder's note: Ma'i, the Coyote, is not to be confused with the Great Coyote or Wolf. This is the Coyote called First Angry or the Scolder, and appears in Zuni and other myths.

[85] This is the same in Zuni myths, etc.

THE AGE OF THE GODS, OR THE STORY OF THE TWINS

THE PEOPLE OF THE STONE HOUSES

Now a certain group of people had already built their houses of stone. They were known as the Blue Bird Clan People. The person at the head of this clan was a woman.[86] She had in her keeping the rock with the 12 months and the seasons marked on it. This rock had been given to her; and by it she was able to know the seasons, the months and the days of the year. Having this rock gave her the knowledge of what is beyond the blue sky, what is under the earth, and what is in the air and the water.

First Man spoke to this woman to whom had been given the Calendar Stone. "I shall go now," he said, "but my work is not yet finished. You will hear of me later." He was thinking that later he would form another tribe which would be called the Dîne'.

At this time all the people lived in peace; and all the work that First Man had done was good. He told the different peoples to go over the world and to live as each had been directed. Then he left them.

So it came about that people, human beings, went to the mesa country and built their homes in the caves in the cliffs. They grew to a great number. These people knew how to plant and to care for corn. They learned how to build great houses. They had all that they wanted on the earth. There was plenty, and there was no need to travel afar. It was because of this that they built their houses of stone.

At this time they grew in great numbers and they became a very strong people. But many of them practiced black magic; when they left their homes they traveled in the forms of the coyote, the bird, or the wildcat. It was while in these forms that they began to kill each other. Evil grew among them. They planned to kill First Man.

They learned to build ceremonial rooms, round in form and covered, with the entrance in the roof. They made a ventilator shaft to admit air. These round rooms or kivas were their meeting places, their places of prayer, and also, where some practiced black magic. They set a time when they would go into the kivas and hold meetings. This was the plan of First Man, but they did not know it. Now many of these people did not practice black magic; they were good people. These good men gathered together and formed a plan. They ground

---

[86] Informant's note: Esdzan at' a' was the medicine woman who was his Hopi ancestor. She belonged to the Blue Bird Clan. Her people lived in Blue House. Other people lived across the river. The mesa above the ruin of Blue House is today forbidden country for the Navaho. Ki'ndot liz is the name of Blue House.

a lot of chili,[87] and they dried and ground bile from eagles, hawks, mountain sheep, and mountain lions. This they mixed together to use as a poison. When the time came to go into the kivas, they, the good people, threw the mixture into the fire, and their relatives closed the smoke hole outside. The bad people were killed and the good ones remained unharmed. Now when the relatives of the bad people found what had happened they turned against First Man. They said that it had been his plan. "Now kill us," they said, "for we have lost our brothers and sisters." First Man heard them and he sent diseases which killed still more of the wicked ones. After the fourth plague was sent among them almost all who practiced black magic were destroyed.[88] The good people went south and grew their corn in other canyons; but after these evil things passed away many of the good people returned to the mesas to live.

THE STICK RACE [89]

It was at this time that they first played the game of the kicking of the stick. The people of the canyon came to play against the mesa people. The mesa people cleared a track on which they were to hold the stick races.[90] There were eight men from the mesa and eight men from the canyons; young men, and good runners all. Each team had four sticks, about a finger-length long and rubbed very smooth, which they kicked. There was always heavy betting. They bet arrows, corn, pottery, turquoise, shell and stone beads, arrow points, and, in fact, everything they owned. First the runners were barefoot; but one cheated and got the stick between his toes and kept running. After that the runners had to wear sandals. The soles of these sandals were of woven yucca fiber and the tops were of buckskin. They covered the soles with a kind of pitch. These running sandals were the first moccasins.

PRAYER STICKS [91]

One time the chief medicine woman, or her successor, looked at the Calendar Stone and told them what she had seen. She said that

---

[87] Informant's note: Chili, aze di chi lichi igi, the red, sharp medicine.

[88] Informant's note: First and second occupation of Mesa Verde. Also, destruction of a culture, see Lummis, 1910, Pecos myth, p. 137–146, note p. 137: "It was, indeed, the largest pueblo in New Mexico, having at one time a population of about 2000."

[89] Stevenson, M. C. (1904, p. 318).

[90] Informant's note: The race track was north of Spruce Tree Camp, Mesa Verde, Colo. And the winning house was one of the Far View Group of Ruins.

Recorder's note: The spring after these myths were recorded, Sam Ahkeah, the interpreter, and my son Deric O'Bryan, traced this track north from Far View House. Knowing what to look for, it was quite clear to follow. Also, some years before, Dr. J. Walter Fewkes, who excavated Far View House Ruin, said that the site must have belonged to a rich people, as there was so much turquoise, etc., found there.

[91] Recorder's note: For further data on prayer or medicine sticks, see page 141, this bulletin.

the people were to have prayer sticks. She showed them how they should be "dressed". She said the people must use them when they prayed. They should use them when they prayed for rain; they should plant them near springs and in their corn fields. Prayer sticks should be used with the sacred corn pollen. They were both holy.

WEAVING [92]

After the medicine woman told the people about the prayersticks she told them that there was a place in the underworld where two rivers crossed.[93] It was called ni tqin'kae tsosi, fine fiber cotton (Indian hemp).[94] There were two persons who brought the seed of that plant, they were spiders. They said that the people were to use the plant instead of skins for their clothing. So this seed was planted in the earth.

When the seeds were planted, the plant ripe, and the cotton gathered, the people shaped a little wheel, 3 or 4 inches in diameter, and they put a slender stick through it. This was used in the spinning of cotton. When they began spinning they pushed away from the body toward the knee. Then the chief medicine woman said: "You must spin towards your person, as you wish to have the beautiful goods come to you; do not spin away from you." For it was in their minds to make cloth which they could trade for shell and turquoise beads and she knew their thoughts. She said: "You must spin towards you, or the beautiful goods will depart from you."

There were two names given to the spindle, yudi yilt ya'hote, meaning, turning or shooting around with the beautiful goods. This the Spider Man suggested; but his wife said: "It shall be called by another name, ntl is yilt ya'hote, turning with the mixed chips."

After they had spun the thread they rolled it into good-sized balls. They brought straight poles and laid them down; one down, one opposite. They tied two other poles at the ends, making a rectangular frame. They rolled or wound the thread on two of the poles as the sun travels, east to west, over and under the poles. The Spider Man said that the ball of thread should be called, yudi yilt nasmas agha, rolling with the beautiful goods. His wife said: "No, it shall be called ntsli yilt nasmas agha, rolling with the mixed chips."

---

[92] Matthews (1884, pp. 371–391) ; Lummis (1910, p. 125) ; Amsden (1934, pp. 154–175).
Recorder's note: Matthews (1884), Whitman (1925), Parsons (1923), Lummis (1910), all refer to the Spider Woman.
[93] Informant's notes: See page 4. The Third World, Tqo alnaosdli, the Crossing of the Waters.
[94] Recorder's note: "Cotton" used as a name for all fibrous plants.

After the loom was finished the cross poles were erected and other poles placed on the ground to hold the loom frame solidly, and the loom was stretched and lifted into place.   Then the Spider Man said: "It shall be called yata ilth na dai'di, raising with the beautiful goods." His wife said: "It shall be called nil tliz na dai'di, raising with the mixed chips."

There is a notched stick running across, with a notch holding every other thread.   The Spider Man said: "It will be called yote biltz nes thon, looping with the beautiful goods."   His wife said: "From henceforth it shall be called nil tliz biltz nes thon, looping with mixed chips."   Then they used a narrow stick about two and a half feet long, and they wound the yarn or thread over it, and where there is no design they ran it along.   That was given the same name as the ball of thread.   The Spider Man held that it should have the same name as the ball; but his wife said: "No, it shall be called nil tliz nasmas agha." [95]

Then they used the wide flat stick for tapping down the thread. The Spider Man said: "It shall be called nil tliz na'ygolte"; but his wife said: "It shall be called nil tliz na'ygolte, twining with the mixed chips".   When they got this far with the weaving, the threads of the warp mixed together and were too near or too far apart.   So another kind of stick was used.   It had long, narrow teeth.   It was also used for the purpose of tapping down the thread.   The Spider Man said: "It shall be called yote yo'golte, hoeing with the beautiful goods." His wife said: "It shall be called nil iltz yo'golte."

The Spider Man said: "Now you know all that I have named for you. It is yours to work with and to use following your own wishes.   But from now on when a baby girl is born to your tribe you shall go and find a spider web which is woven at the mouth of some hole; you must take it and rub it on the baby's hand and arm.   Thus, when she grows up she will weave, and her fingers and arms will not tire from the weaving."   To this day that is done to all baby girls.

The weaving progressed, and they made all kinds of articles.   They used cotton and yucca fiber and Indian hemp.   These were the thread. They raised turkeys, and they used the feathers for feather blankets. They ate the turkey flesh for their meat.   They killed rabbits and cut the fur into strips, and they made fur blankets.   They wove different kinds of grass into mats for their floors, and also, to hang in front of the openings of their houses.   There were many kinds of weaving. The people lived peacefully and were happy in working out designs in the new art.   They raised great quantities of corn.   All this made them grow in number; they became a very strong people and their past troubles were forgotten; but this was not to last.

---

[95] Interpreter's note: Nil tliz means mixed chips of all stones, beads, etc.   Yote means all goods in a home, skins, blankets, etc.

THE MONSTERS APPEAR

About this time the people learned that two strange babies were born of separate mothers. They grew more rapidly than any baby they had ever seen, for they were giants. They were great, clumsy babies; their hair stuck out roughly; they were dirty and lazy and they acted like halfwits. They were called de baya yid etso. When they were fully grown they began to eat human beings. In fact, wherever they found people they picked them up, carried them to their home, and ate them.

Then there were two more strange babies born. They were like birds. These babies had yellowish eyes; their bills were yellow, as were their fingers; they grew to great size and their wingspread was enormous. They were male and female; and they, also, had separate mothers.

There was another baby born after that. It was like a ball. Actually it was a living rock. It had eyes, a mouth, a nose and ears. It grew to a great size and rolled over the earth. It was harmful to human beings, for it rolled over anyone who came near it.

Now the people remembered their own sins. First Woman had told her maidens what to use when they were without men. Plants were the fathers of the giants, turkey wings were the fathers of the great birds; and stones were represented in the great living rock. These were the fruits of their sins.

The giants made their home on the east end of Top Mesa.[96] The great birds made their home on a peak beyond La Plata Mountains.[97] The rolling rock made its home beyond the Carrizos.[98]

Arrow Ceremony Song for Medicine

In times past I lived long. Naye'nez ghani (the Elder Brother) made it.
In times past I lived long. Naye'nez ghani made it.
From the blue sky he sends the water which I put on the soles of your feet.
He made the pollen which is feared by all evils.
The most High Power Whose Ways Are Fearful, he made the medicine.

In times past I lived long.
Spring Boy, Tqo ba jish chini, made the medicine.
In times past I lived long.
He made a Water Woman.
The dew from the Water Woman I put on your heart.
The pollen he made is feared by all evils.
The Most High Power Whose Ways Are Fearful, he made the medicine.

---

[96] Interpreter's note: Yei tso, the Great Giant, whose father was the Sun, and whose home was on Red Mesa, near Farmington.

[97] Interpreter's note: The Giant Birds home was not Shiprock but on a peak beyond La Plata Mountains. The place is calles Tse'ten iss ka.

[98] Interpreter's note: The Rolling Rock made its home at a place called Knol ghi nee, beyond the Carrizos Mountains.

Recorder's note: The Arrow Ceremony, with its chants and sand paintings, comes here. Certain medicine men know this ceremony.

In times past I lived long.
The boy who was the grandchild of the old woman, Sani natle, made it.
In times past he lived long.
The Mist Woman he made whose dew I put on the palms of your hands.
The pollen he made is feared by all evils.
The Most High Power Whose Ways Are Fearful made the medicine.

In times past he lived long.
The young man, the brother of the Maiden who was turned into a Bear,
Tla'y ya ne ana, from the north, he made the medicine.
In times past he lived long.
The Mountain Woman he made, whose dew I put on the top of your hand.
The pollen he made is feared by all evils.
The Most High Power Whose Ways Are Fearful made the medicine.

(The fifth verse is the same as the first.)

WHEN THE COYOTE MARRIED THE MAIDEN [99]

After the first loom was made the people lived peacefully for about half a century. Then these strange creatures that were born began to eat the people. There is a little hill called tqnts'i'se ko just across the Mancos Canyon, which used to be a house. It was the home of 12 brothers. (On the top of this hill you can see a ruin.) The brothers were great hunters and hunted all over the mesas. They had one sister. The girl grew to be a beautiful maiden, and the holy men came from far and wide to ask her to marry them.

The maiden's name was Ataed'diy ini. When her brothers were away hunting she stayed at home alone. Now the Coyote came to the brothers and called out: "Brothers-in-law." He wanted this maiden to become his wife. Ataed'diy ini told him "No," for only the one who killed the giant would become her husband. The Coyote sat there with his head down for a moment, then he said: "Very well." He left her and went to the home of the giant.

When he saw the giant he said: "Brother, why do people outrun you? Now if you want me to, I can make you run as fast as I can. I have no trouble getting meat. I know of herbs [100] that will clean your system; and I will show you the medicine which I use on my legs to make me run fast."

Now this giant was very clumsy; he just walked along slowly and when people saw him they became so frightened that they were unable

---

[99] Informant's note: "A strong story from here on." Also, it is at this place in the story that the Dead Spirit Arrow Ceremony should come.

Matthews (1897, pp. 92–99).

Informant's note: There is a sand painting here. There are the chants of The Great Fearful Beings, The Holy Young Man, The Chasing of Evils, and The Traveling Darkness Chant.

[100] Recorder's note: Thistle family, *Babia woodhousi* Gray. After a hot tea of the above is drunk, copious vomiting follows. Another emetic: Cone flower, *Ratibida columnaris* Don; and *Ximenesia exauriculata* Rydb.

to run away. Because of this he could pick them up and put them in his big basket. The giant was, however, interested in the Coyote's plan.

The Coyote told the giant to build a sweat house; and while the giant was doing this the Coyote gathered the herbs. He also got a fresh leg of deer. When the sweat house was built and the hot stones placed inside they both entered it. Each took a good drink of the herb infusion the Coyote prepared. Now the drink made them nauseated and they vomited into the bowls each had taken into the sweat house. In the Coyote's bowl were found grasshoppers and lizards; the giant had vomited fat meat; but the Coyote hastily changed the bowls, and pulling aside the door covering and letting in the light, he showed them to the giant and said: "Look what you vomited. These things keep you from running swiftly". The giant said: "I see." They left the sweat house to get cool.

"Now," said the Coyote, "I will give you the medicine for your legs so that you will run swiftly." It was well with the giant. They returned to the sweat house; and the Coyote secretly took the deer's leg with him. The Coyote said: "Now comes the last step. This is very powerful medicine that I use." In the darkness he laid the deer's leg over his own leg and cut it in two. He put the giant's hand over the severed leg and showed him that it was indeed in two pieces. The giant said: "I see." The Coyote then quickly put the pieces of the deer's leg back of himself. He commenced spitting on his own leg and said: "Now get well, get well." After this he made the giant feel his perfect leg. The Coyote told the giant that now all the bad food was out of his stomach, and all the bad blood was out of his leg, and that he could outrun anything he saw. The giant said again, "I see."

After this the Coyote got out his knife and said that he would do the same thing for the giant's leg. He cut off one of them, and the giant groaned with great pain. The giant began to spit on the two parts. He tried to make them grow together. But the Coyote grabbed the giant's severed leg and ran away with it, saying: "I never heard of a bone growing together in a day."

The Coyote took the giant's leg to the maiden and told her that he had killed the giant. But the maiden said that before she would marry him she would have to kill him; and if he could return to life, then he could be her husband. The Coyote hung his head and covered his eyes with his hand for a moment. "Very well," he said, and he went away.

He went a short distance to the east side of the dwelling, and there he formed a little black mountain. He put a tunnel through the mountain, and he traveled still farther to the east. He then took out his lungs and heart and wrapped them in the Black Wind. He returned through the tunnel to the maiden's home. He said: "Now you can do as you wish with me." She got a club and killed him and threw his body on the ash dump. She went into her house, but he followed her. "Are you my wife now?" he asked her. But she said: "I have to kill you twice." So he left her and traveled to the south, and there he built a blue mountain, and he carved a tunnel through it. To the south he took out his heart and his lungs and he wrapped them in the Blue Wind. Only his body returned to the maiden's dwelling. He said: "Now do whatever you wish with me." So she killed him and cut him into pieces and threw them on the ash heap. But he followed her into her house and asked: "Are you my wife now?" But she said: "No, I must kill you three times." He left her and went out to the west, and there he built a yellow mountain; and he cut a tunnel through it; and in the west he left his heart and lungs wrapped in the Yellow Wind. He returned to the maiden and spoke to her as before. But again she killed him and ground the carcass with earth and threw it out. She returned to the house but he followed her. He said: "Are you my wife now?" But she answered: "No, four times I must kill you." This time the Coyote went to the north and built a white mountain. He cut a tunnel, as before. At its end he left his heart and lungs wrapped in the White Wind. His body returned to the maiden. "Now do with me whatever you wish," he said. This time, after she killed him, she cut him into pieces, ground the pieces with earth and threw it in all directions. Satisfied, she returned to her home; but after a little while the Coyote came in and said: "Now are you my wife?" The maiden asked him how he could do these things. He told her that after she became his wife he would show her his magic. She let the Coyote come. He became her husband and she became his wife. Then he took her to the east and showed her the mountain and the tunnel that he had made. And he took her to the south, and west, and north. She learned to do what the Coyote had done. He taught her his ways.

And now she was called Jikai'naazi'li, Tingling Maiden.

After a time they saw the brothers returning. The two were frightened and did not know what to do. The Coyote jumped over a pile of goods (blankets) and his wife covered him. When the brothers entered the house the fire was out, and the girl sat there looking strangely. She was not the same. The eldest brother asked in surprise: "Why is the fire out? Why is there nothing cooking? Why is the home not in order?"

The eldest brother told the others to get wood. The brothers did this and built a fire of cedar wood. When the fire was burning the odor of coyote was strong inside the house. The eldest brother told the others to throw out the wood and to bring fresh wood. A second fire was built of fresh wood, but still they smelled coyote. They threw the firewood out again and they gathered the branches of trees, but it did no good; they gathered the topmost branches, but still the odor of coyote was strong in the dwelling. The eldest brother then cursed the coyote. "The Coyote with his ugly odor is everywhere," he said. Just then the Coyote threw the cover off and came out, saying: "What is the trouble, my brothers-in-law?"

Now the brothers did not know what to say. They sat around the fire with their heads down. In a short time they went out and built themselves a little shelter, and they camped there that night. The house they left for the Coyote and his wife.

The following morning when the brothers went out to hunt, the Coyote said that he would go with them. The eldest brother told the others that from then on they could only expect trouble. "But it is our duty to hunt," he said, "and we must go and hunt today."

Now in those days all was sacred and holy. There was a rainbow, formed like a young man, lying by the canyon's edge. They threw him over the canyon and crossed on him. After the brothers had crossed the canyon they heard the Coyote calling far behind them. The eldest brother said: "I guess that we had better bring him across before he does something worse than howling." So they went back and brought him over the rainbow.

They were on a mesa north of the Mancos Canyon when the Coyote came chasing a big ram. (There were many mountain sheep there at that time.) One of the brothers pulled his bow and aimed his arrow at the ram. He shot the arrow and killed the ram. Now in those days the horn of the mountain sheep was filled with fat, delicious marrow; and all the hunters prized it as their favorite fat. Whoever killed a sheep, to him went the horns. When the Coyote saw that the ram he had been chasing had been killed by one of the brothers he claimed the horns. The brother spoke to the Coyote and told him to behave like a man once in a while. "There was a rule that whoever kills a sheep gets the horns." With this the brother began to cut the pair of horns. The Coyote stood to one side and whispered: "Turn to bone. Turn to bone." The brother cut and cut, but the horn had turned to solid bone. And where he had tried to cut it ridges formed. That is why there are rings on mountain sheep horns today.[1]

The brothers dressed the sheep and rolled the meat into a little ball. They told the Coyote to take the meat to his wife and to tell her to

[1] Recorder's note: In another version of this story, heard some years earlier, it is exact up to the point of the mountain sheep horn. In that respect it was like Matthew's version. The horn was split and the marrow in it was eaten. The Coyote tried to do this but failed. The horn became hard and corrugated. In anger he beat the ground with it, thus forming the many canyons of Mesa Verde.

have it ready for them when they returned. One of the brothers took the Coyote across the canyon. He warned him by no means to put the meat ball down on the way. But no sooner had the brother departed than he put down the meat ball. Immediately it turned into the big pile of meat. The Coyote thought that he could do what the brothers had done. He tried to roll it into a little ball again; but he could not do it. He walked over to the canyon's edge and he saw that way down in the bottom of the canyon a big game was going on. There were people in the canyon playing this game. They were the Swallow People or cliff dwellers. The Coyote called down to them; he said that they were certainly an ugly people—the men and their wives alike. He said that his wife was beautiful and light of skin.

All this made the cliff people very angry, and they decided to get rid of him, to kill him. While the Coyote sat up there calling out insults, two young spider men climbed up the wall of the canyon; and from the cliff's edge they spun a long, high fence strong as woven mats. It was very high and very strong, and it extended for a long way back of the Coyote. After the two young men had finished they returned to the bottom of the canyon. Then all the cliff people went after the Coyote who was still sitting there on the rim mocking them. He insulted them and he kicked at them and he said that not one in all that crowd could catch him. Just as they reached the rim of the canyon, away he went as fast as he could run. But he came up against the spider men's fence and it threw him back. He tried to jump over it but failed. Now the cliff people were very near. He tried and tried to jump over the fence, and the fourth time he fell back among the cliff people. They caught him and killed him. They cut his hide into strips and made headbands of the fur. That is why swallows have a little ring around their heads. They have worn these little light bands ever since they made them out of the Coyote's hide.[2]

THE MAIDEN WHO BECAME A BEAR [3]

When the brothers returned that night they entered the house. Not seeing the Coyote among them their sister went out to look for him; not finding him she asked her eldest brother what they had done with her husband. The eldest brother said: "We sent him back with the meat a long time ago. We thought that you would have the meat cooked for us by now." The woman looked straight at her brothers and told them that they had killed the Coyote. The brothers said: "No, sister, we have told you the truth. We sent him back with the meat early in the day." But she accused them four times of

[2] Recorder's note: There is a pictograph in Navaho Canyon, Mesa Verde. It is believed to be the place where the Swallow People killed him.
[3] Matthews (1897, pp. 90–103); Lummis (1910, p. 200).

killing her husband. Four times they gave the same answer. Then she went to the rainbow path and there she found the meat. From there she tracked the Coyote to the canyon's edge and she found where he had been killed by the Swallow People.

After the woman left her brothers to go look for the Coyote the eldest brother said: "Listen now to my words: our sister is about to do something still more evil."

When the woman returned to the house she told her brothers that the people in the canyon had killed her husband. She would not sit down in the home. She prepared herself to go against the cliff people. First, she took her sewing awls and sharpened them; then she hid her heart and lungs as the Coyote had taught her, and turned herself into a great bear with sharp teeth and claws, and she went forth against the people of the canyon.[4] When she came among them they shot at her with their arrows, but they did not harm her. When she returned home she turned back into her woman form. But every night she went out in her bear form and killed the cliff people with her teeth and claws; however, she did not eat them as a wolf or bear would have done.

It was then that the people moved into the caves in the cliff walls. The Rainbow's strength was their strength. The people, in those days, used a rainbow for their ladder as well as for their bridge. They used it and it was not difficult for them to carry up their goods and to build houses in the caves. For a long time the people abandoned their homes on the floor of the canyon; but the bear woman followed them. She would dig up through the earth and kill them. After that they built their homes of rock in the caves.

Always when she returned to her brothers she was in her woman form. But her name was now Esdza'shash nadle, the Woman who Became a Bear.

Soon she went out even during the day to kill people. She became so terrible that the Spider People, the Lizard People, and the Swallow People built high in the sides of the canyons where she could not reach them. After a time the brothers became frightened. They did not know what to do. But they knew that their turn would come; that she would kill them too. The eldest brother had a plan. He, together with the other brothers, pushed the ashes of the fire to one side and they dug a hole under the fireplace. They hid the youngest brother in this hole which had four sides to hold back the earth. They covered the hole with a slab over which they put earth; they then raked the ashes over it and built a fire. Then they went to the east of their dwelling.

---

[4] Interpreter's note: The pictograph in the Mancos Canyon, Mesa Verde, tells the story.

When the Bear Woman returned no one was in the house. She went to relieve herself and said: "Whichever way the water runs, that is the direction my brothers have taken." It showed east; so she followed in her bear form. She tracked them and she killed the 11 brothers. She saw that the youngest was missing. She returned to the house. Again she went to relieve herself, and she said: "Whichever way it flows there my brother is." But it neither flowed nor fell. So she went into the house and tore the rocks out. She found her youngest brother under the firestone.

The Bear Woman spoke kind words to him. "Come out, my brother," she said, "your hair looks dirty; it needs washing and dressing; let me care for it." The little breeze whispered in the boy's ear: "She has killed your 11 brothers, and now she wants your life." The little breeze stayed on the boy's ear and told him to have weapons ready when she began to comb his hair. It told him also, to loosen the string ties of his loin cloth. "She will place you facing the sun when she starts to comb your hair; but you must sit so that you can see her shadow." The woman made her brother sit facing the sun; but he said: "Sister, the sun is too bright for my eyes." After four times she agreed to let him sit where he chose. He sat where he could watch her shadow. She got the grass brush, which they used for the hair, and she brushed his hair once or twice; and out grew her lips to the shape of a bear's mouth with long teeth. The boy turned and said: "What is it, sister?" She said: "Oh, I am just sleepy." The breeze was now busy in the boy's ear telling him what would happen and what he should do. He was to be saved; but the price paid was the lives of his 11 brothers.

The boy was told that the fourth time that he caught her changing into the form of a bear he must jump up and run as fast as he could to the place where she had hidden her heart and lungs. "About the moment when she is about to catch you, you will jump over a big cactus. She will have to go around it and you will gain ground. The second time you will jump over a big growth of yucca; the third time, over a log; and the fourth time you will jump over a big boulder."

Now the boy watched her shadow, and each time that he caught her changing into the bear form he turned and looked at her and she became the woman. After the fourth time he had his muscles set, and jumped away from her. Sure enough she grabbed his belt; but the tie loosened. She was near him when he reached the cactus. He jumped over it; she ran around it. The second time she was near him he jumped over the yucca; the third time he jumped over the fallen log; and the fourth time, over the great boulder. Then her heart became nervous, and the chipmunk who was guarding it screamed. The heart and the lungs were beating up and down just ahead of the boy. They were covered with oak leaves.[5] The Bear Woman cried out: "Oh, brother, brother, stop! There are my heart and my lungs. There is my life."

Now when the boy saw the leaves beating up and down in fright he jumped over them, and he shot his arrow into them. The Bear Woman fell, and the blood gushed out of her mouth and nostrils. The boy returned near her, and the little breeze told him to stop the blood. It must not flow, for if it met the blood from her heart she would become whole again. So the boy pulled the Bear Woman's carcass away. He was angry. He spread her legs and cut out her sex organs. He said: "You have the sex organs of a woman, and great trouble has come of it." He tossed it to the top of a tree and said: "The people of the earth shall use you henceforth." It became the pitch [6] that is found on cedar and pinon trees. Then he cut off her breasts and said: "You have a woman's breasts and still you have caused great trouble." He tossed them to the top of a tree and said: "The people of the earth shall use you." And they became pinon nuts.[7]

After these things happened many people planned to leave the mesas. They were afraid of the Woman who became a bear. They buried the Calendar Stone; they wrapped their dead; and leaving their belongings, they went away. But before they left they drew pictures on the rocks of all the things that trouble came from.

Now only the Swallow People and the Lizard, Snake, and Spider People remained. All the others said that they would never return to make the mesa country their home. They moved into Montezuma Valley and built their homes around Ute Mountain. Their main dwellings were Yucca House and a place near a spring east of Ute Mountain. They multiplied and their homes covered quite a lot of territory. They moved to places where they found good water, good building material, and where their plants would grow. But always they came to where their chief person lived. This was a place west of Dolores called Sage Brush Spring.[8] They moved their chief, or

[5] Franciscan Fathers (1912, p. 71).

Matthews (1886, pp. 767–777): Oak, *Quercus undulata* Torrey, order Cupuliferae. Tseh chel, or chet chel, is oak. Also, tseh chel ink lizi is hard oak; tseh chel inglizi baka is male oak.

[6] Informant's note: There is a chant here. There is also a chant at the place where the Coyote hides his heart and lungs. The words are the story. They sing this chant in the Fire Ceremony.

Matthews (1886, pp. 767–777): *Juniperus virginiana* L., kat nee ay li, is strained juniper; Kat is *Junipersus communis* L. Kat dil tah'li is cracked juniper, *Juniperus pachyphrea* Torrey.

[7] Informant's note: Pinon is called cha'ol. The pinon nut is called neschi, or nechi bina.

[8] Informant's note: Here is the list of the names of the places where the people of the mesas moved to: Mesa Verde, the great center; Moki Springs ruin, about 2 miles west of Towoac; Yucca House, about 3 miles east of Towoac; McElmo Canyon; Sage Brush Springs, near Dolores; near the foot of Elk Mountain; peak above Hesperus; Aztec ruin; Blue House, above Farmington; ruin under cliff southeast of Farmington; Pueblo Bonito; ruin in canyon due east of Bonito; from there the Jemez people branched off, they moved

head person of their tribe, there. This person was considered sacred, and kept away from the sun and the light all of the time. Where he lived sacred stones were placed at his feet, at his out-stretched arms and head. Prayer sticks guarded his body. Then bluebird feathers were set around him.[9] Whatever he said was done. They lived for a time at Sage Brush Spring; but corn did not grow well there; living was difficult. They moved to the foot of Elk Mountain.

THE STORY OF NOQOILPI, THE GREAT GAMBLER [10]

The giants and the monsters were still in the country when the people built their homes near Elk Mountain. Because of this they were not contented; they planned to travel to the place where they had emerged from the underworld and build their dwellings there. Now, as before, some of the people remained; but the chief and the main body moved on. They built Kin ty eli, Aztec, a great dwelling. But after some time they heard of a land of little snow and plenty of seeds that could be used as food, so the main body of the people moved again and built Kin dotl'ish, Blue House, so called because of its bluish color. It is above Farmington on the San Juan.[11] They built again under a cliff which is opposite the town of Farmington. Then the main body of people moved to the Chaco Canyon and built Tse be'an y i, the Place Where There Are Poles that Hold Up the Rock, Pueblo Bonito, and many other dwellings.

They built Tse be'an y i for their chief who never stepped out into the sunlight. They had plenty of seeds and they grew good crops there. All the beads and the turquoise and the beautiful goods that they got below, where the Two Rivers Cross, they held sacred with their chief.

The Sun seeing this became jealous of this chief whom he had never seen. He wanted to own the beads that belonged to this person, even though he had the perfect turquoise—for he was the Turquoise Boy.

At this time there was a very poor woman living near Tse be' na y i called As san' no ho tlo dei, She Goes Around Gathering Seeds. Another name for her was the Rock Woman. She belonged to the

to Pecos; reoccupation of Bonito; below Shiprock on mesa; south of Little Shiprock; in canyon south of Carrizos; Navaho Mountain; Keetseel; Begashibito; Hopi Villages. This list was checked by the interpreter.

[9] Martin (1936, pp. 46–55). Recorder's note: Fewkes told me that when excavating the ruin called New Fire House, Mesa Verde, Colo., he found the remains of a young girl wrapped in a robe made of bluebird feathers.

[10] Matthews (1889, pp. 89–94): The Great Gambler, Noqoilpi; The Navaho Gambling Songs. Matthews (1897, pp. 82–87: Noqoilpi, He Who Wins Men. Wetherill and Cummings (1922, vol. 14, pp. 132–136). Whitman (1925, pp. 103–117); Noqoilpi, the Winner of Men, of the Great Gambler. Cushing (1923, pp. 163–170).

Informant's note: The Great Gambler became the Mexican, and this explains his calling out "Adios" when he left.

[11] Informant's note: The people of Blue House came to gamble with Noqoilpi. They had two great shells.

clan Hada'ho ni gee, Banded Rock or Rock with Rings. After her there were no more descendants of the clan. Now the Sun secretly visited this woman; and when the people noticed that she was with child, the men joked among themselves. They said: "That is going to be my baby." "No, it will be mine. I visited her first." Or: "She is related to me. I want a gift. What will you give me?" "After the gift is made to me, the child can be yours." And when she brought forth a baby boy the men continued to tease each other; they did not know that the child's father was the Sun.

As the boy grew his mother taught him to run a great distance each morning. When he reached young manhood he was beautiful and tall; but his mother being poor, he was poor also; and when he went about the people laughed at him, and the men still said: "No, he is not your son, I was there first."

There was a holy flylike insect called Dotso, whose face was white, and body hairy. One day this fly asked the boy: "Why don't you go to the home of your father?" Now this fly was all-wise and knew everything.[12] And one day the Sun lowered the rainbow to where this young man stood. The youth stepped on the rainbow and was raised to the home of his father.

Now the Sun, who was the young man's father, had a great plan. He wanted to get hold of all the beads belonging to the people, together with their chief, whom he had never seen. First he gave his son two big, perfect turquoises, the shape and the size of a dollar, for his earrings. Then the Sun began to teach this young man all the gambling songs and chants, and also the chant with which to draw people to himself.

The Sun taught his son also, all the games.[13] In the seven sticks,[14] a game like dice, two sides were black and two sides were white. The young man had two sets of these sticks, one set was all white and the other set was all black. If they turned white it was he who won; if black, they won. He was to use these.

There was the game of rolling the ring.[15] The players threw a ring and ran after it, casting their sticks. The stick closest to the ring won. This was for him also.

Another game was played with a stick the shape of the rainbow. When it fell one way, one side won; and the opposite. It was like matching coins.

---

[12] Informant's note: In the Hand Shaking Ceremony they use the pollen that has been placed on the fly, Dotso, when they want to find the cause of the illness or trouble.

[13] Culin (1907, pp. 92–97, note 9, pp. 346–349, 385–386, 457–460; note 10, pp. 623–624, 668).

Stevenson, M. C. (1904, pp. 317–349); Franciscan Fathers (1910, pp. 478–389).

[14] Whitman (1925, p. 108) follows Matthews. He calls the First Game "thirteen chips."

[15] Informant's note: This game is called nanzoz. There are two long poles, one red, one black, and a single hoop. A many-tailed string, called turkey claw, is attached to the end of each pole. The winner of this game is the one who entangles the rolling hoop in his turkey claw. (See pp. 56, 57, this bulletin.)

The fourth game was that of kicking the stick.[16] There were to be two tracks made, like the tracks on Chapin Mesa (Mesa Verde). One of these was to be for the Gambler; and the other was to be for the people.

The fifth game was that of hitting a ball against a pole,[17] a good-sized pole.

The sixth game was the guessing game.

The seventh game was that of the two planted sticks.[18] Where one stick was planted solidly the other was loose. Two runners run to the sticks and grab the one they think is loose.

The eighth game was the foot race.

When the young man had learned all these games the Sun sent him back to Tse be'na y i. At once he started to gamble. For a time the people tried to buy his turquoise earrings, they were so pretty. But he would always say: "If you can win them you can have them." When he chanted the people came to him. Soon he was called the Great Gambler, for he won all their corn and goods. He even won the children and the women and the men for his slaves. They worked for him and they built a great house for him.[19] He had a great many wives and the men built homes for them also. Everyone worked for him. He won the Male Rain, the Female Rain, the Rainbow, the rivers, the mountains, and all the earth. The rest of the land went dry for it only rained where he lived. He had good corn and beautiful flowers. He even won the wife of the chief and the chief himself, together with his prayer sticks and his beads. There was also a big, round turquoise[20] that stood as high as a man, and it had 12 feathers standing around it. The Sun told his son that when he should win the great turquoise it should be his. It was the most precious of all. It was the last thing that the Gambler won from the people.

Then the Sun came down, and he said: "My son, this is what I want. This is the only thing that I want. Now give it to me." But the Gambler had grown to be a very strong man, and instead of turning the great turquoise over to his father, he said: "You will be the next I will gamble with. Come on."

The Sun was very angry. He said no word, but returned to his home. After he arrived at his home he was still very angry with Nilth wilth dine, the winner of Men, because he had not succeeded in getting the great, perfect turquoise.

---

[16] See pp. 59–60, this bulletin.
[17] Informant's note: This ball game may be played in the ball courts.
[18] Informant's note: This game is called Push-on the Wood, or Planted Sticks.
[19] Informant's note: This is Pueblo Bonito.
[20] Recorder's note: Certain medicine men say two giant, spiral shells; and that the Gambler won these from Blue House and Broad House.
Boekelman (1936, p. 27) ; Matthews (1897, pp. 195–208).

Now over on a mesa near Farmington there lived another people called Hada hun estqin, the Mirage People. There was a woman there, one of the Mirage People, whom the Sun visited. Nine days after he visited her she gave birth to a baby boy. (Later the days became months, and women gave birth to children at the end of 9 months.) This boy grew to be a young man at the end of 15 days. (Later the days became years, and boys begin their manhood at 15 years.)

(Sandoval, the informant, said that chants are sung at this point in the story.)

Now this boy was born because the Sun had another plan. He wished this son to win back all that the Great Gambler had won. After this boy grew to young manhood he was told that his father wished him to come to his home. So the young man went to the home of his father, the Sun. He found his sister there. She shaped him to the perfect form of a man, in fact the perfect image, or twin, of the Great Gambler. (Even today there is a saying: "I come. Will my sister shape me with her bread?" And the answer is: "Have you some pack rat's meat?" (In other words, Do you bring a small gift?)

The Sun made his young son six sticks. They had instead of a white face like the first set, a black face. The seventh stick was red and black. The Sun said: "Now my son, you shall use these against the Gambler. But first, before you begin to gamble, you must make me an offering which shall be a white shell basket with mixed chips of stone inside it. Place it where the bunch grass grows. Place it in the center of a bunch of this grass, and then say a prayer." The Sun taught him the prayer. After that the Sun told him to whom to offer gifts.

The young man was to take the skin of a baby buffalo to the bat as his gift. That is why the bat still wears a furry coat. The young man was to use the bat in the first game to be played with the Gambler.

Next he was to give a present to the Big Snake. His gift was to be a precious red stone. That is why the snake wears the red stone on his forehead, and the female snake, on the ears. The snake which the boy was to use in the ring game, was to take the place of the willow ring generally used. He had buckskin wrapped around him, with two little openings for his eyes. They were to throw the rings and to race after them, stick in hand, so that when the rings were about to stop rolling, they could cast their sticks at them. The snake was to roll over the boy's stick. But the boy must be quick to grab the ring or the Gambler, in anger, would throw it onto the rocks in the canyon. The boy must follow these instructions carefully so that no harm would come to the snake. When the Gambler casts his stick, the boy must cast his stick farther on and say: "Bit ade, bit ade. I will win, I will win." Since that time all gamblers say that when they cast their sticks.

The shape of the stick used in the third game is shown in figure 4. It is called wo nal'gili. The Gambler had weighted one side of his stick so that he would always win. The next step was for the young man to take black jet and present it to the measuring worm, wo'shiyishi. He was to go into the young man's stick and fall opposite the Gambler's side. It is because of the gift of the jet that the measuring worm's head is black.

FIGURE 4.—The stick used in the Third Game.

Next the young man was to take white shell to na'at e'e, the brown rat. This rat was to enter the youth's ball used in the fourth game, so that the ball would roll into the hole. The youth was told not to hit the ball, but just behind it; then the ball would roll into the hole, and he would win.

The sign the Gambler used in the guessing game is shown in figure 5. It was a picture of one of the chief sacred beings that the Gambler had won. Ash'ke chili was his name.[21] He had a bill like a crow, and in his hands he held pretty flowers, four in each. The first four circles are the water jars—the black, the blue, the yellow, and the white. They contain the Male Rain. The next four contain the

FIGURE 5.—The sign the great Gambler used in the Guessing Game.

[21] Interpreter's note : Ash'ke chili, the Guard of the water jars, is the Zuni God of Dew.

vapors—black, blue, yellow, and white. They were the Female Rain. The ninth jar contained all the bad medicine that the Gambler used, his black magic.

Now the Gambler used such a picture for the guessing game. Here the young man was told to make an offering to the little breeze so that he would sit on his right ear, and help him guess all that the Gambler put before him. The gift to the little breeze was the mixed chips of stone.

The next game was that of the planted sticks (fig. 6). The youth was to present the woodpecker, tsil kal'i, a precious red stone, which he still carries with him. He was to be used in this game. Now the cutworm, nada'bich osh, was to dig down and cut loose the roots of the young man's stick, the planted part of the solid stick; and the Black Wind, nlch i dilqil, was to enter the Gambler's stick, the loosened one, and blow and blow until the roots fastened firmly into the ground. A piece of jet was given to the cutworm for his trouble; and to this day he carries a black spot on his head.

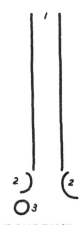

1. THE RACE TRACK.
2. THE TWO STICKS.
3. THE GAMBLER'S HOUSE.

FIGURE 6.—The game of the Planted Sticks.

Now all was ready, all that was to be used by the young man.

By this time the people of the whole country were the slaves of the Gambler; they lived in a great community. They got together all the sacred beings, the Sun as the chief, and they planned to move against the Gambler.

The young man was to have two beautiful maidens to use to bet against the Gambler. They were the daughters of Hasjelti and Hasjohon. These two Yei gave their daughters in the Sun's plan; but they would not consent to do so for a long time. After they agreed they sent the Black Wind to the home of the Gambler to see how he was dressed. They dressed the young man like the Gambler. The young man had already been shaped like the Gambler in the house of the Sun so that he could win the world. Now the Yei dressed the young man like the Gambler from feet to headdress.

The people thought of the rolling ring game. They went to Hasjelti, and they asked him for his ring; but he refused to let them have it. "No," he said, "the Gambler would not look at mine; he has his own rings." But he told them to go to Hasjelbai, also called Tqo'neinili, the Water Sprinkler, who is the Delight Maker or Sacred Clown. He has these two names. He could be found at the end of the trail; and he would have his rings with him. When the messengers found him he was humming: "Han'y ogana, han'y ogana" (All alone, all alone). Away he went after his ring; he cast his stick, and then sat down. He crossed his leg over his knee and put his hand over his mouth. Now he had his rings well soaked, and they were quite wet. He gathered up his rings and gave them to the messengers. When they returned to Hasjelti he said: "The Gambler will not look at these rings; he has his own."

Now everything was ready and they set out for the Gambler's home.

They sent the bat ahead. He was to hide in the home of the Gambler. In the first game he was to catch the Gambler's sticks with one wing and drop the young man's sticks from the other wing. So to be ready for his part, the bat flew out in the night to hide in the Gambler's home.

They were all ready to be on their way when someone came. He was the mountain rat. He said: "I am still here. Why have you kept this secret from me?" They gave him white beads so that he would not feel badly for having been neglected. They were about to start off again when an owl hooted just ahead. He was offended because he had not been included in their plan. They gave him also white beads. All gamblers do this today. They place white beads in rats' nests and in owls' nests. This is to assure them luck when they want to gamble.

They started out again; but one said: "Wait a minute, the Gambler has many spies working for him." They took mixed chips of stone and presented them to the Black Wind. He was to blow dust into the eyes of the spies so that the people could go on their way without being seen.

Now it was the turn of the young man who was shaped and dressed like the Gambler to act. Each morning at dawn the Gambler's head wife came to the spring with her water jar. When the spies' eyes were full of dust the young man passed them, and hid in the spring and waited for the woman. She came to the spring and went down to the water. He followed her. He said: "Give me some water."

She reached down and gave him a gourd full of water, for she took him to be her husband. He sipped some of the water, and then threw the rest over her, over her clothing. She shook the water from her clothing and said: "This is one of your wicked deeds." She took him to be her own husband, and she went and lay down with him. The young man did this to "split the mind" of the Gambler.

When the woman carried the water home she found her husband asleep in their house. She said: "You naughty thing! You made fast time in returning." He jumped up and said: "Someone has been with my wife. Who is he?" She answered: "Someone like you came. I saw him, that is all." "No," he said, "someone has visited you." Now each day that the Gambler gambled he won many men; so he said: "Well, I may find him today. Then I will have him in my power."

When the young man returned to the people the little breeze, which is our life breath today, sat behind his ear, for the Sun had told his son that he would be with him in everything that happened.

They watched until they saw a big dust storm coming. The spies' eyes were filled with dust and they could see nothing. And there was a great crowd at the entrance of the Gambler's dwelling before he knew it.[22]

The young man stepped inside the home of the Gambler. When he entered, the wife of the Gambler, whom he had been with that morning, was grinding corn. Just then she looked up and smiled. The breeze said: "She smiles because she knows that you are the man she met in the early morning." The breeze continued: "The Gambler saw this smile and he is getting up. He is jealous. He thinks that you are the man who was with his wife at the spring." The young man stepped up to the Gambler and said: "My Brother, I came for that big piece of turquoise called ha da thee." Now this was the most precious and the last thing that the Gambler had won, the turquoise that the Sun wanted. The Sun had told the young man that, when he won it, it was to be his.

When the Gambler got to his feet he saw the crowd of people. He said: "Where are those ugly things, the spies, that I placed around this dwelling?" He called them; and when they came to him they said that the dust storm was dreadful. They had seen no one pass.

The Gambler then turned to the young man and said: "Very well. It shall be as you wish; you are the one I will gamble with." With that he brought forth his basket and shook his sticks in it.

---

[22] Informant's note: Different chants are sung at this part in the story. Chants are also used when they dress the young man.

THE FIRST GAME, THAT OF THE SEVEN STICKS

"Now," said the Gambler, seeing the two beautiful maidens that the young man had with him, "we shall bet our wives." He bet all his wives and servants against the two maidens. The young man bet the two maidens and the whole crowd that came with him. After the bets were made the young man said: "Very well. I am willing to lose; but you shall have to throw the sticks as high as the roof beams. You can not throw the sticks knee high, or shoulder high, or as high as a man can reach, but to the roof beams. The Gambler looked up and around and said: "All right, I will throw the sticks up to the roof beams." "Then," said the young man, "we must both look down on the ground, to be able to see the sticks as soon as they fall." The Gambler looked around and then said: "All right. That goes."

The Gambler shook his basket and said: "Mine is white, mine is white." And up he threw his sticks to the roof beam. The bat caught the Gambler's sticks and dropped the young man's sticks. The Gambler grabbed the sticks and swore and said: "This time mine is black, mine is black." The young man called out: "Very well. Mine is white, mine is white." The Gambler threw the sticks a second time; and the bat caught the young man's sticks and threw down the Gambler's sticks. The young man grabbed the white sticks as they landed and said: "You are the loser. You are the loser; and it is by your own sticks that you lose." The Gambler said: "I lost! I lost!"

THE SECOND GAME, THAT OF THE ROLLING RING [23]

The young man's stick is called the turkey feet [24] (fig. 7, *upper*). The name of the Gambler's stick is dot'tloie, meaning hairy (fig. 7, *lower*).

To continue: the young man picked up his stick. The snake was in his ring. The Gambler got his own ring; but the young man said: "No. This time you will use my ring." So the Gambler cast his ring to one side and said: "Very well."

When the Gambler picked up his stick he went around exercising his arms and legs; and all during this time he chanted in a whisper:

> I am walking amid all the beautiful goods.
> A white bead gambling stick is in my hand.
> It is tied with the white bead string.
> I am walking amid all the beautiful goods,
> With the white bead stick in my hand.
> The white bead ring is on top of the stick.
> Today luck is on my side.

---

[23] Culin (1907, pp. 457–460), hoop and pole.
[24] Franciscan Fathers (1910, pp. 482–484).

Then he reached out and turned just as the sun travels; he motioned to all that he saw and he drew it to his body.[25]

After this the Gambler bet against the young man all that he had won, all that he had. Just the one bet. All was ready for the game. The two men were standing at the race track, eager to roll the ring. The young man threw his ring and away they raced after it. The Gambler was in the lead and he cast his stick. The young man cast his stick ahead of the Gambler's stick. The ring rolled over the Gambler's stick and landed on the young man's stick, on the very center of it. Now after the sticks are cast the racers stop and watch the ring. So when the ring turned over the young man's stick, he ran and

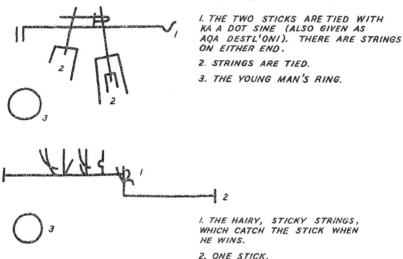

1. THE TWO STICKS ARE TIED WITH KA A DOT SINE (ALSO GIVEN AS AQA DESTL'ONI). THERE ARE STRINGS ON EITHER END.

2. STRINGS ARE TIED.

3. THE YOUNG MAN'S RING.

1. THE HAIRY, STICKY STRINGS, WHICH CATCH THE STICK WHEN HE WINS.

2. ONE STICK.

3. THE GAMBLER'S RING.

FIGURE 7.—The sticks used in the game of the Rolling Ring: *upper,* young man's stick; *lower,* Gambler's stick.

grabbed it. The Gambler was very angry. He made for the ring; but the young man held it behind him with his left hand and pushed the Gambler back with his right elbow. He said: "Wait a minute, Brother, what are you going to do with my ring? All the losers that came up against you did not do this. When they lost, you got them. They were game." So all that the Gambler said was: "All right. We will go inside now."

THE THIRD GAME, THAT OF THE STICK THE SHAPE OF THE RAINBOW

They started for the house of the Gambler. He had lost twice now. Once inside he bet that he would recover all that he had lost and all that the young man possessed in goods and friends. When the bet was settled they entered a room where the Gambler brought

---

[25] Interpreter's note: A splendid example of sympathetic magic.

out the bent stick which he used. But the young man said: "Wait a minute, Brother, it is my stick that we will use today, not yours." The Gambler tossed his stick to one side; and the young man took out his stick with the measuring worm inside it. This stick was made so that when it was tossed up it would hit the ground in an upright position, then fall to one side or the other. When all was in readiness the young man tossed his stick into the air; when it struck the ground it stood up. The Gambler saw this and he was angry, furious, in fact. He jumped for the stick, and was about to seize it, when the young man hit his hand aside with his right hand and picked up the stick with his left. He said: "Brother, this is my gambling stick, not yours." The Gambler was wet with sweat; he had lost three times.

THE FOURTH GAME, THAT OF HITTING THE BALL [26]

The Gambler bet again to recover all that he had lost and all the friends of the young man. When they finished arranging the bets he said: "Now we will go outside." This was the game of the ball that had two tabs like ears; the stick used was curved like a hockey stick. Then the young man brought forth the ball that contained the brown rat. He stood ready with stick in hand, aiming to drive the ball through the hole, which was a house. If the young man made the hole, the Gambler lost; if he missed the hole, the Gambler won. The young man stood exercising his arms as if ready to strike. He said: "My ball, do not miss the hole. Go straight for the hole." The Gambler said: "Miss the hole. Miss the hole." The young man hit the ground just back of the ball; but the ball bounced out and jumped through the hole. The Gambler was very angry. He rushed after the ball; but the young man grabbed him, saying: "Wait a minute, Brother, this is your loss, but my ball." The Gambler cursed the ball and said: "The ball can go to the home of the dead!" The Gambler had lost four times.

THE FIFTH, THE GUESSING GAME [27]

They made their bets for the fifth game; and they covered all that the Gambler had lost and all that the young man had had from the first. When the betting was over they said: "Now we will go inside the dwelling again." This time the Gambler showed the young man the picture of Ash'ke chili on the wall. This was the guessing game. And it was the picture that the Sun had shown the young man. The Gambler said: "Now, young man, you can guess the meaning of this picture that I have drawn." The young man

---

[26] Recorder's note: This game of Hitting the Ball comes as number five in the first list of games given.
Culin (1907, pp. 623–624), Shinny.
[27] Recorder's note: This is number six in first list, p. 50.

said: "That is the picture of Ash'ke chili. He has the beautiful flowers in both hands." The Gambler said: "It is correct, my friend." Then he pointed to the picture of the first black jar. "Now, my friend, can you guess what this is?" The youth said: "That is the black water jar. It contains the black cloud which brings the male rain." "That is it, my friend," said the Gambler. Then he pointed to the picture of the next jar and said: "Can you guess what this is?" The Gambler chuckled after showing the young man each new object. The young man answered: "That is the blue water jar, and it contains the blue cloud that brings the male rain." The Gambler said: "Oh, my friend, you are a good guesser. It is correct." Next came the yellow water jar. The Gambler asked the same question as before, and the young man said: "That is the yellow water jar, and it contains the yellow cloud that brings the male rain." "That is it," said the Gambler. He pointed to the white water jar and said: "Can you guess this?" The young man said: "That is the white water jar that contains the white cloud that brings the male rain." "Correct, my friend," said the Gambler, and he pointed to another black object: "Can you guess what this is?" The youth said: "That is the black water jar which contains the black vapor which brings the female rain." And the Gambler said: "That is it, my friend." And the same questions were asked for the blue and the yellow water jars.

"Oh, my friend, you are guessing all correctly." Then the Gambler pointed to a white object on the wall and said: "Now guess what this is?" "That is the white water jar, and it contains not only the white vapor that brings the female rain but all the beautiful flowers and their pollens included." The Gambler did not laugh now, he just said: "That is it, my friend." There was the last picture, that of a great water jar, on the wall. The Gambler said: "Now, my friend, what is this great jar and what is in it?" The young man said: "That is the gray water jar, and it contains . . ." Then, just then, up jumped the bird which guarded the Gambler's medicine, and out it flew. The Gambler sat with his head down. The young man said: "Well, my Brother, you are the loser. I have won from you." And the Gambler said: "I know. I am the loser." His body was very wet with sweat and he was tiring. He got to his feet and walked round and round.

THE SIXTH GAME, THE KICKED STICK [28]

The Gambler covered all that he had lost and all that the young man possessed. This time they went outside for the game of the kicked stick.

Everyone went outside. Four lines were drawn across the track far enough apart so that a good runner could kick the stick from one

---

[28] Recorder's note: The game of the Kicked Stick is number four in the first list.

line to the other. The Gambler placed these marks on his track. The young man was to kick the stick to the first line, from the first to the second line, from the second to the third, and from the third clean over the house. When all was ready the young man kicked his stick and it reached the first line, for the woodpecker was in the stick. He kicked it again and it reached the second line. The third time he kicked it, it reached the third line. And the fourth time he kicked it, over the house it flew. The Gambler said: "I lose, I lose."

THE SEVENTH, THE GAME OF THE PLANTED STICKS

The Gambler bet again against the young man. He covered everything that he had lost and all the young man had won. This was the game of the planted sticks.

The sticks were planted at the end of the race track. Both men got ready to run. The young man got there first and pulled his stick out first. The Gambler reached for his stick; he tried to pull it out, but it pulled him back. He tried to force it out. The young man returned to the Gambler and pulled at his clothing. "My friend," he said, "you are the loser. Why stay with this stick?" So the Gambler said: "I know that I am the loser."

THE EIGHTH GAME, THE FOOT RACE
(Fig. 8)

This was the last bet. They bet everything, the Rain, the Holy Beings, the Sacred Turquoise which the Gambler had won. The Gambler said: "Now we will run a foot race. If I lose again, my life is included. Kill me. If I win and you lose, your life is included and I will kill you." The young man said: "Very well. I agree."

They circled around a little hill with a ruin on it first, and then they entered the home stretch.

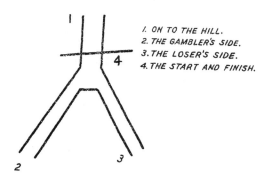

1. ON TO THE HILL.
2. THE GAMBLER'S SIDE.
3. THE LOSER'S SIDE.
4. THE START AND FINISH.

FIGURE 8.—The start and the finish of the foot race that circled the little hill.

As the race track formed a circle the two started from the place where they were to finish. They were to go around the hill and return. Four times the Gambler was in the lead; but the fifth time that the young man caught up and passed the little breeze whispered in his ear: "Jump high, he is going to shoot." The young man jumped high and the arrow went under him. He picked it up. The next time the little breeze whispered: "He is shooting high. Lay flat." The young man lay flat on the ground and the arrow passed over him. He jumped up, ran on and picked it up. Then the little breeze said: "He aims at your heart. Lie down." The young man did this and the arrow passed above him. He recovered the third arrow. The fourth time the little breeze said: "He aims at your head. Press the earth." Again the arrow passed over the young man; and the little breeze said: "He has no more arrows. Now let him get ahead of you; and you must do the same to him that he did to you." When the Gambler passed him the young man took aim and shot him in the leg, just below the knee. The next time he shot him halfway up the body. The third arrow he shot between the shoulders. The fourth arrow he sent behind the head. Then the little breeze said: "Do not run near him. If he catches you he will be whole again, and he will beat you." So the young man circled around the Gambler and ran on ahead.

At the finish line there is a little raised knoll. The young man ran up on the Gambler's or winner's side. The crowd of people cheered and blew their flutes. After the young man had regained his breath up came the Gambler. The young man said: "My friend, you are the loser." The Gambler said: "You are right. I lose. I lose all, even my life. My life is yours." The Gambler entered his house and brought out an ax and laid it on the ground; and he told the young man to kill him while he was still warm. He threw himself on the ground broken-hearted.

Now just as the young man was about to strike the Gambler with the ax the Sun spoke: "Wait a minute, do not kill him, he is your elder brother. Why kill him when he has nothing but his life on the earth." The Sun laid the Black Bow down and told the young man to stand the Gambler on the top of it, and to stretch the cord and let go. It threw the Gambler up into the air. He went up a little way and called out: "Long ago I died in the center of the earth." He went up still farther and called down: "Long ago I died in the center of the earth. My spirit will want to return there. My spirit will want to return to the center of the earth." He went still farther up in the sky and all that they heard was: "Adios." [29]   He was gone.   He went to the upper worlds.

After the Gambler ascended to the upper worlds the young man said: "My Father, there is the Sacred Turquoise that you wanted. There it is.   It is yours."   And the Sun said: "Thank you, my son. I thank you."   He raised the great turquoise and breathed the breath four times.   Then the Sun turned to the Yei Hasjohon and said: "Let us send our two children together to Dzil na'odili.   They shall go above the eight rings of the mountain where there is a changeable house.   That shall be the home of our children, for that mountain is the earth's heart."   So they sent the young man and the maiden, the daughter of Hasjohon, his wife, there.   It was to be their home forever.   The Sun said: "My son, you know our plan."   And the Sun returned to his home.

But before he left the young man went into the Gambler's dwelling and pointed to the jars in the picture on the wall.   He commanded them to move back to all parts of the world.   "From you the people of the earth will have rain and clouds and vapor."   When he left the house he found the people, the Gambler's friends, weeping for they did not know what was to become of them, as they had been the Gambler's slaves.   The young man turned to the people and told them to be cheerful; it was because of the Gambler, not himself, that they were gathered there.   He told them that he was a different kind of person; and that he would send them back to their own countries, or to whatever country they wished.   Then the people came forward and thanked the young man.   "These are the kindest words that we have heard in a long time," they said.   Each took his turn and thanked the young man.   Some said: "We will return to our old homes."   Others said: "We have always wanted to go to a new country.   We know of one.   We will go there."   That day all the people moved away (from Chaco Canyon) [30] to whatever place they had chosen for their home.

---

[29] Matthews (1897, pp. 82–87).   Matthews (1889 b, pp. 89–94): "The Great Gambler went to the Moon and said: 'I am very poor!'   The Moon gave him domestic animals, sheep, horses, pigs, goats, and chickens.   He gave him beautiful goods, more beautiful than those of Bonito.   He gave him a new people—the Mexicans—and then he sent him back to the earth.   (And that is why he said 'Adios' when he left the earth.)   He is now the god of the Mexicans.   It may be that he was the Sun's favorite son."   "He went to Bekolcice, the god who carries the moon. . . . he descended far to the south of his former abode and reached the earth in Old Mexico.   Naqoilpi's people increased greatly in Mexico and after a while they began to move towards the north and build towns along the Rio Grande."
Tozzer (1908, p. 32) gives Orion as the Great Gambler; Rigel as his left hand, and Betelgeuse as his right foot.
[30] Interpreter's note: I went to Chaco Canyon to check the ruins and the race track and to see the pictographs.

THE STORY OF THE MOCCASIN GAME
(Fig. 9)

The Blue Bird Clan people [31] and the people called mai desh kzish ni moved up the canyon and built a house which they called Ken tiel.[32] The rest of the people went in different directions and built new homes. There was another place east of Ken tiel called Sis kit. Above them there is a place called Hada'na y be', the house made of banded rock. The people living there were visited by a giant. He was also the Sun's son.

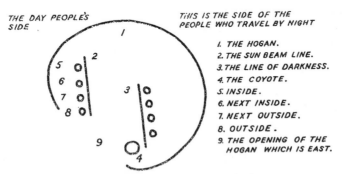

THE DAY PEOPLE'S SIDE

THIS IS THE SIDE OF THE PEOPLE WHO TRAVEL BY NIGHT

1. THE HOGAN.
2. THE SUN BEAM LINE.
3. THE LINE OF DARKNESS.
4. THE COYOTE.
5. INSIDE.
6. NEXT INSIDE.
7. NEXT OUTSIDE.
8. OUTSIDE.
9. THE OPENING OF THE HOGAN WHICH IS EAST.

FIGURE 9.—The chart of the Moccasin Game.

This giant spoke to the people there. "My grandchildren," he said, "let us play the Moccasin Game." They said: "We do not know that game." So he went away; but the next day he returned and said: "My grandchildren, I would like to play the Moccasin Game with you." They told him: "Grandfather, we do not know this game." Again he left them, but on the third day he returned. "My grandchildren, I have come to play the Moccasin Game with you." But their answer was the same. Now after he had left them the third time there came a certain bird called nat tsile gine who said: "This person is called One Walking Giant. When he asks for the game again tell him that we will play the game at a place called a Red Rock where the Big Snake lives.[33] All the sacred People will gather there." [34]

The giant came for the fourth time and said: "My grandchildren, I have come to play the Moccasin Game with you." They said: "All is well, Grandfather; we will hold the game over in Red Canyon

[31] Informant's note : The Blue Bird Clan People were his ancestors.

[32] Franciscan Fathers (1912, p. 228) : Wide Ruin, Kin tqel.

[33] Informant's note: I saw this place in 1896. Today there is still to be seen the large cave with the Big Snake painted above it. The little ball that the giant used is there, as also the stick for pounding the moccasins. It is a sacred place. The little ball and the pounding stick look very old, and again, very new. The black earth is where they built their fire.

[34] Culin (1907, pp. 346–349) : Hidden Ball. Franciscan Fathers, (1910, pp. 485–487).

where the Big Snake lives.[35] The Giant was greatly pleased. "Oh, my children, that is well; that is what I came for." They told him that they would send word to all the sacred people in the world, that in 4 days they would gather in Red Canyon. The Giant was delighted with the plan. And on the fourth day all the people from the clans and the rocks gathered there.[36]

When the holy people from the sacred places came together in Red Canyon they did not know that the Sun had another great plan in which he figured that he would get even for all the mistakes he had made through the Gambler.

At the end of the fourth day, at twilight, the Giant came. Now he had a feather from under the wing of an eagle which he kept laying against the palm of his hand. From the feather in the Giant's hand to the moccasin where the little ball was hidden shone a faint, gray ray of light like an almost invisible rainbow. This would help him win. He had the counting sticks with him, the little ball and the small, curved tapping stick. He brought them all to the Red Canyon of the Big Snake. The counting sticks were 102 in number. The Giant got them from the Sun's 102 trails.

The Coyote came to Red Canyon. He said that as long as he traveled both by night and by day he would be on the winning side, whichever it might be.

All was in readiness. The Giant entered the cave (hogan) and the guessing began.

This is the game:

There are 102 counting sticks in the game. The sticks are tied in a bundle; they are used as counters to pay the points back and forth. When one side wins 102 points they have won the game. Now this game determined the value of everything, all goods and possessions were assessed by this game. If the ball is placed or "buried" in the

---

[35] Interpreter's note: Tse'gie hachee, Red Rock, south of Beautiful Mountain. There is a pictograph of the Snake on the cliff, also of the ball and stick. The cave is in the head of the canyon.

[36] Informant's note: Ten different stories are told here—

(1) The Sun's Plan to Have Night and Day, or the Moccasin Game.
(2) The Finding of the White Bead Baby Girl.
(3) How the White Bead Woman Came to This Country.
(4) The Twins, or the Destroying of the Monsters.
(5) How the White Bead Woman Returned to Form Another People.
(6) The Coming of the Diné.
(7) How the White Bead Woman Told Them About the Most-High-Power-Whose-Ways-Are-Beautiful.
(8) The Story of How First Man and First Woman Left the Earth.
(9) How the Rainbow Trail Was Taken Away, or the Coming of the Horses.
(10) The Beggar's Son.

Then comes the story of the game being taken to the mountain near Zuni, To'waya'lane or Tse'hogan. This is the Hunters' Story. There are chants here, and sometimes other stories are told. After this, strong medicine was taken, and men became as they are today. They must work for their living, and there is much suffering.

next outside moccasin the count is four. It can be four of anything bet, four "bits," four dollars, etc. If the ball is next outside, and the guesser guesses outside, the count is six. It costs the guesser six points. If the ball is inside, and the guesser guesses next inside, it costs him four points. If the ball is next inside and the guess is inside, the cost is six. Now if the guesser taps more than once on a moccasin and the ball happens to be in it, it costs him ten points. One tap means "in there." More than one tap means nothing in the moccasin. If the ball is in the moccasin when he taps once he takes it out and throws it to his friends. It is then their turn to bury the ball.[37]

The Giant explained the manner of betting and showed them the way to play the game. He said: "Now this is not going to be a free game. All those of you who travel at night will bet the night against the day. If I lose there will be darkness always." (Later it was learned that because the Giant's father was the Sun he was sure of winning. And besides the feather he was to carry in his hand, the Giant was given a sunbeam to wrap around the ball. With this he was sure to win.)

The moccasins of the bear and the porcupine were placed on the side of darkness. The moccasins of the gopher and the badger were used for the day peoples' side.

The Giant took a cornhusk, thin as paper and cut at both ends, which had been painted black on one side to represent darkness, and white on the other side to represent day. They were to toss this cornhusk in the air, and when it fell to the earth whichever side showing would have the first chance to bury the ball.

The Giant stood and called out: "All the day people will say 'gray, gray,' and the night people will say 'dark, dark' and I will let the cornhusk fall." He let the cornhusk fall and the white side was up. There was great shouting from the day people.

The antelope had the ball. He sang out: "Gray, gray, gray," and everyone could see him. Now as each animal took the ball he sang. The song is repeated over and over if the opposite party misses the guess.[38]

---

[37] Informant's note: The counting was explained a second time: If the guesser hits a moccasin once, any moccasin, and the ball is in the second one from it, it costs him ten points. If he hits once outside, and the ball is inside, it costs him four. If the guesser taps outside more than once, and there is no ball, and he goes to the next outside and taps more than once on one and two, and he is wrong on three, it costs him four. If he taps, or "kills", more than once on one, two and three and the ball is in three, it costs him six points..

Stevenson (1904), p. 318) recording the games of the Zuni, gives i'yankolo'we as hidden ball game.

Recorder's note: The songs collected by the interpreter are on pp. 66-69.

[38] Informant's note: The songs of the different animals are used in the Moccasin Game.

1. *The Giant's Song*

The big being called the Giant
Is trying his luck
To get the ball,
Crying as he says:
Please place the ball
In the same moccasin next time.

2. *The Beaver's Song*

I follow the river
In quest of a young beaver.
Up the river I go
Through the cut willow path I go
In quest of a young beaver.

3. *The Traveling Rock's Song*

Traveling Rock,
Traveling Rock,
The ball is just beyond
Where you last hit the moccasin.

4. *The Crow's Song*

The crow is a boy
Who got blackened by soot,
And he can not guess
In which moccasin
The ball is placed.

5. *The Diné's Song*

Whom do we hear saying?
Whom do we hear saying:
My friends, my friends,
What fools you are?
I still have the ball in my own moccasin.

The crowd goes to the hill.
The crowd goes to the hill.
What fools!
With foolishness like a little child's.

6. *The Badger's Song*

The badger is lying down.
The badger is lying down,
Growling as he is lying down.
Pretty white stripes on his forehead,
Growling as he is lying down.
His legs have darkish ends,
And the badger is lying down.

7. *The Locust's Song*

The locust, the locust,
He came up through the earth.
He came up through the earth.
The locust, the locust.

8. *The Turtle Dove's Song*

Wosh, wosh!
Adopted, adopted.
The red moccasin is adopted.
The slick head is adopted,
The pretty spot on the body is adopted.

9. *The Magpie's Song*

The magpie, the magpie.
The white feather is for the dawn.
The ball is right down in here.
Now it is dawn, now it is dawn.

10. *The Bear's Song*

A foot,
A foot with toes,
A foot with toes came.
He came with a foot with toes.
Aging as he came with a foot with toes.

Another Bear's Song

He is one who has to do with the grass seeds.
He is one who has to do with the grass seeds.
Now put the ball in the moccasin.
Now put the ball in the moccasin.

11. *The Antelope's Song*

Gray, gray,
Just in plain sight,
There the antelope stands.

12. *The Owl's Song*

The old man owl,
The old man owl.
He is jealous of me
Because I am the only one
Who brings home a rabbit,
Which causes "pain in my neck."

Another Owl's Song

I am the owl.
I sit on the spruce tree.
My coat is gray.
I have big eyes.
My head has two points.
The white smoke from my tobacco can be seen
As I sit on the spruce tree.
The little rabbit comes in sight,
Nearby where I sit on the spruce tree.
I think soon my claws will get into its back,
As I sit on the spruce tree.
Now it is dawn, now it is dawn.
The old man owl's head has two points.
He has big, yellowish eyes.
We see white smoke from his tobacco.
Ho, ho! Ho, ho! Ho, ho!

13. *The Chipmunk's Song*

Chipmunk, chipmunk,
Chipmunk standing.
Pretty and short as he is standing.
His body is striped as he is standing.
Slim of form is his body standing.

14. *The Squirrel's Song*

I can't drag him,
I can't drag him.
His body and his liver together
I can not drag.
His body and all his insides
I can not drag.

15. *Three Bobcat Songs*

The bobcat,
The bobcat has a sore foot.
The bobcat has a sore foot.
Bobcat is walking,
Bobcat is walking.
He walks and he walks and he walks.
He runs down and up the hill,
And then he growls.

I met a bobcat hunting.
I met a bobcat hunting.
And all he was carrying home was his hide.

16. *The Gopher's Song*

The gopher sees the ball in the moccasin.
The gopher sees the ball in the moccasin.
He says: Young Brother,
Keep hidden the moccasin,
Keep hidden the moccasin
Until you get the ball,
Until you get the ball.

17. *The Turkey's Song*

The one who has the turkey for a pet,
The one who has the turkey for a pet,
Down at the foot of the mountain,
Down at the foot of the mountain.
Through the green meadow
He is carrying a load of roseberries,
And a lot of noise he is making.

Another Turkey (Gobbler's) Song

The big turkey gobbler has the ball.
The big turkey gobbler has the ball.
With the help of his wattle he has the ball.
The big turkey gobbler has the ball.

18. *The Horned Toad's Song*

Oh, see what I have killed,
Oh, see what I have killed.
Standing here looking at it,
I place the ball in the same moccasin for you,
In the same moccasin for you.
It is in the same moccasin, the same moccasin.
No, it is in a different moccasin.
The one who carries back the ball
Now places it in another moccasin, an outside moccasin.
The one who carries back the ball
Now places it in another moccasin, an outside moccasin.

A certain bird who had bright eyes rose and suddenly struck the moccasin in which the ball was hidden. He took it and tossed it to the night people. The owl caught the ball and said: "Old man, old man is jealous of me because I am the only one who carries home the rabbit." He sang as he buried the ball. After the owl buried the ball out came the Giant. He wrung his hand and with two fingers pointed down to the moccasins. The gray streak of light shone and he grabbed the ball and tossed it back to his friends.

First one side then the other won until the night was half over. At this time the owl kept the ball in his hand instead of placing it in a moccasin and the Giant missed his guess. Soon the Giant had tears in his eyes and they ran down his cheeks. The owl saw this and said: "Old man called Giant is weeping over his poor guessing, weeping and saying 'Bury the ball where I guess for once.'" The Giant was losing the game. Now the day people had lost one hundred points and there were only two points left. They took hold of the Giant and told him to sit down. They asked the locust to dig into the earth and to go to the moccasins and see where the ball was hidden. The locust agreed. He left his shell there for all to see and he dug down into the earth and when he returned to his shell he said: "There is no ball in the moccasins." (That is why the locust leaves his shell and goes into the earth.) Next the gopher went to the moccasins and found no ball. Then one of the day birds went forward and "killed" a moccasin. No ball was in it. He pretended to strike a moccasin when the owl went for it, but the bird hesitated and said: "Wait a minute, grandfather, keep your hand away." And each time that the bird struck a moccasin the owl tried to reach the next one but his hand was held. At last the guesser hit the owl's hand and out rolled the ball.

It was towards dawn by that time and they heard a curious noise outside. They sent the two Yei, Hasjelti and Hasjohon to see what was happening. They returned and said: "The sound is coming nearer." The people told the two Yei to sit out there, side by side, and to wait and see what this strange thing could be. In the distance the Yei saw two skulls approaching. They were the skulls of two people who had died and returned to the Yellow World. Now they were coming and they intended to harm someone of the assembly. They were given presents and sent away.[39]

Now when the owl dropped the ball all the birds and animals chose whatever designs and colors they wished to wear in the future. The crow and the bear had been asleep. When the crow heard what was happening, in a great hurry he dipped himself in charcoal and went off to his home. They slapped the bear and said: "Wake up. It is day." The bear jumped up and reached for his moccasins, and he made off just as fast as he could go to the mountains. But he had put his left moccasin on his right foot, and his right moccasin on his left foot, and that is why he has strangely shaped feet. Also, as he reached the mountain the first rays of the sun hit his fur, and that is why some of his descendants are brownish.

The Giant's plan had failed. The game had not come out as he had planned, and, as he had not won all the time, it was not always to be day.

The Hada no ege people and the Hada no estine [40] people, Hasjelti, Hasjohon, and Hasjetine came into the cave and started or began their planning: how the Giant should be killed, how the two Big Birds should be killed, how the Rolling Stone should be killed, how the Giant Elk should be killed, how the Twelve Antelope who ate human beings should be killed, and how the Cutting Reeds should be destroyed. These reeds grew at the mouth of La Plata River, below Farmington, and anyone who stepped among them was cut to pieces. There was still another animal with big eyes who killed people by staring at them. There was another being who lived near a cliff and when anyone came near that cliff he kicked him over the edge. And the Swallow People were still warring, even after the woman who became a bear had been killed.

It was a rule that all the different persons who grew to be great powers, once they made a mistake, forfeited their lives. So because the Giant made the mistake of letting the owl outwit him the holy people came together and planned how he, and at the same time all the monsters who destroyed those living upon the earth, must die.

---

[39] They call this Tse tsina tage, the Two Skulls who Came Back. This is the origin of the Dead Spirit Fire Ceremony. Since that time, whenever a person sickens in spirit this is the ceremony used over him. And here all the chants and prayers of the Dead Spirit Ceremony come in.

[40] Franciscan Fathers (1912, p. 127): Hada huniye', mirage; hadahunestqin, heat wave people; and, hadahuneya'nigi, mirage people.

THE STORY OF THE COMING OF THE WHITE BEAD WOMAN [41]

All during this time First Man and First Woman lived on the top of Dzil na'odili, also called Chol'i'i.[42] This is the sacred mountain near Farmington, N. Mex. (See fig. 10.) The circle on top of this mountain is a cloud (fig. 11). Chol'i'i was completely hidden at first, then the bands or clouds rose and the mountain was seen. This is the sacred story which the old medicine men keep to themselves.

Figure 12 shows the cradle and how the baby in it lay. The cradleboard is the rainbow.[43]

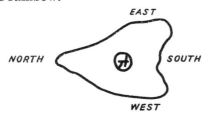

THE POLES ARE IN THE CENTER

FIGURE 10.—The sacred mountain Dzil na'odili, also called Chol'i'i.

FIGURE 11.—The cloud circle on top of the mountain.

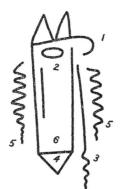

1. THE RING OVER THE BABY'S HEAD.
2. THE BABY'S HEAD.
3. THE RAIN STRING.
4. THE FOOT BOARD IS THE SUN DOG.
5. THE LIGHTNING STRINGS.
6. THE CRADLE BOARD IS THE RAINBOW.

FIGURE 12.—The cradle of the White Bead Baby.

---

[41] Matthews (1897, pp. 104–105).

Recorder's note: He says that two sisters were the mothers of the "Twins"; one, Estsanatlehi, was the Woman-Who-Changes (the turquoise image), and that Yol'kai estan is the White Bead Woman. The Sun and the Water Fall were the fathers of the boys. Lummis, in Pueblo Indian Folk Stories, associates the mother of the Twins with the moon. Whitman follows Matthews. But both the informant and the interpreter agreed that certain medicine men differ.

[42] Interpreter's note: The mountain on which the White Bead Baby was found is sometimes designated as Chol'i', and sometimes as the Mountain of the East, Sis'na'jin.

[43] Franciscan Fathers (1910, pp. 46–47, and 1912, p. 156: natsi'lid, rainbow.

The baby was the White Bead Baby, the female baby, and her cradle is called natsi'lid eta cote, the rainbow cut short. The baby was wrapped in four clouds, black, blue, yellow, and white, and the four vapors, and all the flowers with all their pollens. The baby's head was to the west and her feet were to the east.

First comes the story of the White Bead Baby and of her growth.

One day the mountain Chol'i'i was hidden by clouds and First Man said to his wife: "Now for the whole day we have seen clouds over the mountain. There must be some reason for this." That night when he saw a fire on the top of the mountain First Man said: "All day the clouds have covered the mountain and now there is a fire there. There must be someone there. I will go and find him." His wife said: "No, stay at home. There are many monsters on the earth who eat people. It is not safe for you to go." But First Man said: "I will go. It must be the will of the Most High Power." The next day he started out, chanting as he walked. He called himself the Dawn Boy in the chant. He climbed the mountain, but he found nothing, neither fire nor hogan. All that second day the clouds hung over the mountain, and when First Man returned home that night both he and his wife saw the fire burning on top of Chol'i'. The next day First Man went again to the mountain but he found no fire or home or sign, so he returned to his home. That night when he saw the fire burning brightly he planted two forked sticks and sighted the fire, so that on the following day he could look and see at what point the fire had burned. In the morning, when he looked through the forked sticks, he knew just where to go. He started out as before and he chanted as he walked, naming the mountain toward which he was going, until he reached the top. On the top of the mountain there was a heavy mist. In the center of it he heard a baby crying. Lightning flashed from the baby and First Man saw her on her cradle-board.[44]

First Man picked the baby up and carried her home to his wife. But the baby was tied firmly on the cradleboard and First Woman did not know how to untie the strings. Just at this time they heard a noise: "ho'ho'ho'hooo." Then another noise: "A'ow, a'ow, ho'ho'ho' hooo." And two men entered the home. One said that his name was Ni'hada ho'nigi (he was Hasjelti), the other said he was Ni'ha ha nigi (Hasjohon). They were the two Yei. They told First Man and his wife that the baby had been their plan, and they showed them how to untie the cradle strings and told them what each string meant. Next they told First Man to go out and cut two slabs of wood from a tree, and to mark the tree, and to make from oak the bow for over the baby's head. They told him that he must make a cradle like this first

---

[44] Informant's note: There is a chant sung here.

one. He must gather the soft bark from awae'ts al, the baby bush or cliff rose,[45] and place that on the board before putting the baby on it. So First Man went out and made the cradle as the Yei had directed, for they took away the cradle on which the baby had been found. But before the two Yei left First Man said: "Now she will be my daughter." His wife took the baby and breathed on her four times. "Now," she said, "she will be my daughter." And so the Yei left First Man and his wife.

First Woman washed the baby in a white bead basket, then in a turquoise basket, and in a white shell basket, and in a black jet basket. At the end of the second day the baby laughed for the first time and there came a man, Atse'hashke, the First Coyote, who said: "I was told that my grandchild laughed for the first time." A woman came saying: "I was told that my grandchild laughed for the first time." She was the Salt Woman. First Woman took charcoal and gave it to the Coyote saying: "This is the only thing that lasts." So he painted his nose with it and said: "I shall know all things. I shall live long by it." And First Woman also gave the Coyote salt. He swallowed it and said: "This shall be my meat. It will make my meat taste good." And satisfied with his gifts he departed. It was the Salt Woman who first gave the gift of salt to First Woman. Then the two Yei returned for their gifts. One was given white bead moccasins, and the other decorated leggings. They took them and went away satisfied.

Now that is why all persons present receive a little gift when a baby laughs for the first time.[46] And later, when the White Bead Woman went West to her home she gave the gifts of beautiful flowers, the rain, and the plants bearing fruits and seeds for food.

The third day the baby sat up, the fourth day she walked. When the baby stood First Man put her on his knee and sang:

> The old woman standing,
> The old woman standing,
> The old woman standing.
> The White Bead Girl is standing.

The chant continues. It tells what developed on each day and how the White Bead Girl grew until the thirteenth day when she had her monthly period. (The same things happen to girls now, but the days of the White Bead Girl became our years.) On the thirteenth day she went to her foster-mother and said: "Something unusual has passed through me." First Woman spoke: "That is your 'first race.'"

---

[45] Recorder's note: Matthews (1886, vol. 20, pp. 767–777): Cliff rose, *Cowania mexicana* Don, a way tsal, baby's bed. The soft shredded bark of the cliff rose is used to line the baby basket. Franciscan Fathers (1910, p. 197): awaetsae, baby's bedding.

[46] Informant's note: Origin of the First Laugh Ceremony.

First Woman told her husband that their foster daughter had kin nas ta, her first race (first menstruation), also called her first cake.

They laid different kinds of blankets inside the home. Under them were the white flowers,[47] coyote robes, and such things. The girl lay stretched on these, face down. First Man shaped her all over. He pulled her hair down and she had a quantity of hair. He shaped her face and it was beautiful, and he dressed her in all the beautiful goods, beads, bracelets, and earrings. They let her hair hang down and they tied it at the neck with the rain string which hung down with her hair.

Then First Man and First Woman stepped outside the hogan and told her to run her first race, to go around a cedar tree yonder, as the sun travels, and return home. When she came back she looked from the doorway into the home and said: "You hid the ground with the beautiful goods, you hid the ground with the mixed chips of stones." Now this is what First Man and First Woman had said.

First man commenced planning where they should have the first chant over her. It was decided that it would be in the home on the top of the eight rings of the mountain called Dzil na'odili, at the home which is called hoghan ho'tez sos, Changeable House. The Home that Stretches Out, hogan na' hat tson'e is its second name.[48]

A great crowd gathered the evening of the fourth day. All the different people filled the home and there were 11 rings, or 11 circles, of people around it. As the chant was about to begin some people put their heads inside the home and said: "Why were we not invited?" And everyone said: "Come in. There is room in front for you." These newcomers were the Beautiful Goods People, a whole group of them. They sat in front of the others.

Two hogan chants were sung by the people who planned how the White Bead Baby should be found. Then the White Bead Girl stood up and said that there was something missing. "You have not called upon Tse an no'hoi begay hojone, the Most High Power Whose Ways Are Beautiful," she said. "He should be put into your songs. No one knows his real name, but you must use the one I give you." So all the people sang their chants using the names of the Most High Power and that of the White Bead Girl.[49]

About dawn two men came in and asked why they had not been invited. Their moccasins and leggings were white; they were beau-

---

[47] Interpreter's note: The white flowers are the mariposa lily.

Recorder's note: Mariposa lily, according to Franciscan Fathers (1910, p. 193), altsi'ni, *Calochortus luteus*.

[48] Informant's note: A chant should be sung here. Today, in the chant, "white flowers" is probably used to designate beautiful goods.

[49] Informant's note: Chants are sung here. They tell how the baby was found, about her growth, her first "race" or "cake," and when she went to the West and returned. No one man knows all the chants, only one group of them.

tifully dressed, each having 21 tail feathers for the headdress, and on the top of each feather there perched a beautiful singing bird. They were the two Yei, Hasjelti, the Dawn, and Hasjohon, the Twilight. They received gifts and they came in and sang their chant, and the dawn broke and it was day.

So now each girl at the time of her first and second "race" has this chant held over her. Her cake is made of the different colored corn flavored with a kind of yeast. This latter is made by soaking wheat in water and when it ferments it is dried and ground into powder. It makes the corn cake very sweet.

In the morning the men receive some of the maiden's cake as their gift for their chants.[50] Today the young girl sits in the back of the hogan and the goods or gifts are piled in front of her, symbolic of the Beautiful Goods People who filled the front circle in the "hogan" when the White Bead Girl had her first chant. The young girl, today, has her hair tied with a strip of buckskin from a deer not killed by a weapon.[51]

Now after the ceremony or Night Chant over the White Bead Girl the people went their ways and left First Man and First Woman and their foster daughter to live by themselves. It happened soon after this that this holy girl wished for a mate. Every morning when the sun rose she lay on her back until noon, her head to the west and her feet to the east. From noon on she went to the spring. She lay under the ledge and let spring water drip over her body. This took place each day for 4 days.

THE WHITE BEAD MAIDEN'S MARRIAGE WITH THE SUN

First Man said upon coming home one day: "Over to the east, at the foot of the mesa, there are two different kinds of grass. Their ripening seeds are plentiful." So First Woman and the girl went down to gather the seeds. But when they got there they began to think of the monsters who roamed about the country and became frightened.[52] Looking about them carefully they hurriedly gathered only one kind of seed before they ran back to their home. When they reached their hogan the girl said: "Mother, I want to go back and collect the seeds from the other grass." First Woman said: "No, daughter, you can not go there alone. Some monster might catch you." But the girl insisted. She promised to be careful and to look out for herself.

---

[50] Informant's note: Certain men know the chants of the different people gathered there. There are 8 or 10 groups of these songs.

[51] Informant's note: Today, the hide of a deer not killed by a weapon, for example, by a car, is used ceremonially.

[52] Franciscan Fathers (1910, pp. 189–191; 1912, p. 172).

Informant's and interpreter's note: Two kinds of grasses with edible seeds. These are mountain grasses, tlo'tso and tlo'tsosi, tlo'dahikhali and ndid lidi. Tlo dei is Chenopodium, seeds-falling grass. This is what is called hard seed grass, also pigweed.

After the request was made four times the old woman let her go, warning her to have great care.

The maiden went down the mesa as fast as she could and was soon busy gathering seeds from the grass. All of a sudden she heard something behind her. Looking around she saw a great white horse with black eyes. He had a long white mane, and he pranced above the ground not on the earth itself. She saw that the bridle was white too, and that the saddle was white. And there was a young man sitting on the horse. The young man's moccasins and leggings and clothing were all white. All was as for a bride.

The holy rider spoke: "You lay towards me each morning until noon. I am he whom you faced. When I am half over the center of the earth you go to the spring. Your wish could not have two meanings." He continued:

Go home and tell your father to build a brush hogan to the south of your home. Make ready a meal out of the seeds of the grasses that you have gathered. Put this meal into a white bead basket. Have the pollen from a pair of blue birds (pollen which has been sprinkled over them), and use this pollen to draw a line from east to west across the basket on top of the meal. Turn the hand and make a line from north to south, and a line must be drawn around the outer edge of the basket. Set the basket inside the brush hogan. You and your father must sit there late into the night. He will then go home to his wife and you must stay there alone.

When the White Bead Girl returned home she told her mother of all that she had seen and all that she had heard. That night when First Man came home his wife told him what the girl had related. First Man said: "I do not believe this thing. We are very poor. Why should we be visited by a Holy Being? I cannot believe what you tell me."

Now when the girl told her mother about her experience First Woman asked if she had acted according to this Holy One's directions each day. The maiden had said: "Yes." So the woman told her husband that indeed it was all true, and that he must go and prepare the brush shelter and not argue. When all was ready First Man took the white bead basket filled with the meal, and he and his foster-daughter went into the brush shelter and sat there.

They sat there late into the night, then First Man went home to his wife and left the maiden there alone. The White Bead Girl returned early in the morning, and First Man asked her at once: "Who came last night"? The girl said: "No one came." First Man turned to his wife, "Did I not tell you that it is all a lie," he said. But the girl said: "Wait, I thought that I heard someone, and this morning I found just one track, and some of the meal, that towards the east, had been taken." So First Man went with his daughter to the brush hogan and he saw the one track, and also, that the meal towards the east in the basket was gone.

That night they prepared another basket of meal, and again First Man took his daughter to the brush shelter, and again they sat there late into the night. He left the maiden there alone. In the morning the girl returned to the home and said: "There are two tracks of a man there now. The meal in the south of the basket is gone."

On the third night the same thing happened. In the morning when the maiden returned First Man asked: "Who came?" And the girl said: "No one came." Then First Man became angry. "I told you that this thing is all a lie," he said. But the maiden answered: "But Father, there are three tracks, and the meal towards the west is gone. And I thought that someone touched me last night."

The fourth night they went to the brush shelter as before taking with them fresh meal in the basket. They sat late into the night, then First Man returned to his wife. When the girl entered the home in the early morning her father asked: "Who came?" And the girl answered: "No one." First Man was very angry and insisted that it was all a lie. "But father," said the White Bead Maiden, "The meal towards the north is gone, and there are four tracks. I thought that I was moved by someone, and I was all wet when I awakened." [53]

Now after the maiden was visited the fourth time by the Holy Being she lived with her foster parents for 4 days as they had always lived. But at the end of the fourth day the young woman said: "Mother, something moves within me." First Woman answered: "Daughter, that must be your baby moving." (And it is at the end of the fourth month that a woman feels life.) After 5 more days had passed twin boys were born to the White Bead Woman. (It is so that a woman bears a child in the ninth month.)

Later, much later, First Man and First Woman were sent farther east, farther towards the east than where the Sun dwells.

THE STORY OF THE TWIN BROTHERS [54]

The Twin Boys were cared for like their mother the White Bead Woman had been, each had a cradle, and when they first laughed gifts were given to all who came to the home. Not much is told about them until the fifteenth day. By that time they were young men.

---

[53] Informant's note: Now the story is told in a chant. It was given to the Dîné for their marriage ceremony. The meal basket, the pollen, etc. And because First Woman was not invited to the brush hogan explains why a man must not look upon his wife's mother. This was given to the Dîné (the Navaho) as well as to the Apache, who also have this custom.

[54] Matthews (1897, pp. 105–107; Cushing, (1923, p. 164); Lummis (1910. p. 206); Franciscan Fathers (1910, pp. 359–360).

Recorder's note: The "Twins" appear in Zuni mythology. It is explained that a lightning shaft and a rainbow are brothers to one another. So are the serpent worm and the striped measuring worm; also, the gods of war and thunderstorms. Franciscan Fathers (1910) give the Twins as Naye'nez ghani, Slayer of Monsters, and Tqo bagish chi'ni, Child of Water. Again, medicine men differ: some say the Spider Woman and not Dotso, the All-Wise Fly, was the Twins' guide.

First Man made bows and arrows for his two grandsons, and they played with them. One day when they were on the south side of the mesa they saw a strange animal with a long nose and a long tail, the coyote. Just as they took aim and were about to shoot, the animal went out of sight over the edge of the cliff. They hurried home and told their mother and First Man and his wife of what they had seen. They were frightened. The old ones said: "That was the spy of the Giant Elk, Anaye'tee'leget." Shortly thereafter when they were on the west side of the mesa they were frightened again, and again they hurried home and said: "We saw a great bird with a red head flying towards us, but just as we took aim and were about to shoot it flew back to the mesa." The three older people were now frightened. "That was the turkey buzzard," they said. "He is the spy of Tse na'hale, the Giant Birds who devour people." They scolded the boys for having gone so far from home.

One day the boys returned from the north side of the mesa and they told of having seen a black bird with shining eyes. Just as they took aim it had flown away, they said. The White Bead Woman and her foster parents warned the boys again and said that the bird was the spy of the monsters. And again they scolded the youths for wandering so far. But they could not keep them at home.

Now the boys were afraid to go toward the south, west and north. The only safe place was the east, so they ran eastward chasing chickadees. And someone came to them and said: "Grandchildren, what are you doing?" This was Dotso, the All-Wise Floy who had spoken. He continued: "My grandchildren, your father is the Sun." He told them to ask their mother who was their father.

She will tell you that your father is ga'bege, the single barrel cactus.[55] Ask her a second time. She will tell you that your father is hostage bini', the small bunch barrel cactus. Ask her a third time and she will say that your father is hoish da' gogie, the sour cactus. Ask her a fourth time to tell you who is your father and she will answer: "You are nothing but rock bastards." Then you must tell her that those things which she has named could not father human beings. Tell her that you know that the Sun is your father.

So when the boys asked the questions and received the answers that Dotso,[56] the Great Fly, told them that they would receive, they spoke up and said that they knew that the Sun was their father.

This surprised the three older ones. They were speechless when the two boys said that they intended to go to the home of their father.

[55] Recorder's note : See page 8, this bulletin, regarding cactus.
Matthews (1897, pp. 106–107).
[56] Recorder's note: Matthews gives the Spider Woman, not Dotso, the All-Wise Fly, as the guiding spirit of the Twins.
Matthews (1897, p. 109).

The Twins warned their mother and First Man and First Woman not to look at them as they left. With that warning they started out.

When the boys stepped outside the hogan they stood side by side. Each had lifted his right foot to take a step. They stepped on the rainbow and were immediately on top of the mountain Chol'i'i where their mother had been found. The next step took them to Sis na'jin.[57] Then they found themselves way, way to the east in a country that they did not know, a country of nothing but rolling sand.

They found an old man there who asked them if they were the two boys whom he had heard were on the way to see their father. They told him, yes. The old man said: "My grandchildren, your father is fierce. He kills with many weapons. He will harm you if you are not careful." This old man was Au sayk' giddie, the worm with the sharp tail.[58] He vomited and said: "My grandchildren, take this. You must use it when your father tries you with his tobacco." They took what the old man had given them and continued their journey.

After passing over many difficulties the Twins found themselves way, way, way east standing at the door of a great turquoise house.[59] An old woman asked them where they were going. The boys said that they were going to see their father. She said: "Well, then you are my grandchildren. Come with me." She was the mother of the Sun. She took them to a room, and she wrapped them in the four coverings of the Sky, the dawn, the daylight, the twilight, and the darkness. After a while there was a loud galloping noise. It was the Sun returning home on his big turquoise horse.[60]

When the Sun entered his house he said: "Why is there no one here?" [61] His mother said: "Who would be here? There are only ourselves at all times." After asking this question four times the Sun said: "Why mother, at noon I saw two specks coming here. What are they?" Then came his wife who was a jealous woman. She told her husband that he had always said that he had been true to her during his journey to earth and back. "What you have seen are your bastard children coming here." Then the grandmother brought the Twins out to their father.

The Little Breeze sat behind the boys' ears and told them what to say. They spoke up: "Father, we have come a long way to get help

---

[57] Recorder's note: Here again, medicine men differ. Some say that the White Bead Woman was found on Chol'i'i, others say, Sis na'jin.

[58] Recorder's note: Some medicine men say this is wasek de, the spring caterpillar, which emits blue spittle.
Franciscan Fathers (1912, p. 190): wo'saek'id, tobacco worm.

[59] Matthews (1897, pp. 108–111): The House of the Sun was built of turquoise. It was square, like a pueblo house, and stood on the shore of a great water.

[60] Informant's note: Now the Sun only goes over half the earth and turns back. Another, like the Sun, goes on. The sand painting of the Sun and the Twins comes here.

[61] Matthews (1897, p. 111): "Who are those who enter here today?"

from you." The Sun did not answer them. They repeated their statement four times, but still the Sun did not answer them. He reached up and took down his turquoise pipe. He brought out a sack of tobacco and, filling his pipe, he lighted the tobacco and handed the pipe to the boys. They smoked the pipe until all the tobacco was burned. They shook out the ashes. The Sun filled the pipe again and the boys smoked it a second time. He asked them how they felt, and they said that they felt well. Then their father filled it a third time, and he filled it a fourth time, and they had their fourth smoke. He asked them how they felt, and they answered: "We feel well." The Sun said: "I see you are my sons." He received them as his sons. But still he was not sure that they were his children. He said: "I will take you outside now."

The Sun prepared a sweat house for the two boys and he placed two, big, heated flint stones inside it. The grandmother gave the Twins four feathers,[62] and said: "Your father has not much mercy on you. Put these feathers under each arm when you enter the sweat house." They stripped themselves and went into the sweat house. They sang four sections of a chant. And then they heard someone calling: "Are you warm by now?" They answered: "No, we are not warm yet." The question was asked a second, third, and fourth time. After the fourth time the boys said: "Yes, we are warm now." The Sun turned water on the stones which exploded the sweat house; but the boys, with the help of the feathers, landed to one side. The Sun then knew for certain that they were his sons. He took them inside his house, and calling his daughter, said: "These are your brothers, wash them."

The Twins were washed first in a white bead basket, secondly, in a turquoise basket, thirdly, in a white shell basket, and fourthly, in a black jet basket. They learned that this had taken four days. Each day they had been bathed in a different basket. After this their sister brought them to their father who stood them all side by side, their sister between the Twins. The Sun shaped them, legs, arms, fingers and all, even their faces like their sister's. And he powdered them with white powder [63] and their skins were made white. He put something black in a little bowl. It was hair ointment which he put on their hair.[64] He pulled their hair down to their ankles and they had a great

---

[62] Matthews (1897, p. 109).

Recorder's note: Matthews says that the Spider Woman not the grandmother " . . . gave them a charm called naye'atsos, or feather of the alien gods, which consisted of a hoop with two life feathers (feathers plucked from a living eagle) attached, and another life feather hyina'biltsos, to preserve their existence."

[63] Informant's note: The white powder was probably white cornmeal, as is used in ceremonies.

[64] Informant's note: Mountain sheep fat is the ointment for the body. Ak wol, the marrow inside a deer's hoof, is used for the hair.

quantity of hair. Their sister dressed their hair for them and she dressed their persons.[65]

The Sun showed the Twins over his turquoise house and asked them to choose whatever they wished. One of the Twins said: "Father, we do not wish for anything that you have inside the house." The other brother repeated the same thing. Then they went outside the house. Over toward the East the Sun showed the Twins all the different kinds of horses [66] that he owned. He asked his sons if they wanted the horses, but they said it was not their wish. Toward the South he showed them all the domestic animals, cattle, sheep, etc. He asked them if they wanted these, but the Twins answered that it was not for these animals that they had come. Over toward the West the Sun showed them all the game animals and the birds, and he asked his sons if they were what they wanted. Again they said that they had not made the journey for these. He showed them the North and all the different kinds of stones, turquoise, white bead, red stone, and he asked them if these stones were what they wanted. But they said: "No, it is not for these that we have come."

Now on the outer wall of the Sun's house there hung a weapon. The Twins pointed to this weapon and said that that was what they had come for. The weapon looked like a bow and arrows, but in reality it was the lightning.[67] The Sun asked them what they would do with this weapon. The boys told their father of the suffering on earth, and how men were eaten every day by monsters. They named the monsters, one by one, and they said: "Father, if they eat all the people on the earth, and themselves last, for whom will you travel? What will you receive as a gift for the price of your journey?"

The Sun sat with his head down and thought a great thought for Yeitso, the One-Walking Giant, was also his son. Then he spoke and told the Twins that the Giant was their half brother and that they would be slaying their elder brother. (That is why they say that brothers will sometimes kill one another.)

The Sun explained to the Twins that it was not safe for the people on the earth to possess this weapon they asked for. He said that the boys could use the weapon for a little while, but that he would have to

---

[65] Informant's note: The boys were covered with the blankets of dawn, blue sky, yellow evening light, and darkness by their grandmother.

Matthews (1897, note 116, p. 233): "When they were thus equipped they were dressed exactly like their brothers, Black Thunder and Blue Thunder"; Franciscan Fathers (1910, p. 367).

THE ELDER BROTHER   THE YOUNGER BROTHER

[66] Interpreter's note: In an earlier version given by some medicine men: In the Sun's house they were given the following to choose from:—East, fields of finest corn; South, game; West, domestic animals; North, precious stones.

[67] Interpreter's note: This means what we now call electricity.

reclaim it when they were through with it. "For of a certainty the people on the earth will destroy themselves if they are allowed to keep it," he said. He lifted down the weapon and continued: "Now let us go to the top of the middle of the earth where there is an opening in the sky." The Little Breeze whispered to the Twins: "Now he will ask you questions. He counts on your giving the wrong answers, and he plans on refusing to give you the weapons."

The Sun took the weapon [68] and led the Twins to the opening in the sky above Tso dzil, Mt. Taylor. That is where the guessing took place. If the boys did not guess correctly the Sun's plan was to keep them up there and not let them return to earth.

First the Sun pointed to the East and said: "What is that object way down on the earth?" Then the elder brother began chanting:

> What is that he asks me?
> That is the mountain called Sis na'jin.
> It is the White Bead Mountain.
> It is the Chief of the Mountain.
> It is like the Most High Power Whose Ways Are Beautiful.
> What is that down below? he asked me.

The questions included all the sacred mountains. The questions and the answers were just like, in form, the first verse of the chant, that of the East. The Sun said: "My Sons, your guessing is all correct. I know today that you will kill one of the members of your family." He handed the Elder Brother his weapon, which is the lightning, and to the Younger Brother he also handed his weapon, which is also the lightning. The first weapon is called hat tslin it lish ka', the lightning that strikes crooked. The second weapon is hat tsol ilthe ka', the lightning that flashes straight. They were then lowered with their weapons [69] to the center of the world.

---

[68] Matthews (1897, note 114, pp. 232–233): "Four articles of armour were given to each, and different kinds of weapons were given to them. The articles of armour were: peske' (knife moccasins), pesistle (knife leggings), pese' (knife shirt), and pestsa' (knife hat). The word "pes" in the above names for armour is here translated as knife. The term was originally applied to flint knives, and to the flakes from which flint knives are made. After the introduction of European tools the meaning was extended to include iron knives, and now it is applied to any object of iron, and, with qualifying suffixes, to all kinds of metal . . . Many of the Navahos now think that the magic armour of their gods was of iron . . . the armour was supposed to be made of stone flakes such as were employed in the making of knives in prehistoric days. The Mokis believe that their gods and heroes wore armour of flint."

Interpreter's note: In the guessing game, the four mountains were named as were the rivers. The Male River is the San Juan, the Female River is the Rio Grande.

[69] Matthews (1897, pp. 232–233) gives the weapons as follows: atsinnikli' ska, chain-lightning arrows; hatsilki'ska, sheet-lightning arrows; sa bit lo'lka, sunbeam arrows; natsili'tka, rainbow arrows; and pesha'l, stone knife club.

THE STORY OF THE TWINS AND THE GIANT YEITSO

Yeitso, the Giant, lived at Tqo'sedo,[70] Hot Springs, and the Twins went there and waited for him to come for water. They saw him coming over the hill from the south. The Elder Brother sang two sections of a chant then and other chants as the Giant came nearer.

The Giant went down to the spring and drank four times. He drank all the water, and then he spat it back four times and the spring was as before. He walked back and forth and said: "What are the two beautiful things that I see? And how shall I kill them?" The Twins called back: "What beautiful Big Thing is walking about? And how shall we kill it?" They called to each other four times. Then the Little Breeze, who was with the youths, said: "Ako, look out! Up you go. Jump high in the air." The black knife, the Giant's powerful weapon, passed under the Twins. The Little Breeze said: "Keep low now." And over them passed the blue knife. The youths now got hold of the Giant's two weapons. Now came the time for them to use the sacred feathers that their grandmother, the mother of the Sun, had given them, and when the Little Breeze said: "Jump to this side. Look out!" they were able to do so. This time the Giant had thrown the yellow knife, and it passed them and they recovered it. The fourth time the Little Breeze warned the Twins. "Leap high up now," it said. "Here comes the last weapon." And this time the white knife with the many points passed under them. Then the Breeze said: "He has no more weapons."

The Sun had told the Twins that the Giant should be allowed to act first, for he was their elder brother. When their turn came there was a great, blinding flash of lightning and it struck the giant, but he stood there. The Twins aimed the first knife, the black knife, at the Giant. They threw it, but he stood there as before. They aimed and threw the Giant's own blue knife at him. It struck him, but still he stood up. The third knife was yellow, and they hit the Giant with it, but it did not harm him. But when they hit him with the last weapon, the great white knife, he commenced to fall with a terrible noise.

Then the blood began to flow from the Giant's mouth and the Little Breeze said: "Stop the blood before it runs into the water." So the Twins placed a stone knife and an arrow point between the blood and the water. Today you can see a strange formation where the Giant's blood flowed,[71] and also, where the Twins placed the stone knife there

---

[70] Interpreter's note: Tqo'sedo, hot springs, called Navajo Springs, Arizona.

[71] Interpreter's note: South and west of the San Mateo Mountains there is a great plane of lava rock of geologically recent origin, which fills the valley and presents plainly the appearance of having once been flowing.

is a big, black rock standing. This all happened at Tqo'sedo, beyond Gallup and this (Mesa Verde) side of Tso dzil, Mt. Taylor.

The Twins went to the Giant and cut off his scalp.[72] They saw that he was covered with flint armor [73] or clothing made of stone knives. This covered him from his neck to his feet. They gathered some of the stone knives and threw them towards the East, saying: "From now on the people of the earth shall use you. The Giant's spirit has departed from you." They threw the rest of the knives to the South, West and North, and they covered the whole country.

The Twins, carrying the Giant's scalp, started for their home. When they reached there they hung the Giant's scalp on a pole to the east of the hogan. And when they entered the home they found the three sitting there. First Man, First Woman and the White Bead Woman were very frightened. They had squeezed themselves against the wall for they thought that some monsters had arrived to kill them. They did not recognize the Twins for they had been reformed in the house of the Sun. They were now tall, handsome young men with long hair and beautiful beads and clothing. The Twins called out: "Mother do not be frightened, we, your sons, are here." They called out to their grandfather and grandmother adding: "We have been to our father's home."

The three came forward and looked about them. They were still frightened for the Twins shone with beauty. The Twins said: "We have killed the Giant, Yeitso." First Man said: "No one can kill the Giant." They said: "But we have the Giant's scalp hanging on the pole outside." First Woman went outside and, taking down the Giant's scalp, chanted and danced and then hung the scalp on the pole again. She said: "It was by this that I was made to live alone on earth." For long ago her maidens and her people were destroyed by their sins in the Yellow World.

THE STORY OF THE TWINS AND TEEL GET, THE GIANT ELK

The Twins spoke to the three in the home. "Yesterday our father told us that we must act together." They planted four prayer sticks and four hailstones in the hogan (fig. 13). The Younger Brother was

---

[72] Interpreter's note: El Cabason, the Great Head, the Spanish name, is for the Navaho the head of Yeitso. It is about 40 miles from Mount Taylor.

Whitman (1925, p. 58): "The Elder Brother killed Yeitso, the Younger scalped the giant"; Matthews (1897, p. 116) calls the Elder Brother Nay'enez gani, Slayer of Alien Gods; and the Younger Brother, not To'badsist sini, Child of Water, but is here given a new name: Naid ik isi, He Who Cuts Around, because he cut the scalp from the giant.

Recorder's note: Some medicine men say that he cut the giant's head off, others, that he scalped him.

[73] Informant's note: Twenty songs are sung here, the Nidot'atso gisin. In the ceremony of Hazoni hata'l, near Dzil na odili (also according to Matthews) the Twins met Hasjelti and Hasjohon who embraced them and called them "grandchildren." They sang two songs and then conducted them to their home.

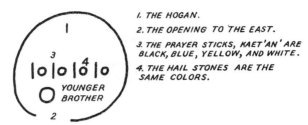

1. THE HOGAN.

2. THE OPENING TO THE EAST.

3. THE PRAYER STICKS, KAET'AN' ARE BLACK, BLUE, YELLOW, AND WHITE.

4. THE HAIL STONES ARE THE SAME COLORS.

FIGURE 13.—The plan of the hogan.

to remain there and watch the medicine sticks [74] each day, while the Elder Brother went out against the monsters. The Elder Brother said: "When you see one of the medicine sticks start to burn you will know that the enemy is getting the better of me. Take the medicine stick in your hand and draw the smoke from it into your mouth and blow the smoke onto the sticks and the hailstones, one by one. And then draw some more smoke from the burning stick and blow the smoke toward the four directions."

After everything was arranged the Younger Brother was left in the hogan and the Elder Brother asked his grandmother where he could find the Giant Elk. She said: "He is to be found over on Bikehalzi'n, the Red Plain, but no one can go near him. When he sees anyone in the distance he charges and catches them and eats them alive. He is very dangerous." Now these monsters had supernatural strength from the rainbow and the lightning, and they were very powerful. But the Elder Brother said: "To all the ends of the earth there is no such place as dangerous." So he went forth to find the animal.

He came to the Red Plain where his grandmother said that the Giant Elk was to be found. When he got to a knoll he gathered a bunch of grass and, as it was tall, he held it in front of himself and crept to the top inch by inch. Just as he reached the crest he saw the Giant Elk, through the bunch of tall grass, quite a distance away. The animal was standing. It was big. It had hair like a moose and a great pair of horns that stood up far into the air. The Elder Brother crept around in a huge circle trying to get closer, and just as he was losing hope an old woman came to him.

She said: "What do you want, my grandchild?" She was the mother gopher. The Elder Brother said: "Grandmother, I am trying to get near the Giant Elk so that I can kill him." She said: "Grandchild, it is impossible. It is impossible to go near that animal. But when my children are cold I can go to him and chew off some of his hair which he gives me for my nest." The Elder Brother said: "Grandmother, you shall have a precious gift if I can have your help."

[74] Stevenson (1891, pp. 242-243). Preparation of sacred reeds (cigarettes) and prayer sticks.

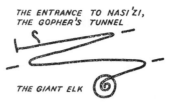

FIGURE 14.—The entrance to the Gopher's tunnel.

She agreed to help him, and she instructed him to wait there while she went into her hole. (See fig. 14.)

When she returned she said that all was in readiness. She had chewed away the hair over the Giant Elk's heart. She told the Elder Brother to follow her; but when he tried to enter the hole which was the entrance to her home he found that it was too small. He hesitated a moment. The mother gopher said: "Raise your right leg." And she puffed into the entrance of her tunnel four times. It was now large enough for the Elder Brother to walk into it. When he reached the end directly over him lay the Giant Elk. He could hear his heart beating: tap, tap, tap. The Elder Brother had with him the weapon which the Sun had given him, the lightning bow and arrow. He aimed and shot. The Giant Elk leapt way up in the air, and when he fell, he fell horns first. He started to tear up the tunnel. The Elder Brother ran back as fast as he could. He ran back to almost the mouth of the tunnel when he heard the Giant Elk drop. Then the Elder Brother walked out onto Bikehalzi'n, the Red Plain.

In those days each animal had certain powers. It was theirs alone. This time the Elder Brother had used the power given the mother gopher. Now after the Elder Brother came out of the tunnel he found the mother gopher with her hands over her heart. She said: "Oh, my heart is sick with fright!" She told him how the Giant Elk acted. "If he had reached the mouth of the tunnel we would have been eaten alive."

Just then a man came up. He was the chipmunk.[75] He came to see if the great animal was really dead. They, the chipmunk and the gopher, were still frightened. The chipmunk wanted to make sure that this was so. He said: "If the animal is quite dead you will see me at the top of one of the horns." The Elder Brother and the mother gopher watched and when they saw the chipmunk at the top of the Giant Elk's horn they went near. The chipmunk had gotten the blood from the animal's mouth and wiped it on his back, from his head to his tail. That is why the chipmunk has dark lines on his back today. The gopher also took some of the blood and rubbed it over the

---

[75] Informant's note: Some say that it is hazai, the ground squirrel, not the chipmunk.

palms of her hands, and then over her face. That is why gophers have dark faces.

The Elder Brother skinned the Giant Elk. He cut the hide and made it fit his body like a coat. He cut holes for his arms to pass through; he cut the belly and made holes for laces. Then he cut out the main arteries and blood vessels and tied them so that the blood remained inside, and he put them around his neck. They hung down over his heart, and he tied them there. Then he removed the coat, placing the arteries, and laces inside it. He took these things, together with the horns, but he told the mother gopher that she could have the rest of the Giant Elk. And so saying, he set out for his home.

When the Elder Brother returned he entered his home and said: "Grandmother, I have killed the Giant Elk." The grandmother spoke up: "That is an impossible thing to do." But he answered: "Look, the hide is outside." The grandmother went outside, and taking the hide she chanted [76] and danced as she had chanted and danced with the Giant's scalp.

Now two of the monsters were killed. The plan of the Sacred People was being fulfilled.

THE STORY OF THE ELDER BROTHER AND TSE NA'HALE, THE GIANT BIRDS [77]

The next morning, after the Elder Brother had returned from killing the Giant Elk, he asked: "Mother, Grandmother, where do the Giant Birds live?" They told him that they were to be found just north of La Plata Mountains, at a place called Tse an' iska', A Tall Rock Standing.[78] "It is a dangerous place," they said. "No one can go near there." The Elder Brother said: "In all the world there is no such thing as a dangerous place." So he made his plan.

---

[76] Informant's note: The chant that the grandmother used was the one that the warriors used. It is sung also before going on a hunting trip. It is sacred. This part must never be told in the summertime—all the stories of the killing of monsters. This ceremony could be used against kin among the Navaho, should anyone be wicked enough to do it. Sometimes it has even been used between brothers and sisters, for the Twins killed their elder brother, the giant, Yeitso. The remedy is to use the chants the Elder Brother sang when going against the monsters. There are hundreds of these chants. By reading the stories one can get an idea of the wording of the chants. The chants always tell the story—the deeds of the holy ones, places, etc.

[77] Recorder's note: Whitman (1925, pp. 66–75) gives Tsenahale as the name of the Giant Birds. There is also an interesting article "An Athabascan Tradition from Alaska, The Giant Birds," by Wright (1908, p. 33).

Informant's note: There are many versions of this story.

[78] Matthews (1897, p. 119, also note 136, p. 235): He says that tse bida'i is the Winged Rock or Shiprock. Franciscan Fathers (1910, p. 357): Tse bida'i Winged Rock or Shiprock.

But both the informant and the interpreter said that this was an error. The name is correct, but it was not the home of the Giant Birds.

He put on the elkskin coat that he had made and laced the front of it. He placed the blood vessels which contained the Giant Elk's blood around his neck and laced the coat over them. Also he placed the two sacred feathers, which the Sun's mother had given him, one under each arm. He carried the black knife and the lightning bow and arrow and one of the horns of the Giant Elk; with these he started out.

When he neared the mountain, at a place where the town of Marvel now is located (this—Mesa Verde—side of Durango), all of a sudden he began to wonder if the Giant Birds had seen him.

The chant is like this:

> I wonder if the lone eyes are watching me?
> I wonder if the lone eyes are watching me?
> I wonder if the lone eyes are watching me?
> I am he who has killed the monsters.
> The lightning is before me.
> All is beautiful behind me.

(The chant continued: "I wonder what the big birds will do to me?" etc.)

As the Elder Brother approached La Plata Mountains he sang two other chants. And as he was singing he saw a black speck over the mountains. It was one of the Giant Birds. It swooped like a hawk after a chicken. The Elder Brother lay, face downward, flat on the ground. The bird [79] scratched the back of his coat but did not get a hold. The elder Brother chanted:

> The Big Bird has missed me.
> The Big Bird has missed me.
> I alone have been missed.
> I alone have been missed.

The big bird circled around again and dived for him. He missed him again, and again the Elder Brother chanted as before. The fourth time he lay on his back, and when the big bird swooped down he caught the lacings of the coat in his talons. Then the Elder Brother sang:

> The Big Bird got hold of me.
> The Big Bird got hold of me.
> I alone shall be saved.
> I alone shall be saved.

He repeated this chant eight times, and he blew eight times on the bird. In this way the Elder Brother was carried to the home of the Giant Birds.

The Giant Bird carried him over a high peak, and over a great smooth rock and there he dropped him. But the Elder Brother landed safely by the help of the sacred feathers and the Giant Elk's horn. There he lay on his back and cut open the blood vessels around his

---

[79] Informant's note: The Giant Birds are called Tse na'hale. They are named after the fashion in which they carry a being to the top of the rock and let him fall against it.

neck, and out poured the blood. The Giant Bird called his two young ones, his two children, and he told them to go and eat. The two young birds approached the Elder Brother and made for his eyes, but he said: "Sash, Sash it!" and they backed away. (That is why an eagle flies backward when he first lands on the ground.) The young birds returned to their father and said: "He is alive, father." The Giant Bird told them to hush and go and eat. This happened four times. Each time the young birds called back to their father that they were afraid because the youth was still alive. Finally the Giant Bird flew away, but before he left he called to the young birds and told them if they were hungry to go ahead and eat.

When the young birds began to cry the Elder Brother told them to hush, that he would not harm them. So the young birds took him to their nest, and the three camped there that night. They had for their cover all the white flowers that grow on the mountains, made like a feather quilt.

The next morning the Elder Brother asked them when their father returned. They answered: "Our father returns when you see the Male Rain begin to fall." So when the Male Rain commenced falling at a certain time of the day the young birds looked up and said: "Our father is coming with a load." The Elder Brother looked into the sky but he could see nothing. He asked the young birds where their father would light, and they showed him the place. He went there and made ready, weapon in hand.

When the Giant Bird flew over the peak he threw a young man on the rock where he had thrown the Elder Brother the day before. The great bird circled and lighted just where the young birds said that he would. Before the Giant Bird's wings were closed the Elder Brother took aim and shot his arrow. The Giant Bird tumbled over with a great roar which was heard at a considerable distance, and then the echo was heard.

The two young birds began to cry, but the Elder Brother told them to hush, that he would not harm them, that he would save them. He asked them when their mother would return. They said: "When the Female Rain falls, then our mother will return." He waited, and he camped that night as before with the young ones. The next day when the Female Rain began to fall the young birds looked up and said: "Our mother is coming with a load." The Elder Brother asked them where the mother bird would light when she came home, and they told him the place. He went to the ledge indicated and sat under it and made ready his weapons. When the mother bird flew over the rock she threw down a beautiful maiden. The Elder Brother saw that she had lots of hair and strings of turquoise for earrings. Now as soon as the Giant Bird lighted the Elder Brother took aim and shot his lightning arrow. The Giant Bird tumbled over the rock with a great noise which was heard over the mountain. The two young birds began to cry, but the Elder Brother went to them and said: "I shall not harm you. You will be saved."

The Elder Brother called to the older of the two birds and said:

Sit here before me. From this day on you will not think as your father thought. The thoughts of your mother have also departed from you. You will forget all that has happened to you, and the spirits of your father and mother will not enter you again. The tribe which is called Dîné shall use you. They shall use your claws, your feathers, your bill, your eyes and your bile.

This he said to the elder bird, and he raised him up and told him to go. The young bird rose and flew up into the sky and out of sight. He was the eagle.

Then the Elder Brother called the younger bird and said: "You sit before me now." He prepared a smoke for himself. He puffed the smoke on his fingers and passed his hand over the bird crosswise. He told him that the thoughts of his father and his mother had departed from him, and that their spirits would not enter him again. "The tribe called Dîné shall use your feathers. When they are out alone and lost you will help them. In case of famine they will eat you for meat. Whatever you say will have a double meaning: it can be taken for a lie or for the truth." He raised the young bird and told him to go. He did not fly high but just over the rocks. He circled around, and the Elder Brother heard an owl hoot. He had said that the owl could be eaten as food. The Giant Birds had big eyes, so are the eyes of the owl.

After that the Elder Brother was alone on top of the great rock. He searched everywhere but there was no way to descend. Now this was the fourth day since he had left his home. The Younger Brother kept watch over the medicine sticks and they were all standing as at first. But the Elder Brother was really worried and lonesome. He sat on the high peak and looked in the direction of his home. He could see a black cloud hanging over his homeland and he saw a black streak of rain and lightning flashing, and the rainbow shone on one side.

This is the chant he sang as he sat there:

Far in the distance the black cloud rises.
I am he who killed the monsters.
Far in the distance the black cloud rises.
The Male Rain rises up from the far horizon.
Lightning rises from the far horizon.
The rainbow rises from the far horizon.
They rise like the Most High Power Whose Ways Are Beautiful.
They rise far in the distance.
I am he who came to earth with the lightning.
The black vapor rises far in the distance.

The Female Rain rises far in the distance.
The lightning rises far in the distance.
The rainbow rises far in the distance.
They rise like the Most High Power Whose Ways Are Beautiful.
They rise far in the distance.

The Elder Brother circled the cliff and he saw the old Bat Woman carrying a basket way down below him. He called down from the top of the rock and said: "Grandmother, take me off the top of this rock in your basket." She mumbled something and hurried behind a rock for she was frightened as she had never heard anyone call from the home of the Giant Birds. He called down again, and she peered out from behind the rock. He said: "Grandmother there is no danger up here for I have killed the Giant Birds." Then he called again: "If you take me down you can have all the feathers from the Giant Birds." Then she called up: "You go over to the edge and dig a hole in the ground and put your head into it and wait until I come up." [81] So he did as she said. He stayed there with his head in the ground, and he heard her singing as she came up. It took a long time until she reached the top of the rock. She then said to the Elder Brother: "Get up, my child. What are you doing here?" When he stood up he saw the grandmother bat with her basket. "You may have all the feathers of the Giant Birds," said the Elder Brother, "if you take me down from this high peak." The grandmother bat said: "Very well. Get into my basket." He saw that it was made of tiny strings woven together, and he said: "Grandmother, those strings are too fragile to hold me up." Whereupon she filled her basket with heavy stones and danced around with it. When she dumped out the stones he got into the basket. She said to him: "You must close your eyes." To make sure of this she wrapped his head in the baby buffalo hide that she had received as her gift when she went to the home of the Great Gambler. So they started to climb down the cliff. It seemed a long time to the Elder Brother who began to open his eyes. He thought: where in the world is she taking me?

The Bat Woman started to fall. She hit over her shoulder with her walking stick and said: "Oh, you foolish-headed boy. You will wander where you do not belong." And she continued to lay on the stick. When they reached the ground the Elder Brother climbed out of the basket and asked: "What happened, Grandmother?" But she just shook her head.

They walked to the place where the Giant Birds had fallen to earth. There the Elder Brother filled the Bat Woman's basket with the feathers, those of the wings, tail and all. He covered the basket with the

---

[81] Interpreter's note: He had to hide his eyes for the Bat Woman wore only a small apron which flapped as she climbed.

hide of the baby buffalo; and he told her that she must not go through the grove of sunflowers with her load. Then he gathered up the wing and tail feathers which he had put aside for himself, and started for his home.

As he had disobeyed the grandmother bat on their way down the cliff she decided to get even with him. She went straight for the sunflowers. A jackrabbit came up to her and said: "Grandmother, what have you in your basket?" He looked in and pulled out two tail feathers which he stuck through his headband. "Now I am quite fine," he said. (And that is why the jackrabbit has long ears.)

When the Bat Woman arrived in the sunflower patch thousands of little birds [82] flew out of her basket. She tried to pull them back, but she lost them all. She called out to the Elder Brother: "Oh, Grandson, look, I have lost all my feathers." But the Elder Brother was well on his way, and he thought to himself: now who will take the trouble to reload her basket.

When the Elder Brother reached his home the Younger Brother met him and said: "I have watched the kethawns (medicine sticks) all the time you were gone. I saw the black stick smoking and I knew that you were in danger; but it went out and I knew that you had overcome the enemy." The Elder Brother left the wing and tail feathers of the Giant Birds outside and the Twins entered the hogan. The Elder Brother said: "Mother, Grandmother, Grandfather, I have killed the two Giant Birds." But First Woman answered: "There is no one able to kill them." He said: "But go and see. The feathers are outside." The grandmother went outside and took up the feathers and danced, saying: "It was for this I was made to live alone." [83]

THE STORY OF TSE'NAGA'HAI, THE ROLLING ROCK

The next morning the Elder Brother asked his mother and grandmother where the big Rolling Rock could be found. They said: "It can be found at a place called Betchil gai,[84] the Shining Rock. But the Rolling Rock is dangerous. It runs after a person and rolls over him. It is very dangerous." But the Elder Brother said: "There is no such place as dangerous on the earth."

He gathered together all his knives and started out for the Shining Rock. When he came near it he took out his black knives and crossed

---

[82] Interpreter's note: All the little birds were created at this time: juncos, nuthatches, titmice, etc. They were called naat'a'gi.

[83] Informant's note: There comes a little chuckle in the narrative whenever the old ones think that they know more than the younger ones.

[84] Matthews (1897, note 152, p. 237) gives the list of 17 places where pieces of the Rolling Rock were knocked off. He gives the place of the Rolling Rock as Tes'espai, as does Whitman (1925).

them and planted them. A little farther on he planted the two blue knives, crosswise. On beyond he planted the two yellow knives, also crosswise. The last to be planted were the two knives with the serrated edges. These, also, he planted crosswise. He came out now in sight of the Rolling Rock. The Rock started for him; and he ran and jumped over the serrated knives. When the great Rock rolled over them a huge piece of it broke away. The Elder Brother jumped over the yellow knives, and when the Rock rolled over them again a big piece broke away. He jumped over the blue knives, and the Rock rolled after him, and another piece broke off. He jumped over the black knives, and when the Rock rolled over them there was only a little piece of it left, and it had very little life in it.

The Elder Brother chased this remaining piece of the Rock westward into the San Juan River. He got a piece of the rock that had been broken off the Rolling Rock and he sat down and told it that the thoughts of the great Rolling Rock had left it and would never again enter it. "The tribe called the Dîné will use you," he said. "They will use you for flint to strike fire from."

The Elder Brother carried the small piece of the Rolling Rock to his home. He left it outside and entered the hogan. He said: "Mother, Grandmother, Grandfather, I have killed the great Rolling Rock." They all answered: "No one has the power to kill the great Rolling Rock." The Elder Brother said: "But you can find a piece of it outside." So First Woman went out and taking up the stone she danced around four times, saying: "It was because of this that I was made to live alone."

So far four kinds of monsters had been killed.

THE STORY OF TSADIDAHALT' A LI, THE TWELVE ANTELOPE [85]

The morning after the Elder Brother returned with the fragment of the Rolling Rock he said: "Mother, Grandmother, where can I find the Twelve Antelope who devour people?" Now these antelope were to be found on the plain surrounding Shiprock. The women said: "They are to be found at a place called Hale gai' e dinla'."

First he made a torch out of bark and then he started for the plain. When the Twelve Antelope saw him coming they all ran for him, but he lit the torch and touched off the dry grass. The antelope circled the fire and the rising smoke, and with his weapons he was able to kill eleven of them. He caught just one. He talked to the antelope and said: "All the thoughts and spirits of your comrades have departed from you. Those thoughts will never enter you again. People will use your flesh for meat. Your head, also, will be used by the people."

---

[85] Franciscan Fathers (1910, p. 358): Jadi nakhidzada, the 12 antelopes fathered by plants.

He let the antelope go. "Your home will be on the plains," he said. "Later the people will use the antelope head, called bea da', when they go hunting." [86]

After the Elder Brother had sent the antelope away he cut off the head of one of the animals that he had killed and turned toward his home. Stepping inside the hogan he said: "Mother, Grandmother, Grandfather, I have killed the antelope." They all said: "No one has ever killed one of them. They are dangerous." But he answered: "But the head of one of the antelope is outside." And again the old woman went out, and taking up the head, she danced around four times, saying: "It was for this that I was made to live alone."

THE STORY OF TSE'TAHOTSILTA'LI, HE-WHO-KICKS-PEOPLE-OFF-CLIFFS [87]

The morning after the Elder Brother returned from killing the antelope he asked: "Mother, Grandmother, where do I find the being called Tse'tahotsilta'li, the Kicker?" Now he was a monster in human form who lay in wait near the edge of a cliff and kicked anyone passing by over the cliff to where his children could reach him and eat him, for they were cannibals. This being lived on Wild Horse Mesa now in the Mesa Verde area. The Kicker could be found on a little neck of the mesa above Ute Canyon. The White Bead Woman and First Woman told the Elder Brother that this being was dangerous, that he kicked people off cliffs, but he said: "There is no place dangerous on earth." [88]

The Elder Brother left his home and journeyed to the top of Wild Horse Mesa. All of a sudden he saw a man lying on his back, his arm doubled under his head. He stopped and said: "Grandfather, is it all right to pass through here?" This person answered: "Yes Grandson, people pass back and forth through here." The Elder Brother pretended to take a quick step forward, but he stepped back instead. The being had kicked. The young man said: "What does this mean, Grandfather?" The being said: "Oh, I had a bad cramp in my leg." The same thing happened four times. Then the Elder Brother hit the being with his long knife and killed him.

The Elder Brother threw the being down over the cliff [89] where his own children were waiting. There was a great shouting below.

---

[86] Informant's note: The tongues of the antelope are black because once upon a time they ate human beings.

[87] Franciscan Fathers (1910, p. 358): Tse'dahidzitqa'li, the one who kicks from the cliff. Matthews (1897, p. 122).

[88] Informant's note: Here there are chants, as there are chants of all the killings of monsters.

[89] Matthews (1897, p. 122; also note 143, p. 236): ". . . he discovered that the being's long hair grew, like roots of cedar, into a cleft in the rock. He cut the hair and the body tumbled down out of sight."

Someone said: "Mine is the head." Another said: "Mine is the heart." And so on, for they wanted different parts of the body. But when the body reached the ground they all stepped back. "This is the body of our father!" They cried. But the mother told them to go ahead and eat.

When the Elder Brother reached them he saw that they were ugly and dirty. First, he told them to eat if they wanted the head and the heart of the monster. Then he talked to the wife and the children. He said that they must all travel to the West. He told them that the thoughts and the spirit of the father had departed from them, that they would no longer think nor act as he had done. But because of the evil that their father had committed they would always be a poor people; they would not have the beads and turquoise as had the other tribes. He sent them toward the west to Natsisa'an, Navaho Mountain. Some later became the Paiutes [90] but others journeyed still farther westward. They were barefoot and the soles of their feet turned black.

After the wife and children had departed the Elder Brother cut off the Kicker's scalp and went home. Stepping inside the house he said: "Mother, Grandmother, I have killed the Great Kicker." They said: "No. No one could kill him." He said: "But, Grandmother, his scalp is outside." So First Woman went outside the home and taking up the scalp she danced about four times, chanting: "It was for this that I was made to live alone."

THE STORY OF LOKA'ADI KISI, THE SLASHING REEDS [91]

The next morning the Elder Brother asked: "Now where are the Slashing Reeds to be found?" They told him that they were to be found at a place called Tse'nee'tlene near the mouth of La Plata River. They told him that they were dangerous reeds, that they cut people to pieces.

The Elder Brother made himself flint armor and started out for the place. When he arrived near them the reeds began to slash about in different directions, but they could not harm him because of his "knife" armor. He lit a torch, which he had brought with him, and burned the reeds. He burned all but one, which he saved, and to this one he spoke. "All the evil actions of the Slashing Reeds you must forget. People will use you. You will be used in the cutting medi-

---

[90] Matthews (1897, p. 123) : "They went to Natsisaan, Navajo Mountain, and became the progenitors of the Pahutes." Franciscan Fathers (1910, p. 400) : Natsis'an, Navaho Mountain.

Informant's note: It is sometimes said that these creatures were turned into birds of prey.

[91] Matthews (1897, p. 110) ; Franciscan Fathers (1910, p. 358), luka digi'shi, slashing reeds.

cine stick, which will be given as a gift to the Sacred People, and also, for the stick itself." Then he waved the reed all around him and planted it in the ground, and reeds sprang up in quantity. He carried one of these home with him.

He stepped inside the hogan and said: "Mother, Grandmother, I have destroyed the Slashing Reeds." They told him that no one who had gotten among them had come out alive. "But look, Grandmother," he said, "one of them is outside."

First Woman went outside and danced and chanted four times with the reed in her hand. She said: "It was for this that I was made to live alone."

THE STORY OF THE BEAUTIFUL, DANGEROUS YOUNG WOMAN

The next is the story of the beautiful young woman called Bet jo'gie etta hi ee',[92] meaning overwhelming sex. She was a wild young woman who thought only of one thing. She was very beautiful and very dangerous, for she went from place to place catching young men whom she harmed. She crushed their sex organs.

The day after the Elder Brother returned from destroying the Slashing Reeds, he asked: "Mother, Grandmother, where is that certain young woman to be found?"

"She is to be found at a place called Tse' et ha' ee, Red Mesa." They told him this and also what she did to a young man if she caught him.

He made his plan, and he fashioned four sticks, each shaped as a man's sex organ. He covered them with the sour juice of a certain plant and he went forth to find the woman monster. He reached the place where his mother told him he would find her, and he saw her fresh tracks. He was following them when all of a sudden he heard a noise behind him and looking back he saw a beautiful maiden coming toward him.

"Where are you from, may I ask?" she said. "Oh," he said, "I just happened along." Coming nearer she said: "You must be my husband. The two of us can live together." The Elder Brother said: "I have never touched a woman." But she told him that she knew all, that he did not have to worry. He repeated the same thing four times, and four times she assured him that she knew all. Then he told her that when they lay together they must both close their eyes, and she was willing. When he used the first of his sticks it was cut in two. He used the second and it was also cut in two. He used the third and it was cut in two; and he used the fourth and she was dead. Her sex organ had its power from the night and the blue haze and the twilight and the black sunbeam.

---

[92] Franciscan Fathers (1910, p. 358) : bijosh yeda'a', the overwhelming vagina. She conceived of cane cactus, qosh naola'li.

The Elder Brother cut out her sex organs and said: "There shall be no more women like you found here. But in cases where a man gets a sickness from a woman, the medicine I use will be used as a cure." [93]

(Here there is a certain ceremony which pertains to this. It is used for either man or woman.)

He took what he had cut out, and her scalp, and returned to his home. And as before, his grandmother danced four times, carrying them, and saying: "It was for this that I was made to live alone."

THE STORY OF THE LAST GREAT GRIEF, THE SWALLOW PEOPLE OF MESA VERDE

There remained the great Swallow People in the Mancos Canyon and beyond. They had been at war ever since the killing of the Coyote.

The Elder Brother said: "Mother, Grandmother, Grandfather, where are the Swallow People to be found?" They told him that they were to be found at a place called Tqo tzosko, Water in the Narrow Canyon. So he started out and traveled to Jackson Canyon.

There were thousands and thousands of Swallow People and he killed them right and left. He killed and killed, and he worked his way to the mouth of Mancos Canyon. Then he began running. He was tired and there were still thousands to be killed. When he reached the second rock near the San Juan River he was very tired. At home, in the hogan, all the medicine sticks were seen burning. The Younger Brother said: "Look, Grandmother, all the medicine sticks are burning." First Woman said: "Hurry and do as your brother told you to do." So the Younger Brother took the smoke from the first stick and blew it on the hailstone next to it, and so on for all four. Then he blew the smoke in the four directions.

A big, black cloud shot out of the sky over the place where the Elder Brother was resting. A great storm broke, thunder, lightning, rain, and hail. This hail destroyed the remaining Swallow People and all the lesser giants who lived in the mesa country. [94]

---

[93] Recorder's note: Probably the sour cactus. But the plants used in the ceremony called be'e kanze, or, be e ganze, for the "itching disease" are: tsil'jin, or, tsil chin, a shrub whose leaves resemble sumac; dit joli, leechee e', and, dit tse de koshi (these are unidentified). The roots of these four plants are boiled and the juice is used.

Informant's note: This ceremony has a chant and medicine sticks, with offerings. The sickness is called dit chit. It is not syphilis. There is a story that tells of one of the Twin Brothers contracting syphilis from a woman. The cure was a plant found on Mesa Verde.

Recorder's note: This plant was identified as Oregon grape, one of the barberries (Saunders, 1933, pp. 88–89.) Oregon grape is gathered; an infusion with salt added is taken. There is also the sweat bath and bathing with the infusion.

[94] Recorder's note: The Swallow People, the people who live in the cliffs, appear in the myths of the Zuñi and Hopi as well as the Navaho. The informant, however, identified them with the Cliff Dwellers of Mesa Verde.

The Elder Brother caught just one of the Swallow People and he told him that from now on he would be of very little use. "You will be harmless from now on," he said. And he let him go. But he took the scalp of one of the dead Swallow People and started for his home.

On his way someone ran after him. It was Mother Earth, herself. She said: "Grandson, you suffered greatly that time, didn't you?" He said: "Yes, Grandmother, I surely did." And she said: "You are in a hurry; but let me sing you this chant." She sang the two chants for the Twin Brothers.[95]

When the Elder Brother returned to his home with the scalp, the Grandmother danced and chanted four times as before.

THE STORY OF TSE'YEINTI'LI,[96] THE ROCKS THAT CRUSH

Now although the Swallow People were the last of the Great Ills, still there were other dreadful beings that destroyed humans on the earth. Way back in Time there was a piece of rock brought up from the underworld; and people were told that at times rocks would hurt them. There was a place called Tse'a haildehe', a narrow place between two cliffs, where, if one started to step over it, it widened or drew apart, and then returned to its first position crushing the person who had fallen into the crevice. This place was beyond Salt Canyon near the head of a canyon having many cracks in the rocks.

The time the Elder Brother went there, there was a distance of about 2 feet between the cliffs. He made as though to step across, but the opposite cliff drew away. When he took a step backward the cliffs drew together. This happened four times. He then placed the Giant Elk's horn across it and it remained in place. He carried a piece of this cliff rock to his home; but before leaving he commanded the cliffs to stay in place and never to move again.

THE STORY OF NAYIE A'ANYIE,[97] OR THE EVIL EYES

The Elder Brother asked his mother and grandmother about the Evil Eyes, and they told him that they lived to the south of their home.

He walked until he arrived at a Rock with a Black Hole, Tse' ahalizi'ni, where these evil beings lived. When he reached the place he built a fire and after it was burning brightly he stirred it. He had brought a bag of salt with him, and, as soon as the whole family of beings looked at him with their many eyes, he threw the salt on the fire and there was a great smoke which hurt their eyes and tears came and

---

[95] Informant's note: The same chants are used here as when a party goes to war.

[96] Franciscan Fathers (1910), tse yi'donahunt'i, impassable creviceffl (1912, p. 182), tse aqae'ndil, stones which clap together.

[97] Franciscan Fathers (1910, p. 358): bina'yeagha'ni, who killed by the charm of their eyes. Whitman (1925, p. 75): Binaye ahani, Evil Eyes.

they could not see. So he killed them.[98] From these beings came the trouble of sore eyes among people. The Elder Brother prayed that there should be no more of such beings formed to harm the people of the earth.

THE STORY OF THE FOUR LAST ILLS [99]

The White Bead Woman and First Woman told the Eldest Brother that the four last ills could be found south of their home.

He traveled southward and he found a ragged old man. He was just a bundle of rags. The Elder Brother was about to kill him when he said: "No, my Grandson, you must not kill me, even though I am Tie en, Poverty, for in six months people will have good clothing, and at the end of that time, called autumn, they will use it for the winter, in order to keep themselves warm." The Elder Brother, knowing that the virtue accompanying poverty is appreciation, let him live.

He walked on and he found an old, old woman. He was about to kill her for she was San, Old Age, but she stopped him and said: "No, no, my Grandson, do not kill me. People will grow old. Know that it will be the old people who will tell the young people what happened in years past. It would not be well if there were only young people on the earth. Every growing thing, including human beings will grow old." The Elder Brother knew that wisdom walked with old age, and he let her live.

Then he traveled on and he found the two E ya a', lice,[100] and he was about to kill them when they said: "No, don't kill us. We shall be seen on animals at different times. When we get on people they will say: 'Sister,[1] there is something on me. Look for it.' Let us live." The Elder Brother let them live, for although they were evils they brought with them compassion.

The fourth ill that the Elder Brother met was a creature of bluish color. "Do not kill me," he said. "I am death, Grandson. Spare me, for if every creature lived there would be no place on earth for youth and laughter." The Elder Brother left him with the others.

---

[98] Matthews (1897, pp. 123–124) says that the two youngest were spared. He changed one into Tsi dil to'i, shooting bird, who gives warning at the approach of an enemy; and the other, Hos to'di, the bird that sleeps in the day and comes out at night.

[99] Matthews (1897, pp. 130–131): San, Old Age, is an old woman who lived on Debentsa, San Juan Mountains. She represents the good element and the increase of people. Hakaz estsen, Cold Woman, lived on the summit of Debentsa. She is given as a lean, old woman who sat without clothing in the snow. The good element: if it were always hot weather the springs would dry up, and the land would dry up and burn. Tie en Poverty, lived on Dzil asdzi'ni. The good element: the joy in having new clothes, etc. Ditsi'n, Hunger, lived on Tlo hadashai, White Spot of Grass. The good: the enjoyment of food. Whitman (1925), in his Navaho Tales, calls Debentsa, Mount Big Sheep.

[100] Lowie (1908, p. 114) ". . . the reflection of a social custom. Picking lice from each other's heads is a sign of mutual friendship and love."

[1] Interpreter's note: This is so that people may know their true relations. The term "sister" is used as one denoting relationship.

He thought great thoughts of the earth and the waters and the sky. If there was no death there could be no new life.

The Elder Brother went to the East and returned. All was well in the East. "There are no more monsters there," he said. And he went to the South and returned. "All is well in the South," he said. Then he went to the West and came back to his home and said: "There are no more monsters in the West. All is well towards the West." Last he went North and he came back from the North and said: "All is well in the North. Mother, Grandmother, Grandfather, there is no longer danger on earth. All is well to the ends of the earth."

The Twins said that now their work was finished. All the monsters who harmed the people of the earth had been slain. Naye'nez gani,[2] the Elder Brother, took off his armor and his moccasins and leggings, he laid down his knives and the lightning weapon that the Sun had given him.[3] Then the Sun came and said: "My son, it is all well now. I shall take my weapons back with me. If I leave them with you, people will use them and harm themselves." But before he left the Elder Brother picked up an arrow and drew two crooked lines and one straight one on the shaft. He did this as a reminder of the sacred weapons. The Sun began to gather the sacred weapons together before starting out. He spoke to the Twins. "I want the White Bead Woman, your mother, to live in a beautiful white shell house in the West. A house like the turquoise house in the East." So the White Bead Woman went to the top of Chol'i'i, where she had been found as a baby. And there she made her plan.

Now up to that time all the things that the Sun had planned had not been successful; but all that the Yei Hasjelti and Hasjohon had planned had come out well. The Sun lost, although he had married the maiden which they had left on Chol'i'i. So power went to the two Yei who had formed the White Bead Baby. Some of the power went to the White Bead Woman herself. With this power she was able to make her people, the tribe called Dîné. This tribe looks upon her as their mother. The Dîné pray to her as well as to Hasjelti and Hasjohon. So it is partly with the power of Wyol gie san, the White Bead Woman, that the monsters were destroyed, and that the tribe called Dîné came to this country and multiplied.

---

[2] Franciscan Fathers (1910, p. 360): The Twin Brothers are named: Naye'nez ghani, Slayer of Monsters; and Tqo bajish chi'ni, Child of the Water. See page 77, this bulletin, footnote 54.

[3] Informant's note: Here there is a chant.

THE WANDERINGS OR AGE OF THE PATRIARCHS

INTRODUCTION: SANDOVAL'S PRAYER

Sandoval sat on the floor. "Now begins the Night Chant of 'All Is Well,'" he said. He chanted and Sam, the interpreter, chanted with him. For them this was sacred. After the chant Sandoval passed his medicine pouch to Sam who took a pinch of pollen and placed it on his tongue and head and threw the remainder in the air to the east. I was told to do likewise. The pouch having been returned, Sandoval placed pollen on his tongue and head. He threw some into the air, sprinkling quite a bit over the manuscript. Then he prayed:

For long years I have kept this beauty within me,
It has been my life.
It is sacred.
I give it now that coming generations may know the truth
About my people.
I give it as the dew falls.
I give it as sacred pollen,
That there may increase a better understanding among men.
My days have been long.
Whoever reads and loves and learns from these stories
Shall profit by them,
And their days shall be lengthened.
I give these in the spirit of generosity
Asking that no harm will come from the Powers
Who have given these stories to us.
May no harm come from them.
May they be accepted as an offering,
As the pollen,
As the dew.

One of the Night Chants, the chant of All Is Well [4]

This covers it all,
The Earth and the Most High Power Whose Ways Are Beautiful.
All is beautiful before me,
All is beautiful behind me,
All is beautiful below me,
All is beautiful above me,
All is beautiful all around me.

This covers it all,
The Skies and the Most High Power Whose Ways Are Beautiful.
All is beautiful. . . .

---

[4] Informant's note: This chant is used to correct all the mistakes that anyone may make. The Tqo'adaline Night Chant comes from the story of the Water Baby. It belonged to the interpreter's grandfather. There are several chants like this one which different medicine men use. They differ slightly.

This covers it all,
The Mountains and the Most High Power Whose Ways Are Beautiful.
All is beautiful. . . .

This covers it all,
The Water and the Most High Power Whose Ways Are Beautiful.
All is beautiful. . . .

This covers it all,
The Darkness and the Most High Power Whose Ways Are Beautiful.
All is beautiful. . . .

This covers it all,
The Dawn and the Most High Power Whose Ways Are Beautiful.
All is beautiful. . . .

This covers it all,
Hasjelti and the Most High Power Whose Ways Are Beautiful.
All is beautiful. . . .

This covers it all,
Hasjohon and the Most High Power Whose Ways Are Beautiful.
All is beautiful. . . .

This covers it all,
The White Corn and the Most High Power Whose Ways Are Beautiful.
All is beautiful. . . .

This covers it all,
The Yellow Corn and the Most High Power Whose Ways Are Beautiful.
All is beautiful. . . .

This covers it all,
The Pollen and the Most High Power Whose Ways Are Beautiful.
All is beautiful. . . .

THE ORIGIN OF THE DÎNÉ

After the bow and arrows of lightning were returned to the Sun,
Hasjelti and Hasjohon came to First Man and First Woman and asked
them what they thought about all that had happened. "What will
take place now will be your plan," they said. "Yes," answered First
Man and First Woman, "Now it must be our plan. We will think
about it." [5]

The Sun brought a turquoise man fetish and gave it to Yol gai
esdzan, the White Bead Woman. She ground white beads into a
powder and made a paste with which she molded a fetish like the one
the Sun had given her, but it was a woman. When it was finished they
laid the two side by side. Then they took the white corn which was
brought up from the Dark World where the First Man was formed and
they laid it beside the turquoise man fetish. And the yellow corn from

---

[5] Matthews (1897, pp. 29–33) ; Hodge (1895, pp. 223–240).

the Dark World, which was formed with First Woman, was laid by the side of the White Bead Woman fetish.

Here the chanting begins.[6] It covers the two fetishes and the two ears of corn and the four clouds and the four vapors. There are many chants sung here. They were sung before the fetishes could move. Then the two fetishes, the Turquoise Man and the White Bead Woman, and also, the two ears of corn, white and yellow, moved.[7]

When they began to move the Coyote[8] came. He jumped on the bodies and put something first up one nostril and then up the other nostril. He said to the first nostril: "You shall be saved by this." To the second nostril he said: "This shall be your shield." The first turned out to be the trickery of men; the second, the lies that they tell. But once in a while they are saved by their own lies. That was what the Coyote had in mind.

The fetishes and the ears of corn moved but they were not able to rise. So word was sent to all the Holy Beings and to the Upper World where the Five Chiefs of the Wind dwelt. Gifts were offered to the Winds and they accepted them. They sent the Little Breeze down, and it entered the bodies of the two fetishes and the two ears of corn. Little, fine hairs appeared over the bodies, for it is through these that air comes out of the body. It was after that, that the four, the two fetishes and the two ears of corn, became human beings.

THE FIRST CLANS OF THE DÎNÉ [9]

Toward the east side of the mesa called Dzil na'odili there is a place named Ta chee. On the top of this small mesa a man and a woman were found. From these two sprang the clan called Tlasch chee, or Tha'tsini, Red Under the Bank. At another place called Ash chee, salt, there arose two persons, a man and a woman. From these two came the clan called Ash chee, or Asi'hi, the Salt Clan. This clan was also called the Beautiful Goods Clan. To the east, toward the mountain called Sis na' jin, a man and a woman arose. From them came the clan called Sis na' jin ee'. Another man and a woman arose at a place called Tse nee tat net tsa. From them came the clan called Tat

---

[6] Informant's notes: A ceremony called na tdan'y analia took place so that the people would multiply. The subject being: how to increase human beings upon the earth after the monsters had been destroyed.

[7] Informant's note: Rarely is much white or yellow corn planted at one time because it is the most sacred.

[8] Informant's note: This is the Coyote called First Angry.

[9] Matthews (1897, p. 138, and note 167, p. 239): 1. Gens of Tse dzinki'ni, House of Dark cliffs (note 167); tse, rock; dzin, black or dark; kin, a straight walled house, not a hogan. Tse, here means cliff: Cliff Dwellers. 2. Gens of Tse'tlani, Bend in a Canyon. 3. Gens of Dzil na odili. . . . . 4. Gens of Haskendine, Yucca People.

nes tsa nee, the home in the side of the cliff with sticks meeting, or joining, in a different way at top.

Now when the two fetishes and the two ears of corn became human beings there were 8 that arose with them, so in all there were 12— 6 male beings and 6 female beings. (There must have been fetishes laid in all the above-mentioned places from which these people came. These 12, forming 6 clans were the first Dîné.)[10]

These 12 people first made their home around Dzil na'odili, which means "The People Move Round Me." After so many years they multiplied. Then there were four who came to them, two men and two women. They came from a place called Tqo toda sihee, which was on the top of mountain Tso dzil. When night came the people gave these four a blanket to sleep on, but they would not accept it. They sat down and, crossing their arms tightly over their breasts, slept that way. From these four started the clan called Bit an he or Bita'ni, meaning, their arms folded under.

There was another people living at a place called Tqo hee tle, where the Pine River nears Ignacio. Here the two rivers empty into the San Juan, and the name of the place is Tqo hee tle. At a place a little above there on the San Juan lived another people. They also came and joined the Dîné. From them came the clan called Tha ban ha, along the water. They were the descendants of the snipe people. Snipe always know where water is to be found. They even know when water will come and will show the high mark of flood water.

By this time there were many people living around Dzil na'odili.

There was a place called Tsa ya hat tso, a large cave lined with red which is southeast of Dulce. There is a black canyon, and farther on there is a cave. The Holy People who planned the White Bead Woman lived there. They said:

There are many people living near Dzil na' odili. They have no guard at the entrance of their home. All others, the Sun, the Mountains, the Plains have guards for the entrances of their homes. Those people down there must have the same as the rest. They must have the red corn and the red banded corn and the dog for their guards.

Here the same ceremony as before was held. There were the turquoise male fetish and the white bead female fetish and the two ears of corn. They call upon the Five Chiefs of the Winds for help and they sent the Little Breeze. Four more people were formed, two men and two women, and from them sprang the clan called Tat chee nee, or Tha'tsini, meaning red lining of the cave.[11]

The Holy Beings formed the dog, male and female. The male dog was dressed with the dawn and he was white. He traveled to the East.

---

[10] Matthews, (1897), p. 137) : Hadahonize asike, Mirage Boy, and Had'ahonestid atet, Ground Heat Girl, married the Corn Boy and Girl.

[11] Informant's note : This is my clan ; and we call our place of origin the place of the old or holy people. This is also the interpreter's father's clan.

The female dog was reddish or brownish yellow and she was dressed with the twilight. On their ears sat the Little Breeze. Their ears were made from the winds, and at the tip of the tail also there is a breeze. So when a dog passes another dog he can tell from the mouth to the tip of the tail. Burned food was put on their noses and they were black. A medicine stick, ke et an'dotishe, was placed inside their stomachs, and they say that is why a dog never gets enough to fill him. As he has the wind at the ears and at the tip of the tail he never gets lost. He knows many things, for he was sent to guard the doorways of the people.

The male dog was sent east of the Carrizos and the female dog to a place now known as Tohatchi. The white dog was a welcome animal. The people were good hunters and they fed him and petted him and he grew fat. But the female dog went to evil people who beat her and threw sticks at her and she grew poor and skinny.

The dogs were told to meet at a placed called Tse ha gaye. There are burning minerals under the ground there and one sees smoke.[12] They met there as instructed, but when they met the male jumped on the female and threw her on the ground. The male dog treated her badly. They fought as dogs do now. Then they crossed. The dog said: "People were good to me and fed me lots of meat." The bitch said: "People were cruel to me. They starved me all the time." So they changed places; the white dog went to the home of the yellow dog, and the female went to the home of the male. And after a time they met again at the same place. This time the white dog had gotten the worst of the treatment and was thin and poor, whereas the bitch was fat. So the two got even with each other.

Then the two dogs started out for a place called Nat ege saka'te, where a lone currant bush grows on a plain south of Fruitland. A little ledge of rock and the lone currant bush are all that are there. When the dogs reached the ledge of rock they sat side by side with their backs toward the people who had been cruel to them. The one dog sent his bad wish with the gas from his stomach, and the other dog sent her bad wish from her backbone to the wicked people. The two then returned to the place where they were made. Later, the people who had been cruel to the dogs sickened. Their stomachs bloated, and they were very ill indeed.

The being who was called Dotso, the All-Wise Fly, came and said: "The only person to make medicine here is Hasjelti (fig. 15) himself; but don't tell anyone what I have said. Keep it a secret." Now up to this time they had used ceremonies over the sick, but they could not cure them. When Hasjelti made the medicine the people recovered.

---

[12] Informant's note: This is a place near Newcomb's Trading Post.

FIGURE 15.—Hasjelti.

This is where the Dog Ceremony [13] begins. The chant is here.

After this Hasjelti took one of the small boys from the clan Tat chee and carried him off to a dance of his people. He carried the boy to a place called Tse'hoghan (To'waya'lane or Taaitalone known as Thunder Mountain near Zuni). When they returned the little boy danced as he had seen those people dance. Hasjelti said: "My grandchild, you will be called Jil yenn taeye, and you must dance like the dancers that you have seen."

Hasjelti said that the dancers must dress in the following manner: 12 tail feathers with little singing birds on their tips for the headdress; the growing corn with a tassel for a nose; the skirt and leggings and moccasins of buckskin with fringe; and a sacred belt with trimmings. Each dancer must hold a sacred fawnskin medicine bag in his right hand.

Now Hasjelti had planned how the monsters should be killed; how the White Bead Woman was to be formed; how the two dogs should be the guards of the people; and how the ceremonial people should dance. He planned the clan called Tat chee. The Tat chee people have fiery tempers, broad faces, and large heads.

---

[13] Informant's note: The medicine used in the Dog Ceremony is for stomach ailments. They are: Informant's name: tse gan il chee; Franciscan Fathers (1910, p. 187), tsigha'jilchi, the dodder, *Cuscuta umbellata*. Informant's name: chil'dily ese; Franciscan Fathers (1910, p. 186), chil dilyisi, dodgeweed, *Gutierezzia euthamiae*. Informant's name: da'e tinda; Franciscan Fathers (1912, p. 77), da'hiqi'hi da', hummingbird food, Scarlet Gilia, *Gilia aggregata*. These plants are boiled together with native salts.

Then Hasjelti spoke to the people he had made and said:

My grandchildren, you are not to live in this part of the country. You must go to other people and join them. I have shown you how this dance must be danced. It will be a sacred dance for you. It will be a holy dance for you. The first four dancers will have four words that they must use. These words will be the names of the corn which will grow from the earth.

He continued:

Secondly, they will name the water, the same being the rain from above. Thirdly, they will name the plants, all the plants on the earth. And last, they will name the pollen.

If a mistake is made in the first dance, it will be an evil thing and people will suffer from it. So the dancers must take great care from the beginning to the end. The first four dancers that come out in this dance will be called "at sal tle." When these first four go out, and the people are well satisfied with them, they will open their medicine bags and sprinkle pollen on their heads as an offering, and they will call on Hasjelti saying: "May it be so from this day on. May we have corn. May we have rain. May we have all the growing plants with all their pollens. May we have the beautiful earth on which we can gather corn, beautiful goods and precious stones and all the animals that we use for food. May the sheep and the horses increase, and may our children increase. May their days be beautiful and may all be beautiful around us. Thus they must pray after the four dancers leave."

THE MAKING OF THE HEADDRESS

Hasjelti said:

The headdress for this dance should be made of buckskin. One medicine man may have 12 or more headdresses which are called tcgich or tqegisch. This includes the hide, the feathers, and the blue fox and swift skins.

He continued:

There are many rules that must be followed. The hide used must be that of a deer not killed by a weapon. The whole hide must be reserved for the headdress. All the different places where the buckskin should be cut must first be run over by a piece of crystal. You must take the sinew from the right side of the spinal cord and use it for the sewing of the right side of the headdress. And from the bone of the deer's right foreleg must be made the awl to sew it with. So with the yellow feathers from the little yellow bird, they must be sewed only on the right side of the headdress. And the whole must be sewed by a right-handed man. Again, from the left side of the back of the deer take the sinew. And from the left foreleg make the awl. Sew the left side of the headdress with the bluebird feathers. And a left-handed man should sew the left side of the headdress. This is how the headdress must be made.[14]

The rattle must be held in the right hand [Hasjelti said]. It represents the Black Water Jar, and the feathers on the right side of the headdress also represent the Water Jar. The feathers on the left stand for the ears of corn. They represent the ears of corn when held in the hand, just as the Corn Father stands.

The face of the mask must be painted a bluish color. The pieces cut out for the eyes and the mouth are tied back on the headdress. The paint used in the

---

[14] Informant's note: There are many chants sung while the headdress is being made for a medicine man.

painting of the face of the mask must be made from a soft greenish mineral like turquoise. And the paint used to mark around the eyes and around the mouth must be made of coal dust.

The dancer is the figure representing the Corn Father. The rattle is the ear of corn, but it is also considered the Black Water Jar containing the rain. The feathers are the growing corn or the corn tassels.

Hasjelti said:

Two willows must be brought from the Mancos Canyon. Only this place must they come from.[15] The male willow must be cut going up the river and the female willow must be cut going down the river. You must use those willows when the patient is put through the Heat Ceremony.[16] The patient must lie down. The willows must be placed standing on either side of the patient while he receives the medicine.

After Hasjelti told the people how to make the headdress and the men had learned the dances and all the ceremony, he said: "My grandchildren, go now to a place called Tat chee'. There you must live. You are to take with you the two ears of red corn." So he gave them the two ears of red corn, full ears with kernels to the tip, and they set out for the place called Tat chee'. After a day's journey they camped for the night. The next morning they started out again. Then the chief, who was called A'gily en'taeye, told them to halt. He said: "I have forgotten something. I left those two ears of corn where we started from yesterday." He sat there with his head bent in great thought for a moment, then he said: "I thought of those as my grandchildren. I am their grandfather." He chanted there with his thoughts:

He called me grandchild,
He called me my young child.
He loved me like a mother loves her child.

He chanted three chants and he said: "Let the two ears of corn return to Hasjelti, their grandfather."

The second day they reached the Red Bank Country called Tat chee'ee. And the people called themselves Tat chee'ee. Now when the Red Bank clan reached their new country they began to multiply. All around them the other people were increasing, so there were many people living to the south of Mesa Verde.

---

[15] Informant's notes: This explains why the Mancos Canyon should belong to the Navaho. It should not belong to the Utes. The Navaho Indians believe that the State line and the Government have nothing to do with it. Cowmen have put up fences, etc. The Navaho have greatly resented this. They have tried many times to have this land returned to them, but they have failed. This area is sacred to them. They feel that it is safe as a National Park (Mesa Verde National Park), but it must not be turned over to the Utes.

[16] Informant's note: A pit is dug and a fire built in it. When the ground becomes hot the fire is scraped out and the patient is laid in the pit and covered with the medicine. Willows stand around. This is the Heat Ceremony.

THE STORY OF THE WATER BUFFALO'S KINGDOM [17]

The Elder Brother spoke: "The World will use me once more. I shall act for the People once again."

There were at that time different places where the water was sacred; but there were other places where people drowned, where people were killed by lightning, while others sank in quicksand or marshes. This is what the Elder Brother was thinking about when he spoke. He went to the Black Yei, who is called Hasjejine, and told him of his plan. Then he traveled to the home of the Water Buffalo.

Here there is a chant:

E'da'ne, e'da'ne, e'da'ne.
I am he who kills the monsters.
With super power I went before the Water Buffalo.
With super power I spoke to the Water Buffalo.
With this super power I told him I had made a plan,
But the Water Buffalo was silent.

So the Elder Brother rolled up the water and went to the home of the Great Buffalo and said: "I want all of my people." The Buffalo said: "No, you cannot have them." The Elder Brother then asked: "Do you mean what you say?" The Water Buffalo answered: "I mean what I say." This was repeated four times. "Very well," said the Elder Brother and he turned and walked away. He then put fire to the water and it sputtered like oil. When the Water Buffalo saw this he went to the Elder Brother and told him that he would have his people returned to him. Now the Water Buffalo had taken all the people who had been drowned, killed by lightning, and lost in quicksand or marshes. In other words he was building himself a kingdom with the people of the earth.

After the people were released from the Water Buffalo's Kingdom the men hugged each other, the women hugged each other, and young men hugged each other as did children, for they were glad to return to the earth.

The water had stopped burning by this time, and the Water Buffalo said to the Elder Brother: "It is well, but I will take some of your people once in a while." So that is why some are drowned, some struck by lightning, and some go down in quicksand or marshes. All this is what the Elder Brother had in mind when he said: "I shall act for the People once more."

THE NAMING OF THE BROTHERS AND THEIR DEPARTURE

All the people from all the sacred places gathered together, and there was a great crowd of Holy Beings waiting when the Elder

---

[17] Franciscan Fathers (1910, p. 359) : Tqe holt sodi, water ox.

Brother returned to his home.   Even the Sun came down from the sky.
When all was ready they decided to give the Elder Brother a name.
They thought of all the names they knew and yet no name fitted, so
they sent for Hasjejine.   He came and said: "Why have you not
thought of a name for my grandchild?   When you knew that he killed
all the monsters that destroyed people did not that suggest something
to you?   His name will be Na'yei na'zone, He Who Kills the Monsters.
And the Younger Brother will be known by the action of his mother,
he will be called Tqo ba'ches chini, the "Spring Boy" (whose other
name was Nai'dikisi, He Who Scalps).[18]

The Elder Brother's body was painted black, like the Black Cloud.
The bow was marked on his left leg, the bow outside and the string
inside.   A bow was marked on his right leg, but the bow was inside
and the string was outside.   Bows were drawn on the arms as on the
legs, and two bows were marked on the chest over his lungs, and two
others on his back.   These bows were marked on him for his protection, for he achieved his greatness by these weapons.

Tqo ba'ches chini was painted red with the red paint, hematite.   He
had the closed cross, queue, representing the scalp drawn upon him
(fig. 16).   They marked the sign of the scalp on his legs and arms,
chest and back, just as the bow had been marked on the Elder Brother.

THE SYMBOL OR SIGN
REPRESENTING THE SCALP.

FIGURE 16.—The scalp.

The Sun asked his wife, the White Bead Woman, where they should
send their sons.   The White Bead Woman answered: "That must be
your plan."   Then the Sun said: "We will send the two boys to the
placed called Toheil'tle.   They will dwell at the middle of the earth.
I shall know all things from them."   And he told the White Bead
Woman: "You too, will know all things from them.   They will
continue to have power as they now have it."

The two boys were first sent to a place called Tqo'bit cloch, the place
where the water hits against a cliff.[19]   There, just above the water level
is the last pictograph.   Right there is a place called Tse'the nee-

---

[18] Recorder's note: In regard to the names of the brothers, Whitman (1925) follows
Matthews (1897).   James Stevenson (1891, p. 281) tells their story.   Franciscan Fathers
(1910, p. 360) gives the spelling of the younger brother as Tqo bajishchini, Child of Water.
[19] Informant's note: Where the Pine and another river empty into the San Juan.

sa′en, a rock in the center of the water.   On the top of this rock there is the footprint of the Elder Brother, and the footprint of the Younger Brother.   Formerly, when no rain fell in the country, a man from the clan called Tqo yali na tline would go there and pray for rain, offering pollen and mixed chips of stone.   This has been long forgotten.   It is not done in these days.

Again the Sun spoke: "First Man and First Woman, the Coyote-Who-Was-Formed-in-the Water and the Coyote called Atse′hashke′, First Angry, these First Four must go to the East beyond the place of the sunrise.   They must travel to a place called To dotsos."   He said that they were to sit there with their backs toward the Sun.   The Sun was not to look upon First Woman again because he had married her daughter.   For even though she had not given birth to the White Bead Baby she was considered her mother.   The Sun said to his people: "This must become your custom.   You must not look upon your mother-in-law.   If you disobey me and you see each other the punishment will be blindness, weak heart, and even death."

After the Four First Beings started for the East, First Woman turned back and said: "When I wish to do so I will send chest colds and disease among the people; when I wish to do so I will send death, and the sign will be the coyote."   (The old men say that when a coyote howls many people cough.   The belief is current that certain appearances of a coyote foretell death.)

So the Four First Ones went East and they took all their powers with them.

The Sun spoke again: "When anyone thinks he sees me he will see me, because it will mean that there is an enemy in the country.   The people will suffer from enemies."   And the Sun returned to his home and he took all his powers with him.

And Hasjelti and all of his Holy People said: "If anyone sees us it will also be a sign that an enemy is coming into the country.   If he hears us call, that same person will be killed by an enemy before the day is over."   And so saying they all returned to their homes and all their powers went with them.   They were never seen again.   (Now if anyone thinks he sees one of the Holy Beings it will not be for the good of the people.   It is considered a bad omen.)

THE DEPARTURE OF THE WHITE BEAD WOMAN [20]

Then the time came for the White Bead Woman to depart. Before her stood two persons, one was Niha oni gay hasjelti, and the other was Niha oni gay hasjohon. There were also 12 male beings, the De'n'yeinaki zatana queye hahoni'gay denae e, the Four Rain Clouds, and all the flowers, and another 12 persons, female beings, and with them were the Four Vapors. The White Bead Woman spoke to these people. She said that it was her plan to have all tribes, other than her own people, move beyond the sacred mountains. She said that she wanted her children to live on the land within these sacred mountains. Then she rose up in the clouds and went to a place called Ta'delth hilth tzes taan Ta'dottliztzes taan, and with her went all her power, and there was no more of her power left on the earth. Now people have to work in order to live; they know hardship.

After that time the White Bead Woman's [21] home was called the Floating White Bead House, also, the Floating Turquoise House. Around her home is flat country called the White Bead Plain. To the East of her home is the Most High Power to whom she goes and becomes young again, and by whose power she knows all things. In the four directions from her house she undergoes a change. She comes out of her house an old woman with a white bead walking stick. She walks towards the East and returns middle aged; and she carries no walking stick. To the South she walks and she returns a young woman. She walks to the West and comes back a maiden. She goes North and returns a young girl. She is called the White Bead Woman, Yol'gai esdzan. She has three names, and the second is the

[20] Informant's note:

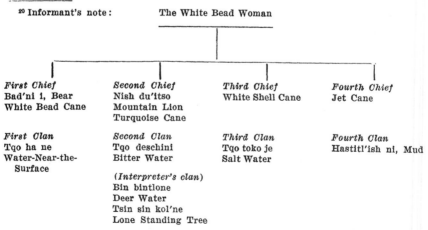

The White Bead Woman

First Chief	Second Chief	Third Chief	Fourth Chief
Bad'ni i, Bear	Nish du'itso	White Shell Cane	Jet Cane
White Bead Cane	Mountain Lion Turquoise Cane		

First Clan	Second Clan	Third Clan	Fourth Clan
Tqo ha ne	Tqo deschini	Tqo toko je	Hastitl'ish ni, Mud
Water-Near-the-Surface	Bitter Water	Salt Water	
	(Interpreter's clan)		
	Bin bintlone		
	Deer Water		
	Tsin sin kol'ne		
	Lone Standing Tree		

[21] Franciscan Fathers (1912, p. 88): Esdza na'dle, Changing Woman; Yol gai'esdzan, White Shell Woman; Esdza na'dle esdzan, the Changing Woman, the wife of the Sun.
Whitman (1925, p. 99): The White Bead Woman went West to the Great Water; she went to dwell in her floating house beyond the shore.
Matthews, (1897, p. 133): I want all precious stones, etc., etc., animals (later, horses).

Changeable Woman, Atsan a'layee. The third is Yol'gai atate, the White Bead girl. She has these three names, that is her power. Only one person knows the origin of her power, he is the Most High Power Whose Ways Are Beautiful.

This was the next plan: four coyote chiefs stood in the four directions. The White Bead Coyote fetish stood in the East; the Turquoise Coyote fetish stood in the South; the White Shell Coyote fetish stood in the West; and the Black Jet Coyote fetish stood in the North. When the Coyote called from the home of the First Man and First Woman the White Bead Woman knew what he called for.[22]

Then there were the Four Sacred Mountains.[23] The first mountain was called Yol gay dzil, White Shell Mountain, and the Changeable Wind called Nlchi de zos was placed inside it. Dotl'ish dzil, the Turquoise or Blue Mountain, was the second mountain, and Nlchi'dotl'ish, the Blue Wind was put inside it. The third mountain was De'chili dzil, the White Shell Mountain, and the Yellow Wind, Nlchi litso, was placed inside it. The fourth mountain, called Baa chini dzil, Black Jet Mountain, had Nlchi'dilqil, the Black Wind, placed inside it.

When the first wind, the Changeable Wind, shakes the mountain all the sleeping plants and animals awaken from their winter's sleep. When the Blue Wind shakes the mountain the leaves come out. When the Yellow Wind shakes the mountain all plants become greener and all animals come out of hiding. When the Dark Wind shakes the mountain all the animals are slick and shed their winter coats. This applies to the snakes and lizards.

Inside the home of the White Bead Woman, on a shelf running east to west on the south side, were four water jars. The first was the Black Water Jar which contained the Black Cloud and the Male Rain. The second was the Blue Water Jar which contained the Blue Cloud and the Male Rain. The third was the Yellow Water Jar which contained the Yellow Cloud and the Male Rain. The fourth was the White Water Jar which contained the White Cloud and the Male Rain. On the north side of the home was a shelf running west to east, and on it were also four jars. The first was a Black Water Jar which contained the Black Vapor and the Female Rain. The second, the Blue Water Jar, contained the Blue Vapor and the Female Rain. The third, the Yellow Water Jar, contained the Yellow Vapor and the Female Rain. And last, the White Water Jar, which contained the White Vapor and the Female Rain. Also, there were jars filled with the seeds of plants and all the beautiful flowers.

---

[22] Interpreter's note: Coyotes were as the telephone is today.

[23] Franciscan Fathers (1910, pp. 136–137): The ceremonial names of the four sacred mountains: Pelado Peak, Sisnajini, Yolgai'dzil (East); Mt. Taylor, Tsodzil, Yo dotl'izh'i dzil (South); San Francisco Mountains, Dookoslid, Dichi'li dzil (West); San Juan Mountains, Debentsa, Bash zhini dzil (North).

The White Bead Woman can use only one kind of seeds during a season [24] for the people's use. These are the seeds used for food. It would cause her sorrow if the people did not eat the ripened seeds of plants whose seeds she planted for them. She has all the seeds of all the plants with her. She has great power over the people.

There stand around her house a white bead walking stick to the East, a turquoise walking stick to the South, a white shell walking stick to the West, and a black jet walking stick to the North. Then all the white beads, turquoise, white shell, and black jet are placed under the water, and from them she gathers corn.

The White Bead Woman sent four persons back to the center of the earth to see how her people were getting along, and how the mountains were standing. The Four who went back were Niha onigai hasjelti and Niha onigai hasjohon and two from the same people.[25] They were to travel around the mountaintops and chant as they went. They went first to the top of the mountain called Yol gay dzil. The chant begins there.[26]

1. The First Mountain rises in sight.
   The Mountain Sis na jin rises in sight.
   The Chief of the Mountain rises in sight,
   Like the Most High Power it rises in sight.
   Like the Most High Power Whose Ways Are Beautiful it rises in sight.

Each of the six sacred mountains with their stones are covered in this chant.

2. The First Mountain near you is beautiful as it rises up . . . .
3. The First Mountain near you is a sacred mountain as it rises up . . . .
4. The First Mountain to which we travel etc. . . . .
5. The First Mountain we near . . . .
6. The First Mountain we reach . . . .
7. The First Mountain we climb . . . .
8. The First Mountain we travel over . . . .
9. The First Mountain where we stand on the summit . . . .
10. The First Mountain we camp on . . . .
11. (Just here the first person dreamed a bad dream, and in the morning he had to chant another chant, which comes in here. It is called My Dream Must not Happen or Come into Being.)
12. From the First Mountain we are starting home . . . .
13. From the First Mountain we are going home . . . .
14. From the First Mountain we are approaching home . . . .
15. From the First Mountain we are sitting down . . . .

---

[24] Interpreter's note: This explains why, in this country, each year, there is an abundance of one special plant or flower.

[25] Informant's note: These were the first two persons who stood before the White Bead Woman.

[26] Informant's note: This chant is called Tsun bey dzil gaye a'desdai, the Chant used to travel safely over the mountains.

The four persons reported that all the mountains were just as they were originally. They were beautiful and all the growing plants were beautiful. The whole country was beautiful. People were living peacefully. They had rain.

THE STORY OF THE CLAN CALLED TQO YAH HA'TLINE [27]

There was a certain man named Tse bit la'kal, the Man with the Rock Shirt, who lived near the mountain called Chol'i'i. There is a canyon near this mountain and the place is called Tsen chet dzil. This man was tall, a good hunter, and swift on his feet.

On a certain hunting trip he became thirsty about noon and went to the river to drink. It was at the place where two rivers empty into the San Juan, a place called Tqo yah ha'tline. As he was nearing the river he saw a baby swimming in the water, back and forth it swam. The baby would float on its back, and he stood there for a long time watching it. Then he returned to his trail and out of sight of the river. Later he went down to the river at a different place, drank, and returned to his home.

This man wondered what the baby was and whether it was there in the river every noon. About noon on the second day he went back to the place by the river where he had seen the baby, and the baby was there in the water swimming around. On the third day he went again to the river bank, and again he saw the baby in the water just at noon time. Then he noticed that there was tall grass on the shore to the very edge of the water where the baby swam back and forth. He made a plan. On the fourth day he went to the place early in the day and hid himself in the grass by the water's edge. Just at noon the baby rose to the surface of the water. And when the baby approached the bank the man jumped out, and lifting it out of the water ran, just as fast as he could, away from the river. There was a hill not far from the river which he climbed. When he reached the top he looked back and he saw the water standing high up and falling his way. When the water hit the ground he was over the hill.

When he arrived at his home with the baby he noticed that it was a baby girl. Now his wife, who was from the clan Tse na'jini, Black Streak of Wood Clan, cared for the baby and she grew rapidly. They called her their daughter and she called them her father and mother. When she was 13 years of age she made her first cake and the First Maiden Ceremony was held over her. But after this her foster parents noticed that she neither drank nor ate. She said: "Mother, Father, I long to look on my own country." They were greatly surprised, for they had thought that she did not know where she had been

---

[27] Matthews (1890, p. 103): Co'yet lini, Junction of the Rivers Clan, No. 21.

found. The man said: "You are right, my daughter, I found you in the water. If it is your wish to return to the place where I found you, it shall be our wish also."

Early the following morning she left them, and she returned that night. She told them that, as she was nearing the river, she heard someone chopping wood, but when she reached the top of the hill the sound of the chopping was heard no more. She said that she had walked all around but there was no sign of a track, nor could she see where wood had been cut. She went out again on the second day. This time she was near the river before the sound of chopping ceased. Again she looked all about but she found no sign of any living being. She went out again on the third day, and she was quite near the river before the sound of chopping stopped. On the fourth morning her father gave her a white shell basket and filled it with all the mixed chips of stone, white beads, turquoise, white shell, black jet, and red stone, and over the stones in the basket he sprinkled a shining mineral called deschee. Still over that he sprinkled blue pollen, tqadidin, and yellow pollen, also called tqadidin; then the pollen from the cattails, tgel tqadidin, water flags they call them, and the crystals found along the shore, which are called tqo bit ech'chee'. These last they sprinkled on the very top of the basket.

The girl took the basket and started out for the place by the river, and again she heard the chopping when she neared it. She arrived at the foot of the hill near the water when she thought that she saw someone move. She went to the spot and she found a blue ax standing against some wood. She was standing there looking at the wood when she saw the river water open, like lifting a blanket. Then she saw a young man step out and stand on the bank. He was a handsome young man. He said: "What are you doing here? Do you know that this is not the place for the earth people?" She said: "Yes, but I have longed to come to this place." Then he asked: "Are you the baby who went to the earth people?" And she answered, "Yes, I am that person." Then the young man said: "Very well, come with me." He rolled the river back like a blanket, and there before them was a path into the river, down which they went. The maiden noticed that there was a track in the sand going the same way that they were going; it was the track of a water horse. She thought that this water horse had the hoofs and the horns of a cow, but the mane and the tail of a horse—in fact it was like a horse except for the hoofs and the horns.

The young man took the maiden to the home of the Water Buffalo. Then the maiden presented the basket to the Holy Being. She motioned with the basket as the sun travels and set it at the feet of the Water Buffalo. The Water Buffalo was pleased with the gift and said: "This is what I wanted when I sent for you." And he continued: "There is something that I wish to give you before you return to the earth and become one of the earth people." Then he took the dung of the Water Buffalo and the hair from all the parts of his body where it curled, and the mud from under the water, and he spat on the three and put the four rains and the four vapors on it, and he tied it in a little medicine bag and said: "This will be your medicine. It must be used when the earth people want rain. Your clan will be called Tqo yah ha'tline. Your descendants will be known by that name, and they will be a sacred people. No snakes or lightning will harm them. But I will reclaim two members of your family later. They will return here in your place. Now you must go back to earth, but first I will show you just how a hogan should be built." He told her of his plan of the hogan. This is a special hogan, and inside it a special ceremony must take place.

THE STORY OF THE RAIN CEREMONY AND ITS HOGAN

"The main poles of this ceremonial hogan should be raised with a chant," said the Water Buffalo.

You should pour the water on the poles from the top to the bottom. The water used must come from the sacred springs of the East. This water must be gotten and carried in a water jar. Then the mud from the bottom of the water should be rubbed on the poles from the top down. You must use all growing things, beautiful flowers and all the plants, to finish the hogan. Then only your descendants who know the chants and prayers and have the medicine will enter the hogan. Only they will be able to perform this ceremony. One will be the priest. The mud taken from the sacred water will be rubbed on his body, arms, chest, and back. He must then sit down and make four sounds like a frog. The mud from the sacred water is called tlah la'haddan, gotten from under the water.

He continued to tell them of the preparations for the ceremony. First must enter a young man, bringing in food for the shaman. The food must be made from the plant called quotse, a kind of cactus. After the young man comes into the hogan and places the food before the shaman, those present will say: "Here comes the Black Cloud. Now we have the Male Rain." Next a maiden with a basket of food for the priest enters the hogan (fig. 17). This food is made from the seeds of the plant called tlo de'i, marsh elder. When she puts the basket down the others will say: "Here comes the Black Vapor. Now we have the Female Rain."

Those who wish to attend the ceremony [28] will then enter the hogan, bringing with them the mixed chips of stone as offerings. A curtain will hang in the doorway. The man entering will push it from left to right with his right hand. The hogan faces the East, and when he enters he circles the hogan as the sun travels. A small buckskin

---

[28] Informant's note: The medicine for this ceremony was kept sacred. It was buried at the foot of the Lukachuki Mountains at the time of the Navaho uprising. It rains often there now.

having been spread on the ground, the man places his offering of stones upon it, saying: "I come from the Big Water. I come with the Male Rain. I come with the White Corn." His gift must be turquoise.

Then a woman opens the curtain from right to left, and she circles the fire as the sun travels. She must hold her stones, white beads, over the buckskin and say: "I come from the Big Water. I come with the Black Vapor. I come with the Female Rain. I come with all the beautiful flowers." She must then place her stone offering on the buckskin and go to the north side of the hogan and sit down. The men sit on the south side. After this their children and friends place their stone offerings and sit in the hogan. The stones should be crystal, jet, red stone, or shells. The father or mother must bring those, one for each member of the family.

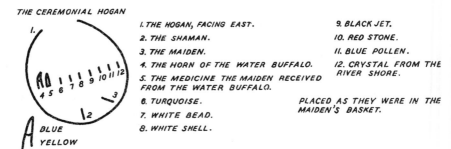

THE CEREMONIAL HOGAN

1. THE HOGAN, FACING EAST.
2. THE SHAMAN.
3. THE MAIDEN.
4. THE HORN OF THE WATER BUFFALO.
5. THE MEDICINE THE MAIDEN RECEIVED FROM THE WATER BUFFALO.
6. TURQUOISE.
7. WHITE BEAD.
8. WHITE SHELL.
9. BLACK JET.
10. RED STONE.
11. BLUE POLLEN.
12. CRYSTAL FROM THE RIVER SHORE.

PLACED AS THEY WERE IN THE MAIDEN'S BASKET.

BLUE
YELLOW

FIGURE 17.—The ceremonial hogan.

There must be no relationship between the shaman and the maiden. They represent the male and the female rain.

The people sit on opposite sides, next to the wall. They chant all during the night until dawn.

Then the man and the maiden both bathe and wash their hair. The man dries himself with white cornmeal, and the maiden uses the yellow cornmeal. Their hair hangs loosely down the back. The maiden should wear a garment of white cotton cloth. The man has buckskin thrown over his shoulders. They leave the hogan and start out chanting. They go either to the top of the Sacred Mountain, Chol'i'i, or to the Place where the Rivers Come Together, or to some sacred spring. The maiden should be a descendant of those Four (the two fetishes and the white and yellow corn). There are very few left. Or she could be of the Beautiful Goods People. The man should be of the clan Tqo yah ha'tline, a descendant of the Maiden.

After they reach whichever holy place is decided upon and make their offering of medicine and the gift of stones, they sit side by side and pray. Should they see flowers, water, clouds, or corn all is well. If they see blood it will be a bad sign.

Then they return and they tell what they have seen.

This is the story of how the Maiden got the medicine, and it is how the clan called Tqo yah ha'tline uses it to bring rain.

THE TWO WHO RETURNED

The Maiden from the Water Buffalo's Kingdom became a mother and a grandmother. There were many people counted as her descendants. They planted corn in the canyon where they lived, and their corn ripened, having tassels and bearing rich ears.

One day the people sent a boy and a girl down into the canyon. Suddenly they looked down and saw a flood coming from above. They called to the children, but the flood carried them away, leaving the cornfields unharmed. These two children were taken back to the home of the great Water Buffalo.

TWO CLANS RELATED TO THE CLAN TQO YAH HA'TLINE

There is a clan called the Mexican clan, Nakai dinae'e.[29] This clan is closely related to the clan called Tqo yah ha'tline because a man from that clan captured a Mexican girl and the Spaniards captured an Indian girl. They planned to take the Mexican girl back to her people because the mother of the Indian girl grieved so greatly. They thought to exchange these girls, but the Indian girl escaped and returned; so they kept the Mexican girl and the clan Tqo yah ha'tline adopted her. She founded the clan Nakai dinae'e.

The same clan captured a Ute girl and her clan was called the Ute Clan, No'da dinae'e.[30] They are related to the two above-named clans.

There were many people all over the country by this time.

THE STORY OF THE PICTOGRAPH OF THE COIL

Now at this time some of the people returned to inhabit Pueblo Bonito and Aztec.[31] They built their homes over the ancient houses. The Blue Bird Clan people went first to Pueblo Bonito, then they moved to Tse dez a', Under the Rock, across from Farmington. From there they moved to the mouth of Salt Canyon.[32] Many seeds were found there, the seeds of many plants then plentiful in the country. The people discovered a rich land south of Shiprock, but they lived there for only a little over 5 years. Then they moved again to south of the Carrizos. They went over the pass, and settled in a cave.

[29] Matthews (1890, p. 103): Nakai (Nakaicine), Mexican or White Stranger Clan or People.

[30] Noca, Ute Clan or People.

[31] Informant's note: The second occupation of Bonito and Aztec.

[32] Informant's note: Salt Canyon is south of Mesa Verde. This had been the informant's forebears' home.

They had the Calendar Stone with them. The medicine woman who kept this stone saw that the people had made a mistake. The people had been making pots that were coiled up like a snake.[33] She saw that at the home of the Five Chiefs of the Winds their water jars were made of coiled snakes. They were the jars which contained the Chiefs of the Winds' medicine: the clouds and vapors, rain and lightnings. The people of the earth were not to copy the jars of the Five Chiefs of the Winds. This medicine woman saw in the Calendar Stone that the lives of all the people were threatened from above. So word was sent to all the people of what she had seen, and of their mistake. They were told that there would come a tribe to their land called the Dinae'e or Dîné. Now some of the people destroyed the pots that they had made; but others just laughed and said: "The wind never told me to make such jars, it was my own idea. I made the jars with my own hands. This has always been our country, and we shall do as we please in our own country."

The Blue Bird Clan people and the different Corn Clan people got together and destroyed their coiled pots. They took all the different kinds of beads and they put them in a big smooth jar, and with them they placed the flint stone, the two feathers of the giant birds, and the Calendar Stone. They placed this large jar on a rock which they had hollowed out; and they sealed it with four slabs of rock and pitch.

After they had done this the hail fell for 4 days, and through some of the hailstones were little young spruce trees. The hail became soft when it fell on those people who had listened to the warning; but the hard hail, and the little spruce trees, like arrows, destroyed those who would not listen. All those who were willing to leave the country were saved.

Now there were some people living at Aztec who were saved, and they were told to remember this story. And there were some people living near the South Mountain, which is called Tso dzil, and the Blue Bird Clan people and the Corn Clan people, who had moved southwest of the Carrizos, who were also saved; the rest were destroyed. Later, the Blue Bird Clan people on and near the Carrizos moved near Navaho Mountain and built their homes there.

There is a story about one of the men who left the party and followed the Chin Lee Wash until he came to the San Juan River.[34] He got into a log that floated him down the river. He went ashore after a long time and he followed the river. He married a snake maiden. They returned to the foot of Navaho Mountain. They had born to them children. One of these children harmed another child of the tribe. The harm was like a snake bite. The people sent the family away.

---

[33] Whitman (1925, p. 88).
[34] Recorder's note: There are both Hopi and Zuñi legends about the young man who traveled down the river in a log.

(Today, their descendants are the people who can dance with snakes, the people who hold the Snake Ceremony.)   Then, while some of the people moved from the top of the Black Mountain [35] and the country near there, others moved farther south and they built on the top of rocky mesas where the Hopi Villages are today.   There is where they made their homes.

Sandoval's grandmother, who was a Hopi Indian, told him that the pictograph of the coil (fig. 18) was the symbol of the Winds.[36]   She

FIGURE 18.—The Great Coil above the Square Tower House Ruin, Mesa Verde.

took him to the different places and showed him how the people had carved the coil in the rock so that people would always remember this story and never make the mistake again.

THE STORY OF THE MOUNTAIN CHANT AND THE FIRE DANCE [37]

There was once a young man captured by a people whose descendants are the Utes.   The peoples were at war and the people of the North carried the young man to their country.   They crossed a big body of water.   There many gathered and they held a dance.   They planned to kill the young man, but Hasjelti and Hasjohon had not forgotten him.   They followed their captured grandson.

Now the Northern Indians had tied the young man inside a tepee. He was sitting there when the two Holy Beings appeared to him. They told him not to be frightened, that he would not be harmed. They made known to him that they wanted gifts.   If he made these gifts to them he would be saved.   They wanted moccasins trimmed with porcupine quills, leggings and shirts of buckskin, fringed, and a headdress with 12 eagle feathers.   Hasjelti wanted these.   Hasjohon wanted the same clothing, all decorated and fringed, but he wanted

---

[35] Interpreter's note : A low mountain range beyond Kayante near Chin Lee.

[36] Informant's note : The great First Wind is the cyclone.   He who travels around, but not the whirlwind.   He is very great.   The great coil above Square Tower House Ruin, Mesa Verde National Park, is an example of him.

[37] Interpreter's note : I think that this story should come after the following story ; but it is not clear just where it should be placed, as medicine men differ.

Recorder's note : I have placed it where the informant gave it.

his headdress to have 12 yellow tail feathers. So the young man, having been untied, went out and found these things and carefully laid them away.

The plan was to kill him the next morning. Before they left him (and before he had collected the gifts) the two Holy Beings told him that he must not sleep on that night. But it was too difficult for him and he dozed. Toward dawn the two Yei awakened him and said: "Grandson, why did you go to sleep?" He could not explain, but he presented the gifts to them. Hasjelti took time to dress, and then Hasjohon dressed. The young man was fearful that the enemies would come and that he would be caught. He told the Yei: "Why, it is day now!" But the two simply took their time dressing and said: "Do not worry, my child, all will be well." Then the three went to the creek near by and it was daylight. When the three reached the water it lifted, and the young man went under it to the home of the otter. The otter said: "The enemy will not come here. You are safe."

The enemy searched the country for their captive but they could not find him. Later he left the home of the otter and set out for his own land. He traveled a great distance, but he went in a circle and he found that he had returned to the place he had started from, and again the enemy had found his track. He ran along, and he cried as he went. Someone called to him from a tree. It was the owl. The owl asked him why he was weeping, and the young man said: "Oh, the enemy is after me. They are after my scalp." The owl said: "Come up here, Grandchild. They do not come up here." The young man climbed the tree, and the owl circled the tree four times; and he used his medicine, schan'dine,[38] which is the rays of the sun, the rays which one cannot see through. The Northern Indians hunted around and around this tree; then they went away.

The young man set out again toward his own country. He traveled very far, but finally enemy Indians were near him, and he found that for a third time he had traveled in a circle. He was running along with tears in his eyes when someone spoke to him. It was the whitish ground squirrel, hasjel'kaeye.[39] This ground squirrel pulled up a greasewood bush and blew four times under it. He went down into the hole and called to the young man to follow him. He held the greasewood bush on top of them, and they remained hidden until the enemy went away. Then the young man came out of the hole and started off again. He traveled for a long time, when, to his surprise, he found that for the fourth time he had lost his way and become turned about. He was running along weeping when a mountain rat

---

[38] Franciscan Fathers (1912, p. 158) : shandin, sunlight.
[39] Franciscan Fathers (1912, p. 188) : hazai, or, tsiditi'ni, squirrel or ground squirrel.

called to him and asked him why he was distressed. He said: "The enemy is after my scalp." The mountain rat said: "Never mind. They never enter my house." He quickly opened his home under the rocks, and after the young man had passed, he sealed the rocks in place. Again the Indians of the North searched all about, but they did not find him.

After the enemies had left the young man again started for his home. He traveled far, living on berries. He reached the San Juan River and the river was high. He walked along the river bank, and he ate the fruit from the little bushes that grew there. He heard someone behind him. He looked around and saw a man of dark color standing there. The man said: "My grandson, what are you doing here?" The young man said: "I have come this far from the country of the enemy. I am trying to reach my home, but the river is high and I cannot cross." The man said: "Shall I take you across?" So the young man climbed on the dark man's back.

A chant begins here:

> I went on top,
> I went on top,
> With the black basket
> Now we cross the big canyon with water in it.
>
> I went on top,
> I went on top,
> With the black basket
> Now we travel across.
>
> I went on top,
> I went on top,
> With the black basket
> Now we settle down on the shore.

Now the two had crossed the river. After he had put the young man down safely the dark man became a black rock hill near the San Juan. He grew and grew and his arms became great wings. He is still there, and is called Tse bit i'ie,[40] the Rock with Wings, Shiprock.

All during this time a ceremony was taking place in the young man's home. A footprint pointing away was made in a basket. When the young man started toward home the footprint was turned. This ceremony that was taking place was the Mountain Chant. And the place was the Beautiful Mountain, Lukachugai. A rock on a peak was the hogan and the rocks around were the bushes. The ceremony was held for the young man's safe return.

The chant sung by the young man who crossed the river on the dark man's back is continued. It is sung as the young man approaches his home. The words of the chant are the same as the preceding chant except for the last line.

---

[40] Franciscan Fathers (1910, p. 357) : Tse bida'i, the Winged Rock, Shiprock.

. . . .
Now his head comes in sight.

. . . .
Now he is standing in sight.

. . . .
Now he is ready to be washed.

He is bathed before he is allowed to enter the hogan with the others. They then sing the last verse:

. . . .
Now he comes inside the hogan.

After he enters the hogan the young man tells all that has happened to him from the time he was taken captive until his return. He is now called the Holy Young Man and there are a great many chants sung here. This is when the medicine men grow the yucca; they grow the cherry; they wash their hands with burning pitch; they swallow the arrow; and—they hold the Fire Dance. This dance is a part of the Mountain Chant. This ceremony is the Earth's medicine, and this ceremony was taken over by the tribe called Dîné.

Now after the Holy Young Man was bathed and entered the hogan, and after he told all that had happened to him, they sang the songs of the Night Chant all the night long. There were a great many songs sung, and toward dawn the chants of the Great Gambler were used.

After that they went to the mountains and gathered the herbs for medicine and the plants whose berries are used for food. They brought them back and ground them together and they boiled them. The Holy Young Man drank the beverage before he was put through the Heat Fire Ceremony. He vomited all that he had eaten among the enemies. This treatment was repeated inside the hogan on four mornings.

After the Fire Ceremony was over they held another Night Chant in which they sang a certain number of chants called One Night Chants. In these they tap a basket with a yucca stick.

They bathed Hashkil zas kaeye,[41] the White Snow Warrior, the Holy Young Man, and washed his hair and dressed him. Feather medicine was tied to his arms above his elbows and on his moccasins. He was given one of two bags made of twin fawn skins to carry. They contained cornmeal. He took this cornmeal to the mountain called Sis na'jin; and, also, he took it to the mountain called Tso dzil.[42] He visited the sacred people living there. He sprinkled cornmeal over them and said: "I have come for your power."

---

[41] Franciscan Fathers (1912): p. 214, warrior, hashkae'he; p. 182, snow, yas, or, zas; p. 218, white (referring to the country to the north), dza'gai.

[42] Informant's notes: Sis na'jin, Pelado Peak; Tso dzil, Mount Taylor. The sacred mountains of the East and South.

Now another young man was sent out as a messenger. Tla testine'e was his name. He was dressed exactly like the Holy Young Man. He was sent to Dook'oslide and Debe'ntsa.[43] He went to the sacred people and he told them that he had come for their power. He was never to jump over a stream, but always to go to the head of it.

When they started out the first young man went to the East, and the second young man to the West. One carried one fawn skin filled with cornmeal, and the other took the other one. When they returned, they arrived at the same time.

In these days they dress two young men as the messengers and they send them to two medicine men whom they wish to take part in the Fire Ceremony. The Holy Beings that the first two young men carried the cornmeal to, as an invitation, were to come and take part in the Fire Ceremony on the last night.

The making of the sand paintings took 3 days. These were made before the last day. On the evening of the next to the last day, the two men (who followed the young man) went to a cleared place; and one of them took corn pollen and sprinkled it around in a large circle. This marked the place where the big brush corral was to be built. When he finished the marking, the corral was built. All the people who came to take part in the ceremony, and to look on, went inside.

On the night of the last day of the ceremony two dancers entered the circle, as the sound of the basket tapping was heard. They began to chant. Six more dancers entered, and with the first two, they danced the first dance. These eight people were considered the same as the four who danced in the other ceremony which is called Atsel tle.[44] After them came the dancers who danced around a great fire. They held feathers in their hands. They burned them, then spit upon them and they were whole again. This they did, and then they went out. This is called ne'gaeye.[45] Later they grew the yucca and performed much magic. The two medicine men who return with the messengers (in these days) perform different tricks of magic. Some grow yucca, some wash their hands with pitch, and so on. The last dance is at dawn. The dancers carry little spruce trees in their hands.

The Fire dancers sing first in a circle. While they chant they chew on a medicine which protects them against fire. This is their chant:

Right where the people come out
There it fell on me.
The Big Blue Star fell on me without harm.
I am tried with the same,
So it fell on me without harm.

---

[43] Dook' oslid, San Francisco Peak; Deben'tsa, San Juan Mountains. The sacred mountains of the West and North.

[44] Informant's note: Atsel'tle, the dance of the Night Chant, is called Yeibitchi.

[45] Recorder's note: The word ne'gaeye is given by Franciscan Fathers (1912, p. 136): ne'gai, local pain.

They first made four torches of cedar bark, from a tree struck by lightning. When the dancers entered for the first time they spat the medicine on the first torch and threw it to the East. This is done in order to spread the medicine. They repeat this for the four different directions. They make a strange buzzing noise as they throw the torch. They dance with other torches in their hands. They posture, they circle the great fire, and they put the burning torches under each other. They have the medicine and they are not hurt by the fire. When they end the dance and retire, the people rush in and gather up the medicine (the ashes fallen from the dancers' torches), which is used when children are burned.

In the beginning, when the dance was over and finished for the Holy Young Man captured by the Northern People, and it was morning, the mother frog and the mother turtle and the mother fish and the mother duck all placed a complaint. "Our babies have been crushed in the dance," they said. So all the people returned and the four babies were restored to life and made whole. The four mothers went away satisfied. A powerful medicine was used. Medicine men can cure animals of certain ailments. But an expectant mother must not see a sandpainting, for it harms the baby after it is born.

This ceremony and the Baby Ceremony were made for the tribe called Dîné. The Baby Ceremony is a very small one; but Mountain Chant, the Night Chant, the Yeibitchai, and others are great chants.[46] They were given to the Navaho People.

THE STORY OF THE FLINT KNIFE BOYS AND THE GREAT WARRIOR OF AZTEC [47]

Beyond Debensa, La Plata Mountains, there is a yellowish colored mountain and near it there is a mountain with shiny rocks on it, this mountain is called Dessos. Now the man who was formed inside the first mountain is called Tso y natlaye', and the man who was formed in Dessos is named Klay ya ne'yan, One Who Was Raised inside the Earth.

There is a 4-day ceremony here called the Arrow Spirit Ceremony.

The first man had no children. The second man had twin boys. These boys were given the names of the First Holy Twin Brothers: the elder was called Na'yei na'zone, but the younger was called La'chee na'yana, He Who Grew in One Day, as well as that of To ba'ches chini. Both boys grew up in one day.

---

[46] Matthews (1887, pp. 379–467; Matthews (1903, vol. 16, pp. 61–64; Stevenson, James (1891, p. 281).

[47] Morris (1921, vol. 26, pp. 115–121). Morris, (1924, vol. 26, p. 192) : "The basketry shield and numerous burial accouterments indicate that the individual occupied a position of unusual importance in the pueblo. Probably this was due in part at least to his great stature."

THE JOURNEY OF THE ELDER BROTHER [48]

The Elder Brother took a long journey. He covered the whole country—mountains, plains, and all. When he was on the side of La Plata Mountains he saw a fire on the mesa, which is a part of Mesa Verde. He saw this fire at night. Now this boy knew of three strong medicines, so when he got to the place where he had seen the fire, and found people living there, he was not afraid, for he had a plan.

Among these people there were two beautiful maidens who turned away many suitors from all parts of the country. The reason was that it was believed that only young men with superpower were to marry the two maidens, and there were no such young men to be found. Their father decided that whoever could shoot an arrow into a little hole far up in the side of the cliff would be the persons to marry his daughters.

All the hunters and warriors gathered there with their bows and arrows. They all tried, but not one could shoot into the hole in the cliff. Then there came two old men, one was the Bear and the other was the Big Snake. The warriors asked: "Where do you come from?" And when all the other men saw the two old men with their bows and arrows they all laughed and said: "Whoever heard of old men shooting that far." But one shot at the hole far up on the side of the cliff and the arrow went into the hole. Then the other old man shot and his arrow went into the hole also. It was decided however that they were too old to have the maidens. The father said: "Whoever shoots an arrow over the cliff will have my daughters." All the other men tried and failed; but the two old men shot at the same time and their arrows went, side by side, clear over the cliff. But it was again decided that they were too old to have the maidens.

Now at that time there was a strong people living at the place now called Aztec. For their chief they had a tall, strong warrior whom everyone in the country feared. He was a great warrior and whatever he said was law.

The uncle of the maidens said: "Whoever kills the Great Warrior of Aztec will have my two nieces." He said that it would be 3 days from that time before they would start the war against the Great Warrior.

At the end of the third day the Elder Brother joined these people. He gathered together a party of warriors and they started out for Aztec. The two old men followed behind them. The people tried to persuade the old men to go back. They said that the two were too old to fight; but the old men would not listen to them.

The first night the two old men camped not far behind the warriors. One slept on one side of the fire and the other on the opposite side.

---

[48] Recorder's note: The story of the Younger Brother was not given.

And on this first night an old woman came in sight of the warriors. She had with her a group of boys. They camped near the warriors, and they made a frightful noise all the night long. The warriors could hear them, but they could not pass them for they sang the chants against the enemy. The second night the camp was again made and the old woman and her boys camped nearby, and the boys made a fearful racket. The two old men also camped near; and one slept on one side of the fire and the other on the other side. On the third night the old woman and her boys camped just opposite the warriors, and the boys played and fought and yelled all the night long. The two old men camped nearby as before, and they slept peacefully.

On the fourth night the Elder Brother and his warriors made their camp, and the old woman and the boys camped just ahead of them. That night one of the boys broke a bough from a cedar tree toward the east side, and he laid it down and said: "May I kill the Great Warrior!" Another boy broke a bough from a piñon tree on the west side, and he laid it across the cedar branch and said: "May I kill the Great Warrior!" Then all the rest of the boys jumped up and taking stones piled them on the two boughs, and each said as had the first two: "May I kill the Great Warrior!" There was a very great pile of stones.

The Elder Brother was angry. He said: "Go kill one of those boys."

But these were Holy Beings, the grandsons of the old Hard Flint Woman, Beshyhl he dot'tlinth, and the boys were the Beshyhl he dot'linthe, the Flint Knife Boys. They came from the land of the Flint Mountain near Dulce.

The next morning the young boys bathed themselves in mud.[49] They jumped off a cliff, rolled down the slopes and had a fine time. Then the boys went to the Elder Brother and said: "Now kill us all." And there was lightning flashing from their toes, knees, sides of the body, arms, head, and tongues. When the Elder Brother saw this he begged them saying: "I was only teasing. It is all right for a grandfather to tease his grandchildren." So they turned and went away.

Soon they were approaching Kin teel,[50] Aztec. The Flint Knife Boys were striking their flint knives and the flashes shot up into the sky. The Elder Brother went against the town and the enemy came out.

The Flint Knife Boys and the Elder Brother and his warriors killed all the enemies and took their scalps. The old woman filled

---

[49] Informant's note: The origin of the Mud Ceremony, which is sometimes given with the Scalp Dance. These Flint Knife Boys are very sacred, and appear in different ceremonies.

[50] Interpreter's note: There is different spelling for this place: Kin teel, Khintqeldae. It is not to be confused with Kin tqel, Wide Ruins, Arizona.

her basket full of scalps before they marched away.   As they neared home they made camp and they lined up all the scalps, but the Great Warrior's scalp was not to be found, nor was the scalp of the warrior chief next in rank among those that they had with them.

Now the two old men had drawn the two great warriors and they had killed them.   Soon they joined the others and they brought out their two scalps.   Everyone knew that they were the scalps of the Great Warrior and of his chief.   They returned home, but still the uncle of the two maidens refused to let the two old men take the two girls.

The people held the Great Scalp Dance.   While this was going on the uncle of the two maidens said to them: "Go to where the young men are singing and choose whichever young men you would like to be your husbands."   So the maidens went to where the young men were singing and they got in the middle of the group.

Now the two old men were camped in a brush shelter, one lay on one side of the fire and the other on the other side.   Toward nightfall they got up and the old man Bear said to the old man Snake: "Our two young girls are in the pot."   (Today they mean a girl dances who has a husband.   The reason a maiden dances, except in certain cere- monials, is that she is ready for marriage.)   So the Bear rolled a cigarette made of a certain herb, and he drew the smoke from it and blew it in the direction of the singing where the maidens were dancing among the young men.   The Snake did the same thing.   When the two maidens smelled the smoke the elder said: "Sister, what a beauti- ful, sweet odor."   The younger maiden said: "Let us go and see where it comes from."   When they got to the place from which the sweet odor had come they found two handsome young men, one on one side of the fire and the other on the other side.   Each youth wore a beauti- ful robe which covered him.   The two sisters thought that these hand- some young men were their husbands, so the elder maiden went to the Bear and the younger went to the Snake.

In the morning, when the elder sister awakened, she had her arm around the Bear's neck, and his arm was around the girl.   He was still asleep and all his ugly teeth showed.   She awakened her sister. A great Snake was coiled around the body of the young girl; their heads were together, and her hand was on the Snake.

The two sisters went through the singing to the four directions, and they went to the river.

After the two young women had crossed the river (the Mancos River) they climbed to the top of La Plata Mountains.   They went to the Bear People who lived there.   The Bear People said: "Where are you from, sister-in-law?"   As the young women were ashamed of ' their acts they said nothing and left.   They traveled on and on until they came to the mountain called Tse dzil. A community of big snakes lived there. They asked the two young women: "Where are you going, sister-in-law?" Again they were ashamed and they left that place also. From there they went to a mountain called Dzil se'he'dzil et. There also lived another branch of the Bear People; and again they were called "sister-in-law."

Now the two old men followed their brides. They used the smoke from their magic cigarettes to tell them which way the young women had gone. Whichever way the smoke drifted, that way they followed.

The sisters traveled to the mountain called Tso dzil, Mt. Taylor, and they were called "sister-in-law" by the Big Snake People who lived there. They left the place because of their shame and they went to the mountain called Tschosh gaeye, above Tqo hache, and there they were greeted as "sister-in-law" by members of the Bear family. It was after this that they decided to part. One went one way, the other went the other way. The old man Bear followed the Elder Sister, and the old man Snake followed the younger one.[51]

THE STORY OF THE YOUNGER SISTER [52]

The younger sister reached a people called Nat at tsele, and there were some members of the Big Snake People living with them who called out: "Where are you going, sister-in-law?" Hearing this the girl left them and fled to the Lukaichukai Mountains. But members of the Big Snake family lived there also, and they called after her as before.

By this time the younger sister was very tired. Her moccasins were worn and her garments nothing but rags. She could see the smoke from the Great Snake's cigarette close behind her. She went on to a place called Tsel tiel, Sage Canyon. She was running along when she saw a slender young man lying on a rock. The young man's face was painted with a bluish paint called tlish dot chee.[53] Now this young man was the racer snake, and he asked her where she was going. She said: "I am being chased by the Big Snake." "No big snake comes here," said the young man. "Take off your clothing and come with me." So she took off her clothing and put it behind a rock, and she went to the young man naked. In the rocks there was a tiny hole. The young man blew into the hole four times, and it was large enough for the young woman to enter. When the Big Snake came to the place he grabbed her clothing and said: "Oh, my wife!"

---

[51] Informant's note: The Younger Sister's story is the origin of the Hojone', or Snake Chant.

[52] Informant's note: Here the story parts, and the story of the Younger Sister is given first.

[53] Franciscan Fathers (1912, p. 170): tlish, snake; and p. 86, dotl'ish, blue.

By his power the young man sent the Big Snake away. After he had departed the two young people started out. They passed through great fields of corn. The young woman had her monthly period, so she made an apron out of the corn husks. That is why some husks are red.

Soon they came to the home of the young man. The maidens there were dressed beautifully. That night the young man was dressed in a beautiful dress, the skin of a snake. But that night the younger sister wished to go out. She started to go forward but there was a throng of snakes ahead of her. She tried again, but there were snakes on all sides of her, so she threw herself on the ground. The next morning the snake people told what she had done when they had coiled and stretched. One snake said: "The sister-in-law is not kind. She stepped on my neck." Another said: "She stepped on my leg." Another complained of his arm, and still another said that she had crossed his body.

Later she had a pain in her abdomen. They gave her medicine and she was quiet. Then came her children. The boy was called Bits is'yenagha'i, male snake, and the girl was called Bits is'quadidin',[54] female snake.

And so whenever the Navaho see these snakes they call them by their names and send them away. They do not kill snakes.[55]

There is a 9-day ceremony held called Hojone hatal', the Snake Ceremony. Rattles are used. There are many sand paintings and many prayer plumes or medicine sticks.

THE STORY OF THE MOUNTAIN TOP CHANT,[56] OR THE STORY OF THE MAIDEN AND THE BEAR

There were 12 young men and 2 young women. The men went hunting and they killed 2 of the Eagle Dancers of Wide Ruin. The Cliff Dwellers were angered over this and they chased the 12 young men to the top of a flat mesa. Now the 12 hunters rode on sun dogs; but the Great Warrior of the Cliff Dwellers and his chief through their power took the sun dogs from them. Soon the flat mesa was surrounded by warriors, and the 12 young men knew that they must make a plan. They cut down a tall cedar tree, and, after trimming off the branches and making it a straight pole, they tied eagle feathers to

---

[54] Franciscan Fathers (1912, p. 67): bits'is'ye osho'shi, ceremonial name of the female snake.

Matthews (1898, pp. 228–235), pre-Navaho myths, many from Moquis and Zuñi.

[55] Recorder's note: Many writers recording myths of Hopi and Zuni have come upon the serpent legends. Parsons (1933, pp. 611–631).

[56] Recorder's note: This story was given to me by Sam Ahkeah, the interpreter, with full approval of its inclusion here by his uncle, the informant. He said that the Mountain Top Chant, Dzil quigi, has its origin in the story of the Elder Sister and the Bear.

the top of it.   When it was ready the 2 youngest brothers climbed to
its top, and the 10 other brothers dropped it over the side of the cliff.
The 2 young men landed safely.   They gave the call of the owl, which
told the others that they were safe.   Now the owl heard this and said:
"But the 10 on the mesa top must die."   And it was so.   The Great
Warrior of the Cliff Dwellers killed the 10 young men.   Before they
died these brothers gave the coyote call, and the 2 who had been saved
knew that they would have to kill the Great Warrior of the Cliff
Dwellers and his chief.

Now these two warriors of the Cliff Dwellers lived under the
ground.   They wore strings of shell and turquoise around their necks
and their arms and their legs.   On their heads they wore large caps
shaped like shells [57] with turquoise and white shell beads tied to the
middle of them.   They would crawl through a little hole in their
dwelling and come on top of the ground only when the Cliff Dwellers
were at war.   After the latter were successful the warriors would
crawl back under the earth.

The two brothers traveled far to the great ocean of the West, to the
home of the Woman Who Changes.   She told the brothers that they
must get the help of the Flint Knife Woman who lived on the mountain called Tso dzil, that the Flint Knife People were great warriors
and would help the two brothers fight the Cliff Dweller People.   The
brothers journeyed to the home of the Flint Knife People, and they
promised to give their two sisters, who were beautiful maidens, to
the two warriors who would kill the Great Warrior and his chief.

The brothers and Flint Knife Warriors started out for Kin teel.
It was night when they arrived near it.   The Flint Knife men made
a fire and held a Fire Dance.   They used sticks that made a curious
whirring sound.   "The enemy will see this," said the brothers.   "No,
for they will believe it to be stars," said the Flint Knife warriors.
The next morning they still danced, and the huge fire sent a great
smoke cloud into the sky.   Again the brothers said: "The Cliff Dwellers will see this."   But the Flint Knife warriors answered: "They will
think that they see a storm cloud."

Then the two brothers and the Flint Knife warriors went near
Kin teel and they fought the Cliff Dwellers.   They took many scalps
the first day.   That night they looked them over, but the scalps of
the two great chiefs were not among them.   They waited 3 days and
they again fought the Cliff Dwellers.   Then they waited for 5 days.
At this time two old men appeared.   They were the Turtle and the
Frog.

These two old men went to the water hole or spring where the
women came for water.   They took stone axes and they killed all the

---

[57] Recorder's note : This cap is undoubtedly the cap worn by the priests of the bow in Zuñi,
as is shown on ceremonial pottery.   It is also the old cap of the warriors of the Navaho.

people who came for water. They took their scalps and they tied them to a pole. (This is the origin of the pole in the Scalp or Squaw Dance which now has branches representing scalps tied to it.) When the Cliff Dwellers learned of the killings at the spring they rushed there and prepared to kill the Turtle and the Frog with their stone axes. "Now they will kill us," said the Frog. The Turtle said: "Be not afraid. Come, get under me." So the Cliff Dwellers struck the Turtle, but their blows glanced off his shell, and they were not harmed.

The Cliff Dwellers said: "Now we will burn them." The Turtle said: "This time they will kill us." But the Frog answered: "Be not afraid." And after they were thrown into the fire the Frog made water and put it out. "We will boil them," said the Cliff Dwellers. They brought out a huge pot and filled it with water. This time it was the Frog who was frightened, but the Turtle reassured him. And when they were thrown into the pot the Turtle expanded his shell and cracked the pot and they were free. Finally the Cliff Dwellers decided to drown them. They threw them into the river where they swam off to the opposite shore.

Now when the Brothers and the Flint Knife warriors counted the scalps on the pole which the Frog and the Turtle had made they did not find those of the Great Warrior and his chief among them. So on the seventh day they prepared to attack again.

Then two old men came and sat on a rock. One was the old man Bear and the other was the old man Snake. "Where do you come from?" the Flint Knife warriors asked. "I come from the mountains," said the Bear. "I come from the plains," said the Snake.

While the warriors were fighting, the Bear said to the Snake: "Let us look around." So they climbed into the cliff dwelling. Presently they saw coming toward them two creatures crawling on their hands and knees. Taking up a stone, the Bear struck them and killed them. The Snake split their skins and took them, covered as they were with turquoise and shell beads. Then the two old men went back to the rock and waited.

Again when the Flint Knife warriors and the Brothers returned and counted the scalps they did not find those of the Great Warrior and his chief. Then the Bear and the Snake threw the two skins on the ground, and the others saw what they were. They asked who had killed them. "You killed them," said the Bear indicating the Snake. "No, you killed them," returned the Snake.

The Cliff Dwellers cried aloud and wept, as they knew that now they would all die.

The two Brothers were greatly troubled when they thought that they must give their two beautiful sisters to the two old men, the Bear and the Snake, so they stopped many times on their journey to their home and held games. Each time they held the games they promised that the winners would have their sisters, and each time the Bear and the Snake won.

At last they came to the place where the two maidens waited. They prepared to give a great Scalp and Squaw Dance. The two maidens were dressed in ceremonial robes; and the warriors of the Flint Knife People were also dressed in ceremonial attire. The brothers said: "Now we will let the maidens choose their own husbands." Soon the dance began and the maidens danced and danced with the young warriors.

Now the two old men, the Bear and the Snake, climbed to the top of a nearby mountain. They bathed and clothed themselves, and they appeared as two handsome young men. They took their pipes and filled them with certain herbs from their medicine bags and began to smoke quietly.

About this same time the maidens grew weary and were covered with sweat. The elder sister said: "Come, let us go apart and bathe." And they went to a little stream, and the elder maiden took the water in her hand and threw it into her mouth, and the younger sister cupped her hand and so drank. After they had bathed and drunk and were refreshed the older sister said: "I smell a sweet odor." "Let us find out what it is," said the younger maiden. And they went in search of the origin of this sweet smoke. They had no idea that it came from the pipes of the Bear and the Snake.

The maidens climbed the mountain, and when they reached the summit they saw the two beautiful youths there smoking. "Where did you come from?" asked the elder maiden. "I came from the mountain," said the Bear. "And I came from the plain," said the Snake. "Give us also something sweet to smoke," said the younger sister. The two youths gave them their pipes, and after a few puffs the maidens fell asleep.

When the maidens awakened they found that they had slept with a Bear and a Snake, for the two creatures lay there beside them.

Being very frightened, the two sisters started to run down the mountain path. "Wait," said the Bear, "if you return your brothers will kill you." So the Bear and the Snake gave the sisters each a basket with feathers tied to the outer rim. "Place the basket on the ground and step into it if you are in trouble or in danger," said the Bear, and the Snake repeated this advice. And so they let the sisters go on their way.

When the sisters came to the place where their two Brothers and the Flint Knife people waited they saw at once that they would be killed. The warriors tied their hands behind them and prepared to beat them to death. The elder sister said: "If we are to die we should be allowed to stand in our baskets." And as soon as they stepped in the baskets they disappeared.

Now the two sisters landed on the summit of a mountain. And as soon as they stepped from their baskets, they sent them back to the Bear and the Snake by the Wind. Almost at once they saw the Bear and the Snake coming towards them. "We must separate," they said. The elder sister stayed in the mountain, and the younger sister ran down to the plain. On and on they traveled. They became thin and almost without clothing.[58]

The elder sister came to a great cave, and, being very weary, she wished to enter it. She saw two bears guarding the entrance. They were fierce and she knew that she could not pass. Just then she heard a whistling and she saw a chipmunk. He said: "Follow me." She did this, and he whistled so lively a tune that the two bears listened to him and let her pass. Next they came to a second cave, and guarding the entrance were two dlo'ee,[59] animals with faces like dogs, one was white and one was yellow. The chipmunk whistled his tune again, and again they passed unharmed. The entrance of the third cave was guarded by two cranes, male and female. From there the elder sister and the chipmunk went into the big kiva of the Yei'bichai. Four men and four women in ceremonial robes came forward to meet her. The women took her aside and bathed her; they rubbed her first with cornmeal and then with pollen and she was beautiful. They dressed her in ceremonial robes and led her into a room lined with fur. And there her little baby girl was born. The child had little tufts of hair back of its ears and downy hair on its arms and legs.

After the child was born the Yei instructed the people to give the Mountain Chant.

They all went to the hogan of the old Mountain Woman (which is the mountain near Taos.) There they ate yellow cornmeal. They left the baby in the home of the old Mountain Woman. Then they went to the great flat plain towards Taos, and there they ate white cornmeal. The old Mountain Woman and the Elder Sister, or the Bear Maiden as she was now called, traveled together. A great Squaw Dance was given and the Flint Knife Warriors came. The Turkey Maiden ground the corn into meal while the Squirrel sang and played the flute. The men liked the old Mountain Woman and the Bear Maiden best, because the Turkey Maiden had pimples on her long neck, and the Dove Maiden rolled white lids over her large eyes, and the Rattle Snake Maiden had long, sharp teeth.

---

[58] Informant's note: From here the narrative follows the Elder Sister. The Younger Sister's adventure is another story.
[59] Franciscan Fathers (1912, p. 84): dlu'i, weasel.

After that they traveled to the Black Mountain near Ignacio, about 40 miles from Durango—the Turkey Clan lived there. They had snowshoes on their feet, the snow being deep. Here another dance was held. And the old Mountain Woman and the Bear Maiden danced with the young men. Then they took them into the mountain and they either starved to death or sickened and died, having sores on their bodies.

Later the Bear Maiden married a man and lived with him in his hogan. There a son was born. But a famine came and everyone left. The Bear Maiden left the little baby tied on his cradleboard hanging from a beam.

Now an owl flew by and she heard the baby crying. She planned to take the baby home for food for her young. When the owl had carried the baby safely to the nest he cried so pitifully that she felt sorry for him and she decided to bring him up with her own children. The boy grew rapidly, being half holy or sacred. The owl fashioned a bow for him; and she made arrows, using her own feathers for the shafts. Soon the boy could shoot everything the owl needed for food. Then the owl became frightened and said: "Soon he will kill me and my children. I must kill him." But she had forgotten that she had taught him to understand what the Wind said. Now the Wind had heard her and he told the boy that he must leave the owl and go to his own people. The sticks in the nest told him that he must follow the Mancos River eastward.

The boy started out at once and came to the place of an old campsite. He saw a little burned stick which told him to go on. The next day he came to another campsite, and there a little potsherd told him to go on. Each time he traveled and came to an old camp, something told him to go on: first a little stick, then the piece of a bowl, then an itching on his arm told him, then a hiccup, then a buzzing in his ears, and lastly a tickle in his nose. Finally he came to some hogans. An old man and an old woman were there, and a boy and a girl ran about. But the Owl's Boy as he was now called, thinking that they were strange animals, shot them with his arrows. The people came out of the hogans and chased him, and he fled toward the North.

The Owl's Boy needed more arrows. He cut the branches of the mountain mahogany, tses'gizie,[60] and the chokecherry, did se,[60] for new shafts. And each time he cut a branch there sprang into being a person. Some were male and some were female. Some had red lips and some had blue lips. This was the origin of the No'daa', the Ute tribe. And today, some have red lips and some blue.

Now the boy came to the Montezuma Valley, and an old man, da'sani, the porcupine, saw him, and as the boy was very tired he took him on

---

[60] Franciscan Fathers (1910) : tse'es dasi, mountain mahogany (p. 198) ; dzidze, choke- cherry (p. 197).

his back to the foot of the mountain called Dzil na'gine.[61] There they entered a hole in the ground. And only just in time, for the warriors were after them and they came and stuck their spears in the hole and almost touched the boy. The old porcupine was so frightened that the boy soon left. But he took with him the old one's medicine which, by its magic, made any burden light to carry.

In his travels the Owl's Boy met the Rat and then the Spider, and he gave them gifts, and they taught him many things. When he was 24 years of age he married the daughter of a great chief and he was known as a medicine man. They had born to them two daughters. Now after the two little girls were born his wife's sister came to live with them. Now this girl he wished to marry and he made a plan.

He pretended to be very ill. He told his wife that he would die. He had them build a frame of four upright poles and poles crosswise on top. Branches were piled on the poles and a fire laid under it. He told his wife to take the three young girls, their two daughters and her sister, and to leave that place after she had lighted the fire. He told her that she must marry her sister to the stranger who would help them. Then he climbed to the top of the structure and lay there, apparently dead. His wife lit the fire, and taking the girls, departed.

But this man rolled off the burning frame and, screened by the smoke, got away. He followed the woman and the girls for about a year. He would kill a deer and eat, and soon he grew healthy and young. He dressed himself in buckskins. He went hunting, and killing a deer he carried it to the woman's camp. They were in need and they gladly accepted the gift. This he did several times, always coming after dark. The woman remembered her husband's words, and she married her young sister to the man. The young wife lived with the man for some time before she discovered that he was her sister's husband. She told the first wife, her sister, who beat him for his wickedness. But after that he lived with them both. When the young wife bore him a son she hid the baby in the bushes. This baby was found by the Bear.[62] [63]

1. With beauty before me,
   With beauty behind me,
   With beauty above me,
   With beauty below me,
   With beauty about me,
   With sacred pollen the White Bead Woman circles her foot.
   With sacred pollen I circle my foot.

---

[61] Interpreter's note: Dzil na'gine is Sleeping Ute Mountain.

[62] Informant's note: The Chant "With Beauty" was sung when this part of the story was told.

[63] Recorder's note: The informant held a short ceremony here. He chanted "With Beauty . . ."

[The last lines alone change in the verses.]

2. With the sacred pollen the White Bead Woman circles her ankle.
   With sacred pollen I circle my ankle.
3. . . . her knee.
   With sacred pollen I circle my knee.
4. . . . her thighs.
   With sacred pollen I circle my thighs.
5. . . . her breast.
   With sacred pollen I circle my breast.
6. . . . her arms.
   With sacred pollen I circle my arms.
7. . . . her hands.
   With sacred pollen I circle my hands.
8. . . . her head.
   With sacred pollen I circle my head.

THE STORY OF THE SUMMER DANCE

The younger of the Twin Brothers,[64] the sons of the Man Raised in the Mountain, also traveled over the country as had his elder brother. He was a great hunter and he always carried his bow and arrows. One day, on one of his journeys near Dzil na'odili, he came upon a hogan. He left his bow and arrows on the outside of the dwelling and entered. There sat a beautiful maiden; she was lovely to see. She was making a pretty dress of buckskin and decorating it with porcupine quills. After the youth entered the home he heard someone coming. In came an old man with his bow and arrows in his hand. He said: "My daughter is narrow-minded, son-in-law. My daughter is all alone and she needs male help." Then again the young man heard someone coming. It was the girl's mother. The old man called out to his wife and said: "Your son-in-law is present. Now don't be foolish." So she ran away from the hogan.[65]

Now the old man's name was Tloth ilth ine', One Who Looks at a Fish. He spoke to his son-in-law: "We are a poor family. We have nothing. Let us go out and see what we can find." So just before dawn they went out and they traveled to where people lived near Pueblo Bonito. They sat down, weapons in hand. The old man said: "I will sit here. You go farther on and sit there." It was not long before two beautiful maidens walked toward them. They wore beautiful dresses and had many beads around their necks and earrings in their ears. The maidens did not stop by the youth, but went on to the old man. The old man killed the two girls and took their scalps, their clothing, and their beads. Then he returned to the home.

On the second morning the old man said: "This may be your lucky day, my son-in-law. Let us go out again." They went out as before.

---

[64] Recorder's note: See p. 126 "The Story of the Flint Knife Boys," etc.
[65] Recorder's note: Mother-in-law taboo.

The old man sat down and the young man went farther on. Again two beautiful maidens came toward them, and again they passed the young man and went on to the old man who killed them and took their belongings.

When they returned the young wife took her husband aside and said: "I will tell you what my father uses. He has a strong medicine. My father has the medicine of the enemies, the medicine from the Giant and the medicine from the Bear. You have nothing. He has the enemy's spinal cord, a short piece, dried, and the enemy's heel cords; and he has the unborn baby. He has all these for his medicine. Go and kill an antelope and also find a gopher heavy with young." The young man went out and did as his wife told him. She took the cord from the antelope, and the unborn from the gopher, and she made them look the same as her father's medicine. She exchanged them for the real medicine which she took home to her husband. Then she taught him the chants which her father used, and the prayers also.

The next morning the old man said: "Son-in-law, let us go out again. It may be your luck this time." The young man said: "Since this is to be my luck I will sit down first and you must go farther on." The young man chanted as his wife had taught him. Then came two beautiful maidens with turquoise beads, earrings, and dresses of beautiful goods. They passed the old man by and came toward him. He killed them and took their scalps, their beads, and their clothes.

Now the old man felt bad because he had lost all of the turquoise. He did not know that his medicine had been changed, and that he carried the imitation medicine.

On the fourth morning again the young man sat down first and the old man went farther on. The young man chanted, and again came two beautiful maidens. They passed by the old man and they came to the young man, who killed them and took their scalps, beads, and clothing. Then the old man came to him and said: "My son-in-law, by what medicine do you do these things?" And the young man answered: "I have nothing." The old man drew his body away from the young man and said: "Without a chant and medicine it is impossible. You alone cannot draw anyone." Now the old man's real medicine which the young man had in his possession was the same medicine with which the old man Bear had drawn the Great Warrior of Aztec and killed him. He took this medicine out and showed it to the old man who examined it closely. He sent for his own medicine. When it was brought to him he laid the articles side by side and said: "They truly look alike." Then he shook them in his hands and took the real medicine himself, but the young man said: "Mine is the oldest because I had the using of the last power. I had the medicine on me." So the young man recovered the real medicine.

After this the young man went after all the enemies he wished to capture. Those that he drew, he killed. Soon his home was full of turquoise, beads, and beautiful goods. But after a while the young man and his wife sickened. The cords of their legs drew up, and their heads ached as did their stomachs. They chanted all the chants that they knew but none helped them. Only Hasjel na' yei nazone,[66] the Black Yei, knew of the proper medicine.

Hasjel na'yei nazone was to be the shaman. The friends of the young man took the skin of a deer not killed by a weapon to the Yei, but he would not look at it. Then the young man sent two buckskins, but the Yei would not accept them. He sent three, four, but Hasjel na'yei nazone would not look at them. Then the same person who told them that Hasjel na'yei nazone would act as shaman came and said: "My children, did you use him?" The young man and his wife both said: "We sent gifts but he would not look at them. We do not understand." So then Dotso, the All-Wise Fly (and here given as the old Man of the Mountain) showed them how to make the medicine stick to take to Hasjel na'yei nazone. They did this, and they took it and presented it to the Yei. Then he asked: "Who thought of the medicine stick?" They said: "We did, ourselves." He said: "No. Only Dotso could have thought of it. He is the only one who knows. Nevertheless I will come tomorrow." They begged him to come that day, but he said: "No. Nothing shall happen. I will come tomorrow."

Then he showed them how to make the jar drum, and what to use. He said that he had his own jar drum and the stick with which to pound it.

The next day he started out. He camped quite a way from the hogan of the young man and his wife, but they could see his fire. Different ones went to him and asked him to come at once; but to them all he said: "No. I will come tomorrow, in the morning."

Now by this time the two were very ill and they needed the Yei immediately. But he kept saying: "I will come tomorrow. Nothing shall happen to them." Then he told the friends of the young man to kill a young buck for him and for his friends. The buck must have two points on his horns. The next morning he arrived, but not before he stopped and demanded his meat.

They brought the deer, which they had killed, to him and there came buzzards, crows, coyotes, wolves, and all the creatures who had eaten the bodies of the enemies. They ate the deer which had been killed.

After this Hasjel na'yei nazone entered the dwelling of the sick couple. And their friends stood outside and beat the drum and

---

[66] Franciscan Fathers (1910, p. 44) : The Black God or Fire God, Hashchezhini.

chanted and called out the names of the sick ones, as also the name of Hasjel na'yei nazone. Then others came out and placed beautiful goods, symbolic of the spoils of the enemy, over their shoulders. And inside the dwelling the Yei burned the barks of the piñon and the willow trees, the bladder pod and the sage, and the sheepgrass and the radishgrass. These they burned while Hasjel na'yei nazone chanted and sprinkled the ashes of these plants over the persons of the two sick ones.

Many chants were sung here and during the decorating of the medicine stick (fig. 19). Today the chants are those of the Two Brothers, the twin sons of the Man Who Was Formed in the Earth or Mountain. From the Elder Brother come the Mountain Chant and Dance (the First Mountain Chant comes from way back in the beginning, the Bear being the last to add his medicine to the old ceremony) and the Snake Chant and Dance. From the Younger Brother comes the Summer or

THE SUMMER OR SCALP OR SQUAW DANCE

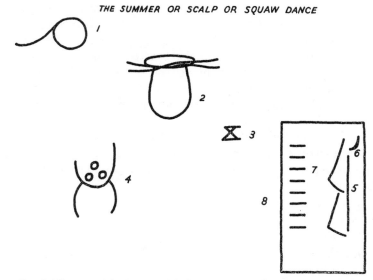

FIGURE 19.—Artifacts used in the Summer, or Scalp, or Squaw Dance and designs on the Medicine Stick. 1, The Rainbow stick to beat the drum with. Today an oak stick is used. The enemy is pounded into the ground symbolically. When the ceremony is over it is straightened out and, with a chant, is taken to the mountains. 2, The jar drum. Inside it are all the sacred waters mixed with the blood or spittle of the enemy. It is covered with skin and tied with rain strings. 3, Scalp of the monsters. It is behind the stick. 4, The skin of a fawn not killed by a weapon, and two strings. Used as a covering for the jar drum. It has a face, eyes, and mouth. The strings hang down. 5, On the medicine stick: the bow of Hasjel na'yei nazone, the Black Yei. 6, On the medicine stick: an opening in the bow and a little object that represents a knife. 7, The rain, the narrow black streaks of rain. 8, The medicine stick is (was) taken from the root of a reed growing from one bank to another across a stream. Today a cedar stick is used.

Scalp or Squaw Dance (fig. 19) and its chants.[67] From Hasjelti came the Yei'bickai. Hasjelti is the god or Yei of the East or Dawn; Hasjohon is the Yei of the West and Twilight. Yolgai esdzan, the White Bead Woman is Nature or the Mother goddess. These three are the chief actors.

The one who holds the jar drum must stand with her eyes and mouth turned away from the drummer. In the first Dance the Black Cloud was used to cover the jar. Today they use a goatskin. Today, also, they use all kinds and colors of yarns around the sticks carried in the Summer Dance. They used the seeds of the columbine and the seeds of the sweet-smelling grass. They were blown on the medicine stick after it was finished.

Today the Dance is as follows: On the first day the medicine stick is taken to the person representing Hasjel na'yei nazone. They sing and dance all of that night. The second day the person representing Hasjel na'yei nazone goes only part of the way. They sing and dance at the place all of that night. The morning of the third day they come near and make camp not far from the hogan of the sick person. Food is then taken to the party, the gift of the sick person. After they have eaten they go to the hogan. On the fourth and last day, while the visiting party stand outside chanting, the women relatives of the sick person go out and distribute presents such as calico, ribbon, and candy. This is an old custom. (The gifts are given in the spirit of our Christmas gifts.)

To continue the story: at dawn Hasjelti came and sang three chants. There are no words, only the tune. Then came Hash chel bai,[68] the Yei known as the clown, also called Tqo'nenili, the Water Sprinkler. He was the last to sing.

> Yo ho, yo ho, ye hi,
> Ha'he he, he'a,
> He'ya ena.

That was the last chant, and after he had finished singing everyone went his way.

Today the Summer Dance is performed in this manner but without the chants. The ceremony takes 3 days. It is held a second time over a person.

Now after the first ceremony was held over the young man and his wife they recovered. The young man went out again and killed more enemies. After a time again they both sickened. Dotso came and told the young man that when he went out and killed the enemy the blood of the enemy was upon him when he returned to his wife. That

---

[67] Tozzer (1908), p. 337) ; Matthews (1894 a, p. 203) ; Parsons (1919, pp. 465–467) ; Franciscan Fathers (1910, p. 289).

[68] Franciscan Fathers (1910, p. 384) : The Water Sprinkler, Tqo nenili, also called the Gray God, Hash chel bai.

accounted for her illness as well as his. Therefore the ceremony was held a second time.

This second time Hasjel na'yei nazone told them they must use the small branch of the cedar,[69] but it must not have two points at the end. On the east side of the branch, he who cut it must so mark it: there must be drawn a bow with an opening, and a scalp on the opposite side. Then the stick must be painted red. It must then be blackened with the same medicine which they burned. They must blow on it the seeds of the sweet-smelling grass and the columbine. Yarn or cotton cloth or red flannel must be tied to the stick, and these must hang down like rain. This medicine stick must be taken to Hasjel na'yei nazone.

But this second time, on the last day, the White Bead Woman came and made the medicine. The herbs she used would heal the patient. She gave a beverage to the young man to drink, but the wife took her medicine outside the dwelling. The Crow stood between them. The Crow represented the third person, and is always shown between a man and his wife. Now after the young man drank the medicine he took a little string from the yucca and drew it away from the tip of his heel. Then he laid it down. He took another and another and drew them, separately, away from all parts of his body. When a medicine man draws the yucca string away from the body of the patient, the Crow, outside, calls, and another medicine man, sitting near where a scalp has been buried, puts ashes over it four times. All this was added to the second ceremony.[70]

Today a wife goes through the same ceremony with her husband. The sick man remains in the hogan. Then they throw over her shoulders the robes, buckskins, belts, long strips of velvet, calico, red flannel, ancient squaw dresses, etc. These are the gifts of the friends and family of the husband. She takes them and gives them to her relatives one by one. She keeps nothing; everything is given to her relatives.

THE STORY OF SAN'HODE'DI'BEGAEYE, THE BEGGAR'S SON [71]

Now after the Great Gambler had been sent up into the sky the Sun wanted the people to know about the medicine that the Gambler had used and had taken up into the sky with him. So he made a plan.

---

[69] Informant's note: A small branch of cedar is the sign of a medicine man.

[70] Informant's note: If a man kills an enemy before his child is born, that enemy's spirit will harm his child afterward. It is said that the scalp, or spirit, of the enemy killed would have this power. If the child becomes ill the ceremony, with its medicine, is held over the child.

Sandoval, the informant, said that his father had killed an enemy before he was born. When he reached middle age his legs "drew up." He was sick and vomited blood. He could not smell tobacco. This ceremony was held over him and he recovered.

[71] Pepper (1908, pp. 178-183).

There is a place called Gaeye net be'e at the foot of the mountain called Tso dzil, Mount Taylor. At this place there lived a poor woman who worked hard for her living. Now the Sun had visited this woman secretly, and she brought forth a baby boy. After the child was 10 or 12 years of age he ran a race each morning around Tso dzil. He thus became a great runner.

The woman and her son left Gaeye net be'e and went to live at Tse be' an y i, the Place Where Poles Hold up the Rock, Pueblo Bonito.[72] At this place the people had the custom of making many turquoise offerings between the split cliff rocks. The woman discovered this place of offering. She picked up all the pieces of turquoise that she could find, then she went to the people and exchanged them for food. After the second time that she went to them the people began to ask among themselves: "I wonder where the poor beggar woman gets her stones?" Then they guessed that the turquoise must be the offerings made to the rock. They went to the place and found her tracks and where she had picked up the turquoise. When they reported that she had been taking the offerings to the rock, the head of the people decided to kill both the woman and her son. But the two heard of the plan and quickly left that part of the country.

From there they went to a place opposite Farmington. People were living under the big cliff at that time. While they stayed there they lived on what they could find. Some of the people gave them food, but others drove them away and were cruel to them. It was not long before the woman discovered the sacred places where the people made their stone offerings. These offerings she gathered and traded for food. She was caught and the people planned that the two should die. But someone told the woman of the plan that they were both to be killed. The beggar woman called to her son and they left.

They followed a ledge of rock so that their tracks could not be found. They stopped at a place opposite Fruitland and they built themselves a little home there. All around that place the seeds were plentiful. They ate those and once in a while they killed a rabbit or a rat. After a time the people discovered them. They were no longer safe and they left that place. They traveled to the Hog Back Mountains and they built a little house there. (Today they call this place Kinda ligene, the Little Ruin on the Side of a Rock). They made grass mats for the floor and matting to cover themselves with. They also made robes of rabbit and rat fur. These robes were at first small, about the size of a saddle blanket, but later they were larger.

By this time the boy had grown into a youth.

They had thought that all was well, but they were discovered again. They left their home and passed Shiprock; they traveled to the other

---

[72] Franciscan Fathers (1912, p. 228): Tse biya hania'hi, Pueblo Bonito.

side of the Carrizos. Today you can see a ruin high up on a rock. It is called Kine'gauge'. It was the house the youth built for his mother. He was a good builder by that time. But soon the seeds from the plants got scarce, and the mother told her son that they must leave and go south of the Carrizos near Beck shi'bi tqo, Cow Springs, were a people lived at a place calle Kiet seel.

When they climbed to the top of the mountain called Dzil li'jin, the Black Mountains of Arizona, they came, all of a sudden, upon a man who was gathering wood and wrapping it in a bundle. They frightened the man so that he nearly lost his breath. Now this man was the head or chief of the little village called Kiet seel. The man tied up a bundle of wood for the woman and one for her son, and on the top of each bundle he put some loose pieces. When they reached the village the man collected the loose wood and laid it near his house. He carried the three bundles of wood inside. Then the man brought a quantity of food for the woman and her son. He told them to burn the pieces of wood he had left outside the house that night. They built a fire and ate and lay down and slept.

They were no sooner asleep than some boys, and even grown men and women, came and threw sticks and stones at them. They threw mud and water and ashes. They bothered them all through the night. The next day they prepared to leave, but they returned the wood that they had used, for the mother said: "The man who gave us the food must be a kind man." They brought the wood to the house, but the food that they received was only barely enough. So that night they camped farther away from the house. Again they received cruel treatment at the hands of the people. The next morning they brought more wood, but this time they were given but one piece of food each. That night the same people came and bothered them again. However, the following day they brought more wood to the man's house, but this time they received nothing at all for their work.

They left that place and traveled toward the South to a place called Ya'kin. When they neared this place they came upon a man gathering wood. This man, as had the other one, tied the wood into three bundles and placed loose pieces on the top. He also carried some. That night the mother and her son made their camp outside his house, and they received all that they could eat. But that night the boys came and pulled their hair and burned them with burning sticks. These boys played every mean trick they could think of on the two strangers. At dawn they left them. That day and the following the woman and the youth carried wood to the man's house and received a little food; but on the fourth day no food whatever was given them; and each night they had received wicked treatment.

They left that place and journeyed to a place called O'zeye. Near there they again found a man gathering wood. He seemed very pleased to see them. He tied the bundles of wood for them, and the three carried the wood back to the village. They were taken inside the man's house and given lots of food to eat, and even some to carry away with them. They were told to camp outside the house. That night, as in the two other villages, the boys and then the people came and treated them in every cruel way they could think of. The two cried and hugged each other all night long. They carried wood to the man on the second day, and the food they received for their trouble was barely enough. That night they camped at a distance, but the boys found them and teased and tormented them all during the night. The third time that they brought wood they received no food. They camped far away and slept until dawn before the boys found them. Fortunately their wickedness lasted but a short time.

Then they went to a place called Tala hogan.[73] There they made themselves a shelter out of the bark of trees. This time young girls came out each day and teased the mother and her son, saying: "We want a husband to gather wood for us." Now they teased the pair because they were so poor. One girl said: "He is to be my husband." And another: "No, I chose him for my husband first."

To avoid meeting these girls the youth would start out early each morning and hunt for rabbits or rats or whatever he could find. One day when he returned to the shelter his mother told him the following:

I was sitting here today when all of a sudden everything inside our shelter turned white. I looked and someone stood out there. It was a man who asked about you. I told him that you stay away all day because the girls come and tease you. He asked me about our food and about our bedding. I had baked four little seed cakes. I showed him those four and I told him we ate seed cakes and the rabbits you killed. I showed him the woven grass mats which we use for bed and cover. The man then took a piece of the bread and ate it and said: "This is my food also."

The woman continued: "I turned my head for a moment, and the man was gone. But there was only one track outside. The piece of seed cake he bit into is here." The youth told his mother that he did not believe this story. "It is foolish to think that any people as poor as we are would be visited by a Holy Being. It is you who have bitten the bread and made the track."

The next morning the youth went away as usual. That night when he returned his mother told him that at noon that day she had again seen the Holy Person, and that he was a handsome man. "This time he ate half the bread cake. I looked away for a moment and he was gone. I ran outside and looked about, but I saw only two tracks in the sand." Then the youth told his mother that she had eaten the cake and made the tracks.

---

[73] Fewkes (1898, pp. 527, 595–603). Brew (1949, p. 22): "There is also a Navajo name for the town . . . Talla Hogan, Talla Hogandi, Tally Hogan."

The third day the youth went hunting as usual, and in the evening, when he returned to his home, his mother told him the same story. But this time the man ate almost the whole seed cake, and there were three tracks outside.

The fourth morning the youth left again. When he returned his mother told him that she had again seen the Holy Man. And that this time he had eaten the whole piece of bread. "And this is what the man told me, my son: he wants you to wash your hair in the morning, and to bathe your whole body, drying yourself with cornmeal and pollen. Then you are to get some water in the jar, and sit beside it in the shelter. You are to sit there and keep looking into the water. After he had departed there were four foot prints outside."

The next morning the young man did all that his mother had told him to do. She sat beside him looking into the jar filled with water. He became restless and doubted her. She said: "Son, the Sun is at noon."

At that moment all outside and inside the shelter turned white. In the midst of the glow there stood a young man. This Holy Being told the woman that he was going to take his younger brother, her son, but that he would return. The poor mother said: "No, you can-not take my child. He is all that I have in this world, and I would starve to death without him." The mother was asked to let her son go four times. Then the youth said: "Let me go, mother. Did you not hear him say that I would come back to you?" So the woman gave her consent.

A white rainbow flashed to the youth's feet, and the Holy Being told him to raise his right foot. With the first step they were on top of the mountain called Sis jin de'lea. The second step brought them to Natsi'lid be'tqo, Rainbow Springs. From there they went to Bitda'ho chee, Red Mountain, then to the top of Tqo jin whee tsa. There they stepped into a house whose first room was filled with trash. They entered another room and someone called out: "Um-m-m, I smell earthly people." And this person added: "The fool-hearted youth must be bringing someone home." When the two young men got to the fourth room they saw a man, a woman, and a girl. They were called Tqo jin whee tsa hastin, Tqo jin whee tsa esdzan, and Tqo jin whee tsa chike'. They were the people of the mountain, the man and his wife and daughter.

They washed the youth, and the maiden gave him a white bead basket. He was washed four times. He was also given a turquoise basket, a white shell basket, and a black jet basket. And each time that he was washed he was dried with corn pollen. Then he was trimmed and formed like the maiden herself. She put her head beside his and he was formed like her, all except the feet. He had big feet.

Then the Sun came.

Now the Man of the Mountain wanted to dress the youth, and his wife wanted to dress him. But the Sun said: "No, he is my son, and I will dress him myself." Then the White Bead Woman came, and she said: "If he is the son of the Sun he is my son also. I will dress him myself." The four Holy Beings had different minds. Their thoughts were changeable. There are four sections to the chant sung while he was being dressed by the White Bead Woman.

The White Bead Woman's Chant

She dressed me with her white bead moccasins.
She dressed me with her white bead leggings.
She dressed me with her white bead garment.
She dressed me with her white bead bracelets.
She dressed me with her white bead earrings.
She dressed me with the perfect white bead called ha'da tehe which she had on her forehead.
She dressed me with the perfect crystals of pollen, the beautiful goods pollen, which were her words
And with which I can call for beautiful goods and pollen and they will come at my word.
She dressed me with the turquoise feather
On top of which sat the blue bird with his beautiful song.
I am dressed like the Most High Power Whose Ways Are Beautiful.
All is beautiful before me.
All is beautiful behind me.
All is beautiful around me.
All is beautiful everywhere.

This chant is repeated, and then sung twice with this difference: "I am all dressed . . . ." instead of "She dressed me . . . ."

After this the Sun and the White Bead Woman returned to their home.

The Man of the Mountain gave the youth blue gum,[74] and he gathered four herbs for his medicine. From the east side he gathered a plant called tlo cho ae tso [75] which had black flowers. From the south side he got a plant called cholchin ilt ai,[76] which had white flowers. The plant from the west was called aze bi'ni i,[77] medicine of the mind.

[74] Informant's note: The powdered petals of a flower are used with pinon gum to make blue gum.
Matthews (1886, pp. 767–777): tha'di'thee do tllj', blue sacred powder, *Delphinium scaposum* Greene.
[75] Informant's note: Tlo che whee tso is a small mountain below San Francisco Peak where these plants grow.
Matthews (1886, pp. 767–777): tlo ta hi tso, great tlo ta hi, *Chenopodium album*.
[76] Franciscan Fathers (1912, p. 73): cho'hojilyai, Jimson weed, thornapple, *Datura stramonium*.
[77] Franciscan Fathers (1912, p. 44): aze bi'ni i, medicine of the mind, in reference to its bewitching effects. Akin to locoweed.

It is a very poisonous medicine herb which is said to make them insane. It is akin to locoweed. The plant from the north is called aze tlo' hi; [78] this plant had yellow flowers. The flowers from the north had their mouths open, and if touched they laughed. It was called the laughing medicine. It was the medicine the Gambler had used, as were the others. The youth now learned the chants the Gambler had used. After that the Mountain Man got pieces of all the beautiful goods which were inside the mountain, and he tied them in a little bundle and gave them to the youth. All the trash that he had seen on entering the first room was now piles of beautiful goods and food. The youth was then told that he must climb to the top of the mountain called Dzil nit chee, Red Side Mountain; there he must shoot an arrow into a deer bush, into four different bushes eaten by deer. This he did. He was instructed to draw the arrows out of the bushes and to place them pointing back to the place he had come from. This was the price he had to pay for learning the chants and for the medicine.

From Red Side Mountain the Rainbow carried him back to the doorway of his mother's home. When he entered the dwelling she ran out; she looked about but saw no one else. Then the old woman grabbed him and said: "What have you done with my son? Did I not tell you that you would take him away from me? Where is he?" The young man said: "Mother, it is I." She did not hear or understand, and she asked the same question, shaking him. She did this four times, becoming more and more excited. The young man said: "Mother, don't you hear? I am your son." Then she fixed her eyes and looked long at him. He had changed, he was different. His hair fell to his ankles. She asked again four times if he was indeed her son.

The youth chanted the chants that he had learned and he chewed the blue gum, and he blew to the East, South, West and North, and they found themselves in a home like the home of the Mountain Man. Then he heard the maidens coming for their wood. When they opened the door of the house he blew toward them with the blue gum and they all fell back. He heard them whispering about all the beautiful things that they had seen inside his dwelling. He went out and led them to the forest; and he cut wood until each had her load. They carried the wood home, and they were ashamed of themselves, but also glad that he had helped them.

The chief of the village had two daughters. Their names were To chine'e and O chine'e. These maidens were well guarded and their father kept watch over them. The elder daughter went to the spring

---

[78] Matthews (1886, pp. 767–777) : a zay tlo ee, medicine hay, *Arenaria aculeata.*
Franciscan Fathers (1912, p. 45) : aze tlo'hi, bluegrass, *Sysyrinchium mucronatum.*

for water early in the morning. Now each time the maidens went to the spring, when they returned their father asked them to make water. So early one morning the young man went to the spring and waited for the elder sister. She came, but she did not look at the young man while she filled her water jar. The young man asked her for a drink and she filled a dipper from the spring and gave it to him. "No," said the young man, "I want the water from your jar." She threw the dipperful away and dipped out the water from her jar and gave it to the young man without looking up. He drank some of the water and threw the rest on her. She brushed the water from her clothing without looking up. Then she began to fill the water jar, but he blew with the gum on the jar and it tipped over. She filled it a second time, and she filled it a third time, and then she looked up and just a little smile came to her lips. She filled the water jar a fourth time, but he blew on it with the gum and it tipped over. After that she smiled and said: "How do you do this?" And he said as he gave her a piece of the gum: "This is how I do it." She put the gum in her mouth. She filled her water jar and blew and it tipped over. She did this a second time. Then she let the young man become her husband.

After that she returned home and her father told her to make water. When he saw that she had been visited by a man he went to the spring, and he measured the man's foot track with a stick. He called all the men of the village together and measured their feet. Every measurement of the men's feet were short by a long way. He next went to the neighboring villages and measured the men's feet; he even traveled a long way from where they lived, but all the men's feet were smaller. He returned to his home and he wondered whose foot track he had measured.

Now the Little Breeze told the young man that the father would never guess where to go after he got home. So the young man used the chant, that he had learned, that drew people, and then the father remembered the son of the poor woman. The Little Breeze told the young man that the father was coming, and he chanted until the father came to the door. The father entered and sat down, and the young man lay on his back. The father measured the young man's foot, and the size was exactly that of the stick. The father said: "My son-in-law, do you know that you are an expectant father?" He told the young man that his daughter was soon to have a baby.

When the father returned to his home in the village he saw that many people were about his house getting ready for the birth of the baby. A baby boy was born. And the people made ready to carry the baby and gifts to the young man. They carried a basket filled with meal. They chanted many chants as they walked, and the songs that they sang at that time are the songs that should be sung during the birth of a child. When the people were near the young man's home they wrestled with each other and laughed. The baby was brought into the house and placed on the young man's lap. Then they washed the baby.

The words of the chant that they sang are these:

I am the Sun's son, into my hands he is given.
I am the Sun's son, into my hand he comes.
He has for his moccasins the turquoise moccasins, into my hand he comes.
He has for his leggings the turquoise leggings, etc.
He has for his garment the turquoise garment, etc.
He has for his earrings the turquoise earrings, etc.
A perfect turquoise is placed on his forehead, it comes to my hand.
He has for his feather the turquoise feather, it comes to my hand.
He is the turquoise boy and he comes to my hand.
Nothing can harm him as he comes to my hand.
Like the Most High Power Whose Ways Are Beautiful he comes to my hand.
For all is beautiful before, behind, above and below, and it comes to my hand.[79]

The people gave their gifts to the young man, and they brought his wife to him. The young man, in his turn, gave them gifts of venison. They carried home a quantity of meat. After the people left they found that they had brought the younger sister also to be his wife. He had a baby and two wives. He went to the home of his father-in-law. There he was given a longhouse. His mother remained behind where they had lived. There also remained all the beautiful goods.

The next morning he drew a woman with his chant. She gave him her leg wrapping, and he told her that she would see old age. He made a beda [80] like an antelope. The young man laced it with the woman's leg wrapping. Early the following morning he got up and counted the doorways of all the houses in the village, then he went to where there was a herd of antelope. He could do this, for he wore the beda that he had made over him. He killed as many antelope as there were doorways. When he returned home he told the people that one man from each doorway should go out and carry home an antelope. When they brought the meat home, the people said: "Our son-in-law is very great. He must have two longhouses."

The next morning he went out and killed two antelope for each doorway; and he told the people to send two men from each doorway to bring home the meat. He was given three longhouses.

On the third morning he killed three antelope for each doorway. And when he returned to the village he told the people to send three men from each dwelling. He received four longhouses. The fourth day he killed four antelope for each doorway, and four men from each house went out for them. He was given five longhouses. Then all

---

[79] Informant's note: This is the song that is sung as they wash the baby; but not all know about it.

[80] Recorder's note: A beda consists of the head and hide of an animal. It is explained in the second hunting story.

the people said: "Our son-in-law is very great. We will have plenty of meat.

On the fifth day San'hode'di', the Beggar's son, set out for the home of the Mountain People called Tqo che o whee tso. He started to hunt, as before, but when he neared an antelope herd, a coyote hit him with his hide and blew four times upon him. The coyote then took his beda, the antelope headdress, and placed it on his own head. He went away after the antelope, while the poor young man was left behind in the form of a skinny coyote.

Now the coyote was unable to kill one antelope, even with the beda. He took the discharge from his eyes and laid it in a row and stepped over it four times and it turned into fat. This he took to the two young wives. But the younger of the two sisters told the elder that the man who came to them was not their husband.

The Beggar's son in the coyote's skin turned to the East and lay that night under a cedar tree.[81] He ate the berries of the cedar tree. The second night he traveled to the South and he laid under the bush called kin jilth ie',[82] and he ate its berries. The third night he went to the West and he stayed under an iron bush.[83] Its berries are called maida to this day because he ate them. He traveled to the North on the fourth day, and he lay under a wild-rose bush [84] that night, and he ate its berries.

After the fourth day he went out and fell down for he was almost dead by that time. Now the person called Dotso went to the place called Tqo che o whee tso and told the people living there that the young man had been hit by the coyote's hide, and that he lay in the open almost dead. Then the same Holy Young Man, who had called him brother in his mother's home, went to him. When he found the skinny coyote, he said: "What are you doing here, Tqo che o whee tso tsel kee?" The poor coyote got to his feet and tried to say something, but all he could do was howl like a coyote. Then his "brother" made a ring out of a young cedar, big enough so that he could push the coyote through it. When he pushed the coyote through the cedar ring the skin ripped open and the head of the young man could be seen. Then the Holy Being made a ring out of the bush called kin jilth ie and the hide fell down and exposed half of the young man's body. The third ring was made from the iron bush, and after it was passed over the young man the skin fell down to his knees. The fourth time the ring was made from the wild-rose bush, and this freed the young man.

---

[81] Informant's note: The berries of the cedar tree are called dit tse.

[82] Franciscan Fathers (1910, p. 198): kinjil'ahi, currant, *Purshia tridentata*.

[83] Franciscan Fathers (1910, p. 198): ma'ida, coyote food, or iron bush, the wild cherry, *Prunus demissa*.

[84] Franciscan Fathers (1910), p. 197: cho, or chu, the wild rose, *Rosa fendleri*.

Now all this took place in order that the people might have medicine for another wrong that they would do. The Beggar's son was instructed about this thing. In cases where a brother and sister cohabit one or both persons will sicken. They usually become mad. There are several sicknesses, however, that come from this. It was necessary for the Beggar's son to go through this black magic transformation so that he could make known the medicine. There is a certain kind of plant,[85] with pretty flowers, that attracts both moths and butterflies. They fall dead if they light on it.

While the young man was being told what should take place in the ceremony by the Holy Being they saw the coyote with the beda going by. So the young man was told to go and hit him with his own hide and to blow four times upon him. This he did and the creature resumed his true form. The headdress, however, was an awful looking thing, for the hide had spoiled it. But the young man, even so, was able to kill one antelope before going home.

On the way he met a little creature coming out of the ground. This person said: "I saw that you had a hard time." The young man answered: "I had a hard time of it, Grandfather." The person said: "You were given power from the Sun and the White Bead Woman, and also from Tqo che o whee tso hastin, the Mountain Man; but there are one or two things that they did not tell you. That is why you have had all this trouble. Come home with me." He raised a greasewood bush and blew four times into the hole, and they went down into the opening.

Now this person told the young man that he had heard that the Earth People's tobacco was very sweet and he longed to taste it. So he rolled four cigarettes made from the young man's tobacco, and each time he smoked one he killed little animals and brought them back to life. He said: "I see, my Grandson, your tobacco is very good." He then told the young man of the ceremony that was not before made known to him. He taught him all the chants and what was to be done. After this the person wanted a gift, so the young man gave him the antelope hide. He put it over the little creature and blew four times over him, and it became his coat. He is known as ha zeylth gaeye,[86] the ground squirrel. He was well pleased.

There was in this ceremony, the young man learned, a prayer from the East, a prayer to begin way in the East and come home. It is called

---

[85] Informant's note: His father showed this plant to him. It was large and covered with many flowers of different shades of purple color. Around it lay dead moths and butterfies. Recorder's note: The Hopi call it the butterfly flower because it attracts them. The Navaho name is chil aghani, poison weed.

Franciscan Fathers (1912, p. 72): chil agha'ni, killing plant, fatal to flies, moths, etc.

[86] Interpreter's note: Ha zelyth gaeye is a member of the chipmunk family.

Franciscan Fathers (1912, p. 188): hazai, or tsidit i'ni, the rock or ground squirrel.

tche'whee a te'he'. This prayer is told from the East, from the home
of the four plants of Tqo che o whee tso. It is also told from the
South home, from the West home, and from the North home; but it
is called "From the East back to the home of the Tqo che o whee tso
people and the four plants." They say that it comes from the South,
from the home built with cholchin ilt a'i; [87] from the West it is from
the home built with aze bi'ni i; [88] from the North it is from the home
built with aze tlo'hi,[89] the laughing medicine. This was the prayer
of the White Bead Girl, and this prayer is very long. This prayer
was given by the White Bead Girl herself and was to be used for
any person who became possessed or insane. It was also to be used
over any young man or woman who became mad over drink, gambling,
or sex. They were the medicines of the Great Gambler, and had only
now been made known to the young man. They were the medicines
that the Great Gambler had used against the people.

Then the Beggar's son went to a place called Tse jinjede lia. At
this place he went through another prayer ceremony. It is called
the prayer of the Turquoise Boy, Des chee del ja. It was the Turquoise Boy himself who gave it to the young man for his protection.

Then the young man was made so that nothing in heaven or on
earth could harm him, and he was ready to return to his home.[90]

When San'hode'di' begaeye returned to his home the younger sister
recognized him and said: "Did I not tell you that the other person
was not our husband? And you answered me and said that there was
no other person like him." His father-in-law came out and said:
"Did I not tell you that that person (the coyote) ate a whole lot more
than my son-in-law?" The father of the two women commanded
that the children begotten by the coyote should be killed, but the young
man said: "No." They took them down to a place called Tqo che eko,
and they became little animals somewhat like a coyote, but with black
faces, short tails, webbed feet, and they climbed trees. They lived
along the water and were called tapan mai, along-the-shore or water-
edge coyote.[91]

By this time the son, San'hode'di's first-born, was a youth. The
Beggar's Son called to the youth and said: "Come here, my son, and
stand before me. You will now go to the mountain called Taho chee,
and you will live there. You will be over all the game. And because
of you the People of the Earth will have game forever." When he
began his chanting his son started out on his journey. He went first

---

[87] Franciscan Fathers (1910, p. 189) : cholchinilt'ai, *Geranium incisum.*

[88] Franciscan Fathers (1912, p. 44) : aze bi'ni i, medicine of the mind, akin to locoweed.

[89] Franciscan Fathers (1910, p. 184) : aze tlo'hi, sandwort, *Arenaria aculeata.*

[90] Informant's note: There are some medicine men who specialize in these ceremonies.
They know all of the chants and prayers.

[91] Informant's note: There is a saying among Navaho men that if a man marries a
girl not a virgin, "The young man has gotten a coyote."

to Rainbow Springs, and he circled the springs four times as the Sun travels. Then the antelope of the plains came and circled around the youth. After this he ran ahead of the antelope and they all went to the mountain that San'hode'di' had told his son about, and they all disappeared out of sight into the mountain.

The Beggar's Son then went to his mother's home. His two wives wished to go with him but he told them that they were to remain in the village. However, after he left, they said: "We have nothing to do here now. We will follow him." So they trailed behind him until they reached his mother's house. Once there, by his magic, he gathered all the beautiful goods together and made them into a small bundle which he put in his bag. Then the four started out. They visited all the places where the beggar woman and her son had received ill treatment. Now in every village where the men and the boys had treated them badly the Beggar's Son took their wives. This was done to get even with them. When they arrived at a place at the mouth of Tse gee (Sage) Canyon they found that his two wives had worn out their moccasins. There was a small rock at this place. He stood the two sisters on top of it side by side. He placed his flute on their feet, but first he made their footprints on the rock. Then he began to chant. In this way he sent them back to their father's house on the flute, and the flute returned to him.

Now he built a house up in the canyon, and the two lived there, the man and his mother. The house which he built is called Kin'nee nii gaeye, the house with the white bands.[92] At first he called his mother "Mother," but as he was a Holy Being and remained young and she grew old, he called her "Grandmother." The woman said "My son," then she said "My grandson."

During the time that the Beggar Woman and her son lived in the house in the side of the cliff San'hode'di' begaeye went out each day to the people of the canyon who had been cruel to them, and he visited all their wives. Then he told his mother that they would return to all the other places where they had been ill treated. They left their house and followed the top of the canyon. They crossed the head of the canyon called Tse he'lain and traveled to a place called Tsin tlo heyan', and from there they went to a place called To'jo'hogan. While they were camping at this place for the night, a little dog came near them. He

---

[92] Informant's note: He said that he had seen this ruin once. It is now known as White House in the Canyon de Chelly. A very long time ago he went to see a regiment marching through the Reservation. They marched up Tse gee Canyon and camped there. When he (Sandoval) reached the camp the chief officer decided to go up the canyon and look around. The White House was way up in the side of the cliff. It had a white center band around the house, and yellow above it. They tied two poles together and the officer climbed to the first ledge. The officer threw a lariat over a pole sticking out of the house. The officer climbed to the ruin and was there a long time. When he came down he asked who had built the house. Sandoval knew that this was the place where the Two had made their home. He had heard that the footprints were there, but he did not see them.

was a pretty little dog, black with brown legs and brown around the eyes. Each time that the man tried to catch the little animal he ran away. The next morning the man went after him, but he jumped just when he was about to be caught. That night when the little dog came into camp again the man tried to catch him; and all the next day the dog managed to stay only a little way ahead of the man. He would jump for the dog, but the dog would always run. In this way the dog led him to a lake called Tqo' del tqo'.[93] When they got near this lake the dog ran and jumped into the water. And the man saw the water rise up into the air. Then he ran, just as fast as he could, back on his own tracks. Just as he reached the summit of a hill near the lake the water fell just behind him. And the water ran back into the lake. When he returned to his mother he said: "Mother, Grandmother, the dog was from the lake called Tqo'del tqo'. The water nearly caught me. The water is cruel there."

From there they traveled over the pass called Besh el chee'beage.[94] They went from there to a place called Cha bin i'ee, Beavers' Eyes. There is another lake there, and in it lived the Water Buffalo. When they neared this lake the water rose again, but they ran to safety. The water hit the ground just behind them. They left there and went to a place called Whee cha'. They camped on a little hill. They planted the turquoise walking stick on the East side; a white bead walking stick on the South side; a white shell walking stick on the West side; and a black jet walking stick on the North side. That night, near their camp, they heard chanting and the sound of a basket being pounded. They listened. These were the words of the chant:

I am the White Corn Boy.
I walk in sight of my home.
I walk in plain sight of my home.
I walk on the straight path which is towards my home.
I walk to the entrance of my home.
I arrive at the beautiful goods curtain which hangs at the doorway.
I arrive at the entrance of my home.
I am in the middle of my home.
I am at the back of my home.
I am on top of the pollen foot print.
I am on top of the pollen seed print.
I am like the Most High Power Whose Ways Are Beautiful.
Before me it is beautiful,
Behind me it is beautiful,
Under me it is beautiful,
Above me it is beautiful,
All around me it is beautiful.

[93] Informant's note: Tqo' del tqo' is near Crystal, N. Mex. It is now a dry lake. The bank broke a few years ago (1936).
[94] Recorder's note: The road near Drolet's Trading Post, and over the mountain to Crystal, N. Mex.

The man planted a forked stick to see where the chant came from. He went to the place and found one kernel of white corn. He planted that kernel and it grew. With four chants he started it, before he prayed. He planted it in the center of a flat clearing, and it grew up before him. On his right side grew six white ears standing up. On his left grew six yellow ears standing up. There were 12 ears on the one cornstalk. Then he cut those ears and husked them, the white corn alone, and the yellow corn alone.

In the center of the field he planted the white corn by itself, and he planted the yellow corn by itself. Then he heard people there, and some were laughing. The next morning he saw that the whole field had been planted in corn, and some of the kernels were split open. It grew that way because of the laughing of the planters. On top of the cornstalks and on each side there were ears covered with kernels to the tip. Do'honot i'ni they were called. Then on one side was an ear split into five parts, and each little cob was covered with kernels, and it was called nadan tlane'.

The hill called To whee cha' was to be a sacred hill, and the people were to pray from the top of it from time to time. The Beggar's Son left his mother there with all their beautiful goods and the corn. He left her and he traveled to the place under the high rock across the river from Farmington. There he got even with all the men who had been cruel to them. He visited their wives.

From there he went to a place called Be'he'kitna'ha tzis, a lake hollow. He made little snares with his hair to catch the little gray birds which are to be found on the plains. These birds are called ga'tet lo'he.[95] When he caught a number of them he strung them together and roasted them for his meat.

THE STORY OF THE TWO MAIDENS AND THE WHITE BUTTERFLY[96]

San'hode'di heard that there were two maidens in the village of Ken tiel who were guarded. These maidens were sacred.[97] All the young men who came as suitors were sent away. The Beggar's Son said to himself: "So the young maidens will say: 'Eat my brains.'" He went to the top of the hill and he saw many people from the village gathering wood. Holding the flowers from the plant of many different colors before him he sang three sections of a chant. The first part is this:

When I arrived
I had in my hand these many colored flowers.
I am To che o whee tso dzil kin schleen young man.

---

[95] Pepper (1908, pp. 178, 181) calls them prairie larks.
[96] Pepper (1908, pp. 178, 179, 180).
[97] Informant's note: These maidens were called Do'bede klad, Not Shone On By The Sun.

Now when they look my way
Their eyesight will hold different colors.
The reddest circle of the Sun is my feather.
All the Sun's circles surround me.
The Sun's pollen covers my body.
To che whee tso's pollen covers my body.

The Earth-Traveling-Laughing-Being,
My feather's pollen, affects the mind.
My feather is looked at and is seen as beautiful.
All the beautiful goods in the home are in my hand.

(There are three sections of this chant.)

In the coat of the bluebird, San'hode' di flew over the people.
Then he put on the feathers of the rock wren and went to all the
houses. Then in the form of another little rock bird he went, and
this time he flew to the opening in the roof of the house where the
two maidens sat. The hole in the roof was for the purpose of letting
sunlight into the dwelling.

(There are chants to tell just how he entered.)

He looked down through the opening and saw that the two maidens
were sitting facing each other with their legs together. They were
trimming a dress made from the skin of an antelope. Their legs were
as shown in figure 20. The skin was spread across their knees.

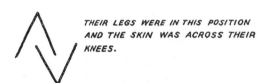

FIGURE 20.—Position of maidens' legs.

The man laughed, and the younger of the maidens said: "What a
beautiful laugh!"

(Here the chant continues.)

The young man said: "What a beautiful laugh down below." And
he named the one who had laughed. Then the two maidens looked up
to where they had heard his laughter, and he told them his name and
that he had laughed.

After this he stepped into the form called ho no gaille,[98] the butterfly. It was a large one with many beautiful colors. He sat between
the two maidens. The elder said: "Sister, what a beautiful thing has
come to us. Look at all the beautiful colors. Right there is our
design. We will use it for our pattern." The younger sister said:
"No. Leave it alone. It might not be good for us."

---

[98] Franciscan Fathers (1912, p. 45) : kalu'gi, small butterfly; kalugi ya'zhe, large
butterfly.

(Here the chant begins with: "Sister, what a beautiful thing has come to us.")

The sisters tried to catch the butterfly. He flew this way and that, and all the beautiful coloring, the dust from his wings, filled the room. The maidens stumbled over their water jar and over their food in their effort to catch him. He flew through a crack in the door, and out they came after him.

> She ta'ge, younger sister,
> Lo la he'he, lo la he'.

The maidens ran outside and looked all about for the butterfly, but he had disappeared. A little yellow bird passed them and they ran after it. The little yellow bird hopped here and there in the pumpkin field.

The elder sister felt very bad because the butterfly had gone. She was very sorrowful. So San hode'di left the form of the yellow bird and entered the form of another insect. This insect is called alt'an e, the ripener. It is small and greenish in color and looks somewhat like the locust when it is still in the ground. This insect sings a pretty song: "Tlo-o-o-o-o-o," in a high key.

(There are two sections of a chant here.)

The two maidens tried to catch this beautiful little insect. When they were among the pumpkin vines San'hode'di resumed his own form and stood up. The maidens felt ashamed and stood there looking down and twisting their bodies and feet, for he had asked them why they had followed him.

The elder sister turned to the younger and said: "Sister, let us go back." But the younger sister said that she had advised leaving the butterfly alone in the first place. "But now that we are here," she said, "we will stay and see what comes of it."

The man took the two maidens to his camp. He fed them the meat of the little birds he had caught with his own hair. When the elder sister tasted the meat of the birds she spit it out. The younger tasted the meat of the birds and swallowed it. She told her sister that it was not bad.

That night the two maidens sat down and slept hugging each other. The man jumped into the water and rolled in the feathers from the little birds and slept that way. He told the maidens that that was how he lived. He said that they had made a sorry mistake coming after him.

In the morning he started out for his mother's home. Before leaving he told the maidens that, should they wish to catch birds, by no means to break the hair snares. But when they caught a bird the hair tangled and the snare broke. And San'hode'di got soaked with the rain that poured down on him. When he returned to his camp he found the maidens cold and hungry.   He told them that it was because they had had no fears that they were out there.

On the fourth night he lay with each of the maidens.   And on that night he chewed his blue gum and he sang his chant.   He blew to the four directions, and at once he had a beautiful home with all the beautiful goods inside it.   He covered both girls with beautiful robes. When the elder sister awakened she did not know where she was.   She shook her sister and said: "Sister, look where we are.   We are in a home now, a home better than our old home ever was."

San'hode'di told the maidens that they should return to their own home, for their father was cruel and so was their mother.   He gave the elder sister the feather that had come from the Sun's mother; and he gave to the younger sister the top of the cattail rush.   He told them that if they were in trouble they should use those two things.[99]

He placed the two sisters on the rainbow and they found themselves standing in the center of the courtyard back of their house.   But before they started out they asked themselves where they should place the feather and the cattail rush.   One suggested that they place them in their hair.   The other thought that the place to hide them should be their moccasins.   The sisters knew that when they returned to their home they would be stripped of their clothing and punished.   So the last thing they decided upon was to hold their treasures under their arms.

When the maidens were discovered in the courtyard out came everyone on the housetops.   They noticed that the men brought bundles of willow switches.   The sisters were stripped of all their beautiful clothing, not a stitch was left on them, and they were made to march around a circle of men.   These men held the switches and they hit the sisters whenever they wished to do so.   The sisters walked around the circle twice, and toward the end of the third time they could stand no more.   The elder sister cried out: "Sister, where are our feather and cattail rush?"   The younger sister threw down the cattail rush and blew four times at the people.   Immediately they found themselves standing before San'hode'di in his home.

He was sorry that he had let them return and suffer such punishment. So he shot his arrow toward the village and down poured the rain and it thundered and the lightning destroyed all the people.   However, his wives told him that, even though they had suffered, they were sorry for their people; so the man went to the village and made a certain medicine which restored the people to life.   Then the chief, the father of the two sisters, said: "My son-in-law, you have strong medicine.   You are a great man.   All the houses are yours."

_____

[99] Recorder's note: Pepper (1908, pp. 182–183) gives hailstones.

But San'hode'di lived at his home with his wives. He came to the village only now and then. Now one day when the three had been to the village and were on their way home, he sent his two wives ahead, and he went to see his mother, using the rainbow path. When he saw his mother the first thing that she asked him was: "Son, where are your wives?"[100] The young man said: "Mother, I sent my young wives home from the village." His mother told him: "Quick, quick, my son, the White Butterfly will steal your wives if you are not careful."

San'hode'di returned to his home, but his wives were not there. He went at once to the place on the trail where he had left them. There he saw three tracks going East. He saw, too, that the three had kicked off the flowers along the way. He followed after the three until he came to the edge of the water. There he noticed a little home on one side. Smoke was coming out of the top of the home. An aged, red woman, the Spider Woman, came out and asked the young man what he was doing there. He told her that his wives had been stolen and that he was on their track. The Spider Woman said: "It was not long ago that I saw the White Butterfly with two beautiful maidens." The young man was about to start out again when the old woman said: "My son, the White Butterfly is dangerous. You cannot go to his place." But the young man said: "I will follow him; and I will eat his brains when I find him."

The young man ran on and he came upon a man hoeing in a garden. This was the old Frog Man who said: "Where are you going, Grandchild?" The young man said: "My wives have been stolen and I am on their track." The Frog said: "It has not been long, my grandson, since the White Butterfly passed here with two beautiful maidens."

Then the young man wondered and looked at the Frog Man and thought: "What a funny leg he has." The Frog answered though the young man had not spoken a word: "Yes, Grandson, I have a funny leg, and rough, isn't it?" Then the young man thought: "What funny eyes he has, popping out they are." And the Frog said: "Yes, Grandchild, I have funny popped-out eyes." Then the young man thought: "What funny humps all over his body." And the Frog said: "Yes, my Grandson, my body is covered with these funny things." And he continued: "Come inside, my Grandchild. The White Butterfly's home is a dangerous place. I will ask your father first to make all the sacred places known to you. Give me the thing you travel by, the rainbow path."

So San'hode'di let the Frog have the rainbow, and the old man just seemed to walk out of his home and come back. The young man asked: "I thought that you were going to take my story to my father."

---

[100] Informant's note: Whenever San'hode'di returned to his mother's home and addressed her as "Grandmother," he became a young man again.

The Frog said: "Yes, yes, Grandchild, every place is made known. Your Father and the rest of the Holy Beings said that it was time for the White Butterfly to die. You see I sent word with the sunbeam."

The young man was about to start off. "I will go now, Grandfather," he said. "Hold on," said the Frog. "Who will you make medicine to now? The Sun has set." The Frog had shortened the day.

There was nothing to do but spend the night with the old Frog Man. The next morning the Spider Woman, who had received a gift from the young man, brought her two daughters and all the people from the sacred places to the Frog's garden. The Wind had blown over the White Butterfly and he told them just how the White Butterfly was dressed. He had for his headdress a hummingbird plant which was covered with red flowers and a lot of hummingbirds. So they made one like it for the young man. Then the Spider Woman blew her web across the water and the people crossed over on it. The Wind blew and the people outside the village had their eyes filled with dust. So they were on the land of the White Butterfly before he knew it. They chanted against the White Butterfly so that when they reached his home the flowers on his headdress had wilted and the hummingbirds were almost dead. But the flowers on the young man's headdress were blooming and the humming birds were humming and he looked his best.

One of San'hode'di's wives was grinding corn. She was the younger sister and she looked up with tears in her eyes and said: "Did I not tell you that this person (the White Butterfly) was not our husband. There is our husband who has come for us. You have thought that there was no one like the White Butterfly."

It was decided that San'hode'di and the White Butterfly should go through the same games that the Great Gambler used. And the young man won each of the games. The bat was used again at the first. All was the same except the guessing game of the water jars. That was not there. The last thing was the foot race.

When the races started the White Butterfly was ahead four different times. He had with him the weapon like the one carried by the Great Gambler. He threw it but missed the young man four times. Then, believing that he had harmed the young man, he sprinted ahead and told him that it was his last race, and to take his time. But the young man had recovered the weapon and he shot the black magic of the White Butterfly back into his body. This stiffened the White Butterfly and slowed up his pace so that the young man passed him and finished the race first. All the party of his friends were dancing and singing. The people of the White Butterfly were weeping.

Now when the White Butterfly came in he brought forth his ax. He told the young man to kill him while he was still warm. The young man stepped forward with his own weapon and split the head of the White Butterfly in two. Instead of brains his head was filled with all different colored butterflies, and out they flew. The young man caught one, and holding it in his hand he said: "Though you came out of the head of the White Butterfly you will not enter the brain of a man hereafter. You will be of little use to the people. Only when they catch you and put your pollen on their legs and arms and say:

May I run swiftly,
May my days be long,
May I be strong in arm.

Then the same person will live to see old age. But he must let the butterfly go without harm."

Then all the wives of the White Butterfly wept and cried out. San'hode'di spoke to these women: "What are you crying about?" he asked. "The White Butterfly either killed your husbands or made slaves of them."

Now there was a great tower that the White Butterfly had built, and a large house extending from it where he kept his wives. And at quite a distance from this there was another house into which he had thrown the bodies of the husbands that he had killed. The young man discovered this. And afterward he spoke to the people. He told them that they were free and could go to whatever country they wished.

San'hode'di brought back only his two young wives and the two daughters of the Spider Woman who had accompanied him. They came back across the water, but his two wives stopped at the lake to drink. The young man saw that they had tears in their eyes, for they were not happy. So when the two young women stepped down to drink their husband pushed them into the water, head first. All that the man saw was an animal with horns that came up out of the water.[1] The young man said that the father of these two women should offer a prayer to the water.[2]

The two maidens, the daughters of the Spider Woman, were brought back to this country and adopted by the Navaho tribe. Their descendants are many this day. Their hair turns gray early and they also lose their teeth.

It was for this purpose that the young man was born, and the White Butterfly stole the wives and lured their husbands across the water and killed them.

[1] Informant's note: tqo'holtsodi, the water buffalo.
[2] Informant's note: The Hopi and other tribes have medicine sticks planted near this spring and lake.

THE STORY OF SAN'HODE'DI'S MEDICINE

When San'hode'di arrived at his home the person called Dotso came and whispered to him, saying: "There are two more maidens over here who are calling for suitors. Go try your luck."

Before he went to this village he chewed poison ivy [3] and blew some of the plant over his body. Sores broke out all over him. In this way he went to the home of the two maidens. There was a ladder outside the house. He made one step on the ladder when the mother of the maidens stopped him and said: "What are you doing here?" The young man replied in a mild voice: "I have come to marry your two daughters." But when the woman saw the sores that covered his body she told him to go away.

The next day he chewed another poisonous plant called zen chee'e,[4] which has a blue flower and grows about an inch high. It is found on the mesa near Shiprock, and blooms in the early spring. He blew some of this plant on his body and dreadful sores appeared. Then he returned to the home of the maidens and climbed two rungs of the ladder. The mother came to the top of the ladder and said: "What are you doing here again?" He said: "I have come to marry your two daughters." The woman said: "I say no. With those sores! You go away."

The third day he came with still more dreadful sores. They were called na'kit.[5] The sores covered his hands and his body. He came in this condition to the home of the maidens, and he climbed three rungs of the ladder. The mother stopped him again, and sent him away. He said: "However, I am going to marry your two daughters."

He went away, but the fourth time he blew another kind of sore over himself. This is called des chit.[6] With this disease he returned, and he climbed four rungs of the ladder. This time the mother let him come up and he entered the house.

The maidens had a guessing game, and up to this time no suitor had been able to guess correctly, so the old woman felt safe. The maidens brought out their basket with the guessing game in it and sat down (fig. 21). The young man reached into the basket and took the husk pointing East. He unwrapped the husk as the sun travels; and he wiped the juice that was on it, circling the basket with it. He took the turquoise out and swallowed it with a piece of bread.

The two maidens felt for the stone but found none.

---

[3] Franciscan Fathers (1910, p. 182): ish ishjid, poison ivy, *Rhus toxicodendron.*

[4] Matthews (1886, pp. 766–777): azay'ha chee'nee, red body medicine, *Lithospermum angustifolium* Michaux.

[5] Franciscan Fathers (1912, p. 126): na'kidtso, Spanish pock, also called cha'ch'osh, syphilis.

[6] Franciscan Fathers (1910, p. 108): des chit, ishchid, or, qiuichchid, a prostitutional disease. Dideschi, blood poison.

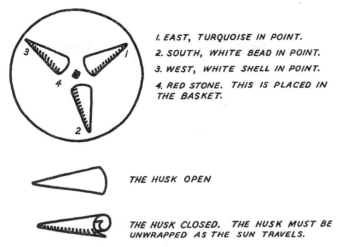

1. EAST, TURQUOISE IN POINT.

2. SOUTH, WHITE BEAD IN POINT.

3. WEST, WHITE SHELL IN POINT.

4. RED STONE. THIS IS PLACED IN THE BASKET.

THE HUSK OPEN

THE HUSK CLOSED. THE HUSK MUST BE UNWRAPPED AS THE SUN TRAVELS.

FIGURE 21.—The Guessing Game.

Then the young man unwrapped the husk that had pointed to the South, in the same way, and he took the white bead and swallowed it. The maidens felt for the stone but they could not find it.

He unwrapped the third husk that had pointed to the West, again in the same way, and he took the white shell and swallowed it. The maidens felt for the shell but it was gone. They had tears in their eyes this time, for the young man was covered with dreadful sores, and this did not please them.

Then the young man took the red stone from the center of the basket and swallowed that also. The maidens felt for it but it was not there.

Now all this happened so that medicine might be made known that would cure poison ivy and the other diseases of the skin. Since then the medicine of the young man is known for these sores.[7]

Now they take four leaves from the poison ivy, East, South, West, and North, and they cut a hole through the four leaves. They chew the leaves of the poison ivy mixed with powder of ground chips of stones. Whoever receives this medicine gets it through the holes in these leaves. Afterward he can travel around poison ivy and other poisonous plants. This was San'hode'di's medicine, and with it he cured himself.

---

[7] Franciscan Fathers (1910, p. 113): "Syphilis was supposedly removed by a beverage (yidla) of syphilis medicine. *Cordylanthus ramosus* (chach'osh aze') and the buttercup (la'etso ilja'e) which were powdered and taken in water every morning."

Interpreter's note: The Oregon grape was also used for this sickness.

Franciscan Fathers (1910, pp. 113, 115): (The Young Man's medicines.) Swellings, nanchad, were removed by applying the plant, nanchad aze, *Thellipodium wrightii*. Sores in general: a liniment made of the leaves and branchlets of the cancer root, ledol'aezi. Pimples, naeetsa, were rubbed with leaves of a plant called naeetsa aze. Also spurge is chewed and used as a liniment for pimples. Boils, chozh aze, a liniment made from *Euphorbia*, khetsi halchi, and, behetsi halchi. Blood poisoning is cured with a poultice prepared from a plant known as ndochi (?).

After he had won the guessing game he took the two maidens to a new home. Each morning when the sisters returned home to their mother their father asked: "Did he touch you?" And the old man wondered where the young man had gotten the power to guess the game.

After the fourth day San'hode'di was as well as before. Then he lay with the two maidens, and they told their father. They told him also that in the morning they found themselves sleeping under beautiful robes, and in a home filled with everything they could wish for. Their father came over and when he saw all he was pleased with his son-in-law and said: "My daughters have wished for many things. I see that they have them all now."

Then San'hode'di departed from there and returned to his mother.

He told his mother that she should live where she was. It is a place called Whee cha'. This Whee cha' is a hill between Gallup and Shiprock. And nearby there is still another hill called Be'es jade'. "You will have the power over the cornfields of the People called Dîné," he said. "Your two homes will be sacred places. The people will bring precious stones as offering when they come to pray for rain. I will return to you from time to time."

Then he went back to the two wives he had sent to their village on his flute.

There is a peak this side of San Francisco Mountain which is called Tocho whee tso. It is near Tlo chee ko. And that is the place where San'hode'di went with his first two wives. He is there. His home and those of his mother are considered sacred places. They say that the Beggar Woman worked for the Dîné, while her son, afterward, went to another tribe.

THE STORY OF THE DÎNÉ [3]

Now all that has been told before this time was about the people living in the country before the coming of the Dîné, the Navaho.

The White Bead Woman wished now to have her own people. She wished to have a people that she could call her grandchildren. They would carry on the lore that she would teach them. They would respect and hold holy the prayers and the chants that she would give them.

She took a white bead stone and she ground it to powder. She put this powder on her breasts and between her shoulders, over her chest and on her back; and when this powder became moist she rubbed it off her body and rolled it between her fingers and on the palm of her hand.

---

[3] Recorder's note: The following are given: Dîné, Dénés, Dinae e, meaning the People. There is Navajo and Navaho. The Early Spanish appellation was Los Apache de Navajoa.

Hodge (1895, pp. 223–240).

Franciscan Fathers (1910, p. 28): Migration of the Dénés.

From time to time a little ball dropped to the ground. She wrapped these little balls in black clouds. They arose as people. She placed these people on the shore of a big body of water.[9]

These people lived there and they brought forth children. These children played along the shore where the waves broke on the sand. The waves rolled up all kinds of shells, big and little ones. The children played with these shells.

Then the White Bead Woman asked the Twelve Holy Beings to lead her children far away from the Great Water. She said that the shells should be planted for corn and for different kinds of food plants. So the people made ready and they moved far inland from the sea.

These people had four chiefs, they were the head men. The names of the four chiefs were: Ba'nee, Ba'nee kosa, Guish to' and Ba'no'-tilthne'.

In the mud of the mountain called Dzil chal'yelth, Night Mountain, a cub bear was found. This cub was brought to the people. Then on another mountain called Dzil yel soie, Yellow Mountain, a young mountain lion was found. These two animals were given to the people.[10] This was all in the White Bead Woman's plan, and the animals were raised by her power.

Then one of the Twelve Holy Beings came and told the four chiefs that they were wanted at the home of the White Bead Woman. They started out. When the five got to the shore of the Great Water, over the sea there appeared a white house with a wide flat land of white bead in all directions. When it settled down and floated to the shore they stepped on it and were taken way out to sea.

They entered the white house and saw a very old woman sitting inside. Now she got up and she went into the east room, and she carried a white bead walking stick in her hand. When she returned she was only a little past middle age. She then went into the south room, and she carried a turquoise walking stick in her hand. She came out a young woman, without a walking stick. She went into the west room and returned a beautiful maiden. She went into the north room, and returned a girl. So she is called the Changeable Woman as well as the White Bead Woman and the White Bead Girl.

Then the White Bead Girl sat down and said:

My grandchildren, I did not create you to live near me. You are now ready to go to a place called Dine'beke'ya, the Land of the People. You will go with two of my children, two of the Twelve Holy Beings. You will go to the mountain called Neilth sat'dzil; then to the mountain called Nit tlez'dzile; and to the

---

[9] Informant's note: The Pacific Ocean.

[10] Informant's note: Now there were two old men who told different stories as to how these animals were raised. The first old man said that the animals were raised on cornmeal; but my (Sandoval's) grandfather said that this was not so. He said that he had learned that, as the animals were formed by the Holy Beings, they were also fed by them.

mountain called Ka'ta'dine dzile.[11] To these mountains you must go. I made
you so that you can live there. I will give you the seeds of different plants for
your food, and I will give you pretty flowers to seed over the whole country. I
will give you rain. Then should another people come crowding into your country
I will do what I think best. Whatever I do will be for your good.

You must go now. When you reach your present home you must start out.
In your travels you will cross the mountain called Yol gaeye dzile, and the
mountain called Yodot ligie dzile, and over another mountain called De chili
dzile, and over still another, Ba'chini dzile.[12] From there you will go to a place
called Tse'ha dole'kon, the place of solid rock. At this place the first chiefs
were made. And as long as the footprints are there I will know that all is well
with my people.

From there the Holy Beings will return to me. After this happens you must
go to a place called Tse'bit e'tine. You must travel on the south side for there
are people living there who are not peaceful. From there you must go to a place
called Dzil ines gaeye. You must go to the north side there. From there you
will see a mountain peak in the distance. It is called Na'ysis an', Navaho
Mountain. You must go beyond that mountain to a place called Tqo da'enet
tine. From there you must follow the range of mountains called Dzil le' gine;
then to the north of the canyon called Tse ji or Segi (Canyon de Chelly). Then
you must go to a place called Tse'hel ne'; and to a place called Tsin tlo hogan.
Follow the range of mountains to a place called Tse'ta je'je, and over the mountains to a place called Ha'ha'tsia. From there you will go on to a plain where
there is a place called Tseast tso'sa'kade, Big Cotton Wood Tree.

The country is good there. You must plant your corn there. When the corn
grows up and ears develop, the lowest ear above the ground will not grow to a
full ear. Break those off and put them into a basket which contains water; and
after you have placed them in the water raise one out and say: "May we have
the Male Rain. May we have the Female Rain." These ears of corn you must
boil and eat.

Then the White Bead Girl brought four bundles of strings and
placed them before her. She took a string from each bundle and
threaded four white beads on it; and she laid the string, with the four
beads, from the first bundle on the first bundle, and in like manner,
the others on the other bundles. She placed the white bead walking
stick on the first bundle. On top of the second bundle she laid the
turquoise walking stick. On the third bundle she placed the white
shell walking stick. And on the fourth she placed the walking stick
of ha'dan'y yei, male banded stone. Now the first bundle went to
the first chief, and the second, third, and fourth to the respective chiefs
as they were named.

Each chief was to take his bundle, beads, and walking stick. The
walking stick was to be used in the country where there was no water.
When the people got thirsty the first chief was to put the white bead
walking stick into the ground and give it one turn, and the water would

---

[11] Informants' note: These mountains are far to the Northwest.
[12] Interpreter's note: The ceremonial names of the four sacred mountains of the Diné:
East, Yolga'dzil, Pelado Peak; South, Yo dotl'izh'i dbil, Mount Taylor; West Dichi'li
dzil, San Francisco Peak; North, Bash'zhini dzil, San Juan Mountains.

come forth.   The second time the second chief was to put the turquoise walking stick into the ground and give it two turns, as the sun travels. The third time the white shell walking stick was to be used; and the third chief should turn it three times for water.   The fourth walking stick was to be turned four times; and after that they had to repeat the whole thing beginning with the first and so on.

Then the White Bead Plain with the house floated near the shore and the four chiefs and the two Holy Beings landed.   They traveled to their home and joined the people.   They all crossed over the first four far mountains named.   By that time the load that they were carrying got very heavy.   They opened the bundles of strings and they found strings of beautiful beads.   They had a great many strings of beads.

When they got to the rock where they saw the footprints, made carefully by the first two chiefs so that they would remain forever, the two Holy Beings left and returned to the White Bead Woman.

The people moved to the next place which was called Tse bit e'tine. They camped there, and in the afternoon they sent two men out to see what they could find.   The men returned and said that there were people living not far away.   They said that they had cornfields and that the corn was ripe to eat.

They remained at this place until they got acquainted with the people.   These people were known as the Ga dine, the Arrow People. After a time some of the young men went to the maidens of this other tribe.   They gave them beads and they took them for their wives. They also gave some of their maidens to the young men of the Arrow People, and the maidens were given different cornfields.

One day when the corn was ripe the chiefs went to the sweat house to take a sweat bath.   While they were inside, Chief Ba'nee' said: "We were not made to live here.   We are going to the country which will be our country.   In two days from now we must move on.   We have made friends and we have exchanged maidens.   Those who wish to go with us will go.   Those who wish to remain will remain."   Then the other chiefs went out and Ba'nee' knew that they were dressing. So they all dressed and went home.

That night Ba'nee' spoke to the people and told them that he planned that they should go on to the land which had been given them. He said that those who wished to go on should do so; and those who wished to stay in this place should remain.   The next morning the second chief, Ba'nee'kosa, made a speech about their leaving.   So when the 2 days had passed they started out.

They made camp the first night, and after another day's travel they made a second camp.   They made their second camp just about twilight. Now the bear, who was with them, pulled up two little spruce trees and crossed them; and they noticed that he sat on them. Then Ba'nee' said: "Now we shall see what my pet will do and what he knows."

The bear chanted:

> Terrifying is my home.
> I am the Brown Bear.
> Terrifying is my home.
> Lightning flashes from my home.
> Terrifying is my home.
> Like the Most High Power Whose Ways Are Terrifying
> My home is terrifying.

There are 10 sections to this chant. And the people heard it sung by the bear. Then Ba'nee' received the chant and it was his.

The next morning, just at dawn, they heard the bear chant two more chants. And these chants went to Ba'nee' and were also his. And Ba'nee' said: "I wonder what my pet knows? There must be something wrong. Now we shall see what my pet knows."

The bear ran around in a circle four times, then to the East he went. Now the other tribe had followed them, but they did not know it. The Arrow People intended to follow them, kill them, and take their beads and their women. During the night they had circled around them. They planned to attack the first thing in the morning; but the Arrow People retreated because of the bear's chanting. They called from a distance: "We have followed you because we have loved you, and we wish to have a talk with you once more." Then Ba'nee' said: "We will not listen to you. You had murder in your hearts when you circled our camp in the night. If you had had peace in your hearts you would have come up in the day time. Now go away while you have a right mind."

Then some said: "We are going back." But by this time some others wished to go on with the Dîné. However, Ba'nee' told the Arrow People that those who wished to go on should join the people in the daytime not the night.

Then the Dîné, with the bear, moved on.

They came to a country where there was no water. Ba'nee' used the first walking stick and the water came forth and the people drank. Because of this the descendants of this First Chief who used the first walking stick were called Tqo a'ha'ne', Near Water Clan.

Then they moved on, and the next time they grew thirsty the Second Chief used the turquoise walking stick. When the water came out of the ground it was bitter to the taste, so the people who used the turquoise walking stick were known as the Tqo tachee'nee, the Bitter Water Clan.

On the third night of travel the Chief who used the white shell walking stick found water that was salty to the taste. His people were then called Tqo te' gonge', the Salt Water Clan.

The fourth Chief used the banded male rock walking stick. He found that mud came first, and then came clear, sweet water. His people were called Has'klish nee, the Mud Clan.

They were now in a country where there was no water and both plant food and game were scarce. After a time they grew hungry. Early one afternoon, after they had made camp, they saw the mountain lion asleep on a pile of goods. Ba'nee' said: "My pet, what is wrong with you now? Is that all you can do, just sleep? Now wake up and see what you are good for." The mountain lion got up, stretched, and disappeared out of sight. When he returned there was a little blood on his mouth. They went at once to see what he had killed, and they saw that he had killed an antelope and that he had eaten only the heart. They brought the antelope to the camp and the people ate it.

The second day the mountain lion killed two antelope; the third day he killed three, and the fourth day, four antelope. At the end of the fourth day they were carrying extra meat. Then the people knew that the bear had been given to them to warn them of their enemies, and the mountain lion had been given to them to get their meat.

About this time the Dîné reached the place called Dzil ines gaeye, the Mountain with White Bands. Here another group of people joined them. The men of this people wore two feathers on their heads and it made them appear as though they had horns. They came from the South. They were the same people who had first come from the White Bead Woman.

The chief of this party carried a basket full of pollen for the Big Snake. The Big Snake killed their meat. When the parties joined they said: "Our pets are equal. So we will be one people and go on together." From these people sprang the clan called Kin ye'a ane, Standing House.

This made five clans.

Then they arrived at a place called Tqo da'enet tine. There was a mesa there, and from this mesa flowed springs. Now, when they got there they found another party of people following them. These were some of the Arrow People who wished to join the Dîné. This they did, and they were called the Ga dine, Arrow Clan. This made six clans.

They had, by this time, passed Navaho Mountain. There were tall, standing rocks near, and around these rocks and through this country were many mountain sheep. So they lived there for some time.

They killed the sheep for food, and they used both the wool and the hides.

One spring they decided to move on. They wanted to name this place. "What shall we call it?" they said. Then they named it Ag'thlan, Much Wool, because they had gathered much wool from the mountain sheep. Then they followed the foothills of the Black Mountains, and the bear found tlochin,[13] wild onion, for them. They ate the wild onions. They also gathered a low plant with little white and red flowers and flat leaves called chas tigee.[14] They dug up the roots and ate them. And they ate the roots of another plant called il se'nee,[15] Mariposa lily.

Then they went to the mouth of the Tse'ji or Segi Canyon and crossed the Tse'hel ne' to Tsin tlo hogan. They made camp in the daytime because one young woman, who was a little lame, got tired, but some of the party pushed on. Now a light-skinned young man came to the camp and slept with the lame girl. The next morning when the party was about to start out they delayed because the young man had taken to himself a wife.

This young man was from Tse ne'e jin, which is just over the Lukai-chukai. The girl was from the clan Has klish nee, but her descendants are known as the clan Tqo tso nee and they are related to the Mud Clan. The young man was from the clan called Ta chee', and he took his young wife back to a place called Tqo tso, also near the Lukaichukai.

Then they traveled to a place where there is a gap between two rocks.[16] They put down a walking stick on one side of the gap and a spring came up; and on the other side as well, a spring appeared. They called the place Al nash'ee tqo (Al nash ha'tline) meaning Opposite Springs. Then they went to Bear Spring, Shash'bitqo, which was later the site of Fort Wingate.

Now this country was not like the country they were told to go to so they crossed over the mountain. Then they moved back to where Tqoha chi is now. The place was called Ba'has tla. They found good ground there and they planted their corn near a grove of big cotton-woods.

When they were living there there were some people among them who quarreled. And over at the foot of Red Mountain, at a place called Dzil lechee, there was a village, and the people there were very strong. The village was so well fortified that the people who marched against it were killed. So the people who made war against this

---

[13] Franciscan Fathers (1912, p. 171): tlochini, wild onion, strong smelling grass, *Allum palmeri.*

[14] Informant's note: Chas tigee, edible roots, a low-growing plant with flat leaves and whitish and reddish flowers.

[15] Franciscan Fathers (1910, p. 193): alt sini, mariposa lily (*Calochortus loteus*).

[16] Informant's note: Na'nzhosh, the site of Gallup, N. Mex.

village said: "These people who have just come from their Grand-mother have for their pet a bear. Now our only chance is to borrow this pet. Some of us will go over to see what they will say." Then some of them went over to the Dîné and asked for the loan of the bear. They told the Dîné how each time they had been defeated when they marched against this village. Their enemies were very strong.

After the Dîné had listened to the chief, Ba'nee' spoke: "My pet," he said to the bear, "these men have come for our help. They wish to make war against the village near Red Mountain. What do you think about it?" The bear got up, stretched, and let his tongue out. It stretched and circled up. He made ugly faces and the hair above his spine stood straight up. Then Ba'nee' said: "I see, my pet, that you agree that we should help these people, and that we should march against this village. We will set out 3 days from now."

They camped near this village. The bear pulled up two little spruce trees, crossed them, and sat on them. Then he chanted. And the first chant he used was this:

> Ponder well what you think of me.
> I am he who killed the monsters.

There are 6 sections of this chant, and 10 sections of the following:

> Ponder well what you say of me.
> Etc. . . .

They were told that the enemy had strongly fortified houses and that their spies were out at all times. So the bear chanted and told how he wished it would be when he went against the enemy. He was not to be seen. He was the mirage. He was the heat waves over the desert. He sang about 20 sections of the chant here. In the last two verses the Bear named only himself. He said that he would take the scalps, that he would carry the scalps.

Then the Bear went forth and there settled a great cloud on the earth. The enemy could not see the Dîné and the others. The bear ran four times around the village, and he killed many enemies.

Long ago when the Big Hail fell there were only three villages saved, and this village was one of them. And now the bear destroyed it.

The sign or symbol of the knife is called A'cha whee tso. The people crossed, as shown in figure 22.

They had sung 75 chants [17] by the time they returned. When they neared their home the bear made a mark.

This was the bear's mark (fig. 23), and they stepped over it. The bear was behind them.

---

[17] Informants' note: These were the Bear Chants. The informant knew them. These chants are used today in the Navaho country in cases of "coughs" or similar illness. They are used against anything that bothers the people, whether enemies or disease. And it is told that every time the Bear chanted he gave the chant to the chief, and it became his.

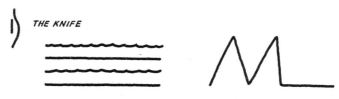

THE KNIFE

WHERE THE PEOPLE CROSSED THE RUNNING WATER,
THE LEVEL LAND, AND THE MOUNTAINS.

FIGURE 22.—Where the people crossed the running water, the level land, and the mountains.

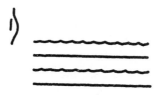

THE BEAR'S MARK

FIGURE 23.—The Bear's mark.

When the Dîné returned from fighting the enemy the bear seemed never to have finished fighting. Whenever he saw an object in the distance he went after it, determined to kill. Chief Ba'nee' said: "My pet, you can never be peaceful again I see. You came from the mountain called Night Mountain, now you must go to the East to a mountain called Black Mountain. You will join your people there." He spread out a buckskin, the hide of a deer not killed by a weapon. It is called do'gi gi. Then he spoke to the bear. "My pet, now sit on this." The bear sat on the buckskin. Ba'nee' tied five white beads in each of six different strings. He tied five beads around the bear's four legs, and then he tied five beads on a string across the chest one way, and the same the other way. Then Ba'nee' took a turquoise, and giving it to the bear told him to put it in his mouth. The bear put the turquoise in his mouth and then laid it on the buckskin. This is called shash biza nas'tan. Then Ba'nee' gave the bear a white bead and told him to put it in his mouth. The bear put the bead in his mouth, and taking it out, placed it with the turquoise. Then he sprinkled corn pollen all over the bear, and Ba'nee' told him to shake the pollen off. The bear did this. The medicine from the bear, or other animals, is gotten in this way. Now men were to use this medicine against all sorts of diseases. It was to be for their protection.
Here is the chant:

De yana he'a now it starts out
De yana he'a,
De yana he'a.
A Big Black Bear starts out.
Now he starts out with the black pollen for his moccasins.
Now he starts out with the black pollen for his leggings.

Now he starts out with the black pollen for his garment.
Now he starts out with the black pollen for his headdress.
He starts out for the Black Mountain plains.
He starts out for the doorway of the two crossed spruce trees.
He starts out on the straight pollen trail.
He starts out for the top of the pollen foot prints.
He starts out for the top of the pollen seed prints.
He is like the Most High Power Whose Ways Are Beautiful.
With beauty before him,
With beauty behind him,
With beauty above him,
With beauty below him,
All around him is beautiful.
His spirit is all beautiful.

There are three sections of this chant: "Now he goes . . ." "Now he is gone . . .". Only one knowing all the chants can possess a bear fetish, among the Navaho people.

Now after the first chant was sung the bear's hair lay down and was smooth. And after the chants were sung he went peacefully on his way.

The plan was also to send the mountain lion back. He had come from the Yellow Mountain, Dzil let'tsoie. He was returned to that place. He was sent back without a chant or a prayer, or without any dress or trimming because he had been peaceful.

THE STORY OF THE TWO BOYS AND THE COMING OF THE HORSES

By this time tassels were coming out on their cornstalks and ears of corn had begun to form.

When some of the silk on the ears of corn had turned red, two girls and two boys were sent to bring in some ears of young corn. Returning they carried the ears of young corn. They poured some water in a basket and placed the corn in it, and then they took the ears out with the water dripping from them and said: "May we have the Black Cloud which brings the Male Rain. May we have the Black Cloud which brings the Female Rain. May we have all the beautiful flowers and their pollens." And then they boiled the young corn and they ate it. They ate this green thing as they had been instructed to do.

After 4 days had passed Chief Ba'nee' sent four more children, two boys and two girls, to the cornfields. He said: "There may be more young corn by now." The children went to the fields, but only the two girls returned bringing the young corn. They told the people that after they had gathered the young corn they were playing hide-and-seek. They could not find the boys. Their tracks ended right out in the open where they had stood side by side. So then Chief

Ba'nee' told the people that he could guess that the boys had returned to their Grandmother. So nothing more was done about the missing boys.

After 4 days passed Ba'nee' sent four more children to gather the young corn. This time a boy and a girl came running back and said: "The missing boys have returned, and they say that they have lots to tell. But first, they want a brush shelter built. The main poles must be touched with corn pollen. You must lay a branch of mountain mahogany,[18] tses ta'zee,[19] and a branch of joint pine, tlo ho'zee'e, crossing each other. And you must make four footprints from the entrance to the inner side with corn pollen."

The people made all those things ready. Then Chief Ba'nee' and some others went out and brought the boys to the shelter. When the boys entered they stepped on the footprints. They stood on the crossed branches and were washed. After this was done they told their story.

When they were playing hide-and-seek, their grandfathers, Hasjelti and Hasjohon, stood before them. They said: "Your grandmother wishes you to come. Now raise your right foot." Just as they did so they were taken to the top of the peak called Chush gaeye,[20] and, with the next step, to a peak called Tsin'beleye. On the top of this latter peak they were washed just as they had been washed in the brush shelter. From there they went to the mountain called Tlo gaeye dzil, and then on to their grandmother's home.

There they stood before the old woman. She rose up, and, with the help of her walking stick, hobbled into the east room of her dwelling. She returned younger, and she went into the south room. From there she came back a young woman. She went into the west room, and she came back a maiden. She went into the north room, and she returned a young girl.

The White Bead Girl told the boys that they were to learn the Night Chant and all the prayers that went with it. For it was by this ceremony that they should live. So the two boys learned all the chants and the prayers that they were to use in the spring when the plants and the flowers and the young animals come out, and at the time of the harvest.

---

[18] Franciscan Fathers (1910, p. 198): Mountain mahogany, tse'esdazi, heavy as stone, *Cercocarpus parvifolius.*

[19] Recorder's note: Tses ta'zee, joint pine, also called joint fir, Mexican or Mormon tea, teamster's tea, canatilla, and popotillo, is *Ephedra.* It was known and grown in China ages ago.

Franciscan Fathers (1910, p. 189): tlo'aze, grass medicine, *Ephedra trifurcata.*

[20] Franciscan Fathers (1910, p. 31): ch'osh'gai, white spruce.

After this the White Bead Woman said: "The Dîné shall have horses." [21]   And the first chant that she sang is this:

From the East comes a big black mare.
Changed into a maiden
She comes to me.
From the South comes a blue mare.
Changed into a maiden
She comes to me.
From the West comes a sorrel mare.
Changed into a maiden
She comes to me.
From the North comes a white mare.
Changed into a maiden
She comes to me.

The chant is divided into two parts, two sections are sung and then four sections.

The White Bead Woman chanted again:

This is my plan:
I am the White Bead Woman.
In the center of my home I planned it.
On top of the beautiful goods I planned it.
The white bead basket which contains the horse fetishes,
They lay before me as I planned it.
All the beautiful flowers with their pollens
And the horse fetishes,
They lay in each other,
They lay before me as I planned it.
To increase and to multiply, not to decrease.
They lay inside (the animals) as I planned it.

There are about 20 sections of this chant.   It changes slightly each time.

After the White Bead Woman's chanting, the four horses began to move, the white-bead horse fetish, the turquoise horse fetish, the white-shell horse fetish and the banded stone horse fetish.   These four stone fetishes were made into living horses.

Life came into them and they whinnied.   Then the White Bead Woman took the horses from her home.   She placed them on the white bead plain, on the turquoise plain, on the white bead hill, and on the turquoise hill.   Returning, she laid out four baskets—the white bead basket, the turquoise basket, the white shell basket, and the black jet basket.   In these she placed the medicine which would make the horses drop their colts.   The White Bead Woman then went outside

---

[21] Recorder's note: The introduction of horses, although apparently of great antiquity as evidenced by the earlier part of the myth, is of comparatively recent origin.   The three-toed horse existed in the Americas and disappeared because of the tsetse fly.   The horse was reintroduced by the Spaniards.

and chanted,[22] and down came the horses from the hills; but instead of four there came a herd. They circled the home, and they came to the baskets and licked up the medicine with one lick. Now some of the horses licked twice around the baskets; so once in a long while there are twin colts. But the horses that licked out of the black jet basket licked more than once, and they have many colts. Then out of the herd there came one with long ears. She snorted and jumped away; and the second time she approached the basket she snorted and ran away. So she was not to have young, either male or female.

It was planned that the fetishes of the horses were to be laid in the center of the earth, in a place called Sis na' dzil, near, or beyond Hanes on the road to Cuba (N. Mex.).

The White Bead Woman told the boys that they were to have the horses in their country; that when she believes it is for their good they will multiply, or again, they will decrease. So they do not always multiply. Some years, when there is poor grass and deep snow, many die.

The White Bead Woman then sent the two boys to the Twelve Holy Beings, the Dîné na' kiza'tana gaeye. They were to teach the two boys more chants. They were to show them how to make the medicine for a male colt and a female colt. They were to run strings through a white bead for a female, and a turquoise bead for a male colt. And they were shown how to tie it in the mouth of a colt and run the string around the lower jaw. The colt must nurse with it for 4 days. The umbilical cord must be tied and left until it dries and drops off. The sacred earth from the mountains must be used for the female, and for the male colt, the crystal. Four turquoise beads must be placed in the medicine bag for the male colt. The same is done for the female, but white beads replace the turquoise. The sacred earth from the mountains and the banded male stone (agate), hada'huniye, are used when there are prayers for horses. And when they ask for any goods or rain this banded stone is used.

Then the boys were told that the horses' hoofs are hada' huniye, the banded male stone. The hair of the mane and tail is called nltsa'najin, little streaks of rain. The mane is called e'alinth chene. Horses' ears are the heat lightning, that which flashes in the night. The big stars that sparkle are their eyes. The different growing plants are their faces. The big bead, yo'tso, is their lips. The white bead is the teeth. Tliene delne'dil hilth, a black fluid, was put inside horses to make the whinny. Should a horse have a white spot on its forehead or a bald face it has been made by the big stars. If a horse has white stockings, he also sees by them.

---

[22] Informant's note: There are 85 Horse Chants. They are to be used for the good of the horses. The interpreter and the son of the informant, Sandoval Begay, know many of them.

Then the boys were taken home by the same way they had come. They went through the whole ceremony, beginning with the bath. In the first Night Chant the boys chanted the songs that they had learned. This lasted all night. They then chanted the chants of the horses in the same manner as the Night Chant.

After they had finished there came a man from near Sis na'dzil.[23] Now this man saw a horse standing in the distance, to the East. He went over to it, but he found that it was only a plant called ga'tso dan, jack-rabbit corn.[24] The next day he saw another horse standing in a place to the South. He went to it, but it was only the grass called nit'dit lede.[25] The next day he saw another horse. This was to the West, and when he went to it, it proved to be only tlo nas tasse, sheepgrass.[26] The fourth time he saw the horse was to the North. And it turned out to be only the droppings of some animal.

Now this man was one of the people who had come from the mountain Sis na'jin. And the person Dotso came to him and said: "What are you doing here, my Grandchild?" The man said: "I saw a horse four times; and each time it turned out to be a plant or something." Dotso told him that he should go to the home of his father, the Sun. When he got there he was asked what he had come for. He said: "I have seen a horse four different times, and each time it turned out to be only some grass or plant."

There the man saw horse fetishes to the East, South, West, and North. Then he was taken to the opening in the sky, to a place called Haya tsa'tsis. He was asked to look back. "From where did we start?" he was asked. Now the Little Breeze whispered in the man's ear: "If you do not tell him aright, what you came for will not be granted." Then the man said: "Way over where the two rivers come together, there is where we started."

Then he chanted:

I am the Sun's son.
I sat on the turquoise horse.
He went to the opening in the sky.
He went with me to the opening.
The turquoise horse prances with me.
From where we start the turquoise horse is seen.
The lightning flashes from the turquoise horse.
The turquoise horse is terrifying.
He stands on the upper circle of the rainbow.

---

[23] Informant's note: That is the place where the Mud Clan claims that they buried the beads and the white bead walking stick. Different ones have searched for them; but they have never been found.

[24] Matthews (1886, pp. 767–777): ga tso dan, or kat so tha, jack rabbit grass, *Eurotia lunata* Moquin.

[25] Franciscan Fathers (1912, p. 136): ndid li'di, mountain rice, *Oryzopsis cuspidata*.

[26] Franciscan Fathers (1912, p. 171): tlo nas tasse', sheepgrass, tlo nastqasi, grama grass, *Bonteloua hirsuta*.

The sunbeam is in his mouth for his bridle.
He circles around all the peoples of the earth
With their goods.
Today he is on my side
And I shall win with him.

This chant is used to thank the Powers for horses. These are the last two sections. The chant was correct as a prophecy, for the horse, or team, is used to earn "goods"—money with which to buy blankets, clothing, food.

The Sun told the man that he must offer a gift to the plant called ga'tso dan that he had seen in the East. He should go to that place and camp. Then he should go to the South and camp, and offer a gift to the grass called nit'dit lede; then to the West and camp for the night, and the next morning offer a gift to the grass called tlo nas tasse. Then he should go to the North and camp, and offer a gift to the droppings of some animal. After that he would see the horse.

When the man returned to the earth he obeyed the Sun. He chanted four sections of the chant that he sang when he went to the four directions.

I came upon it.
I came upon it.
I came upon it.
I am the White Bead Woman,
I came upon it.
In the center of my home,
I came upon it.
Right where the white bead basket sits,
I came upon it.
The basket has four turquoise decorations,
I came upon it.
The white bead basket has a turquoise finishing around the edge,
I came upon it.
The white bead horses stand toward the basket from the four directions,
As I came upon it.
All the beautiful flowers are its pollen,
Black clouds are the water they have in their mouths,
As I came upon them.
White poles for its enclosure (corral)
As I came upon them.
Blue poles for its enclosure,
As I came upon them.
Yellow poles for its enclosure,
As I came upon them.
Iridescent poles for its enclosure, flashing,
As I came upon them.
The rainbow for its gate,
As I came upon it.
The sun closes its entrance (gate of corral)
As I came upon it.
The white bead horses pour out,

As I came upon them.
The turquoise horses pouring out,
As I came upon them.
The white shell horses pouring out,
As I came upon them.
The male banded stone horses pouring out,
As I came upon them.
All mixed horses, together with the sheep, pouring out,
As I came upon them.
As the horses pour out with the beautiful goods,
As I came upon them.
The earth's pollen (dust) rises as they pour out,
The shining dust of the earth covers their bodies,
As I came upon them.
To multiply and not to decrease,
As I came upon them.
Like the Most High Power Whose Ways Are Beautiful are my horses,
As I came upon them.
Before my horses all is beautiful,
Behind my horses all is beautiful.
As I came upon them.
As I came upon them.

From that time the horses were given to men, but the rainbow and all the supernatural powers were taken from them by the Holy Ones. Also, the Holy Beings were not to be seen again by men. The medicine and the chants have been used and learned by those who wished to learn and use them. Those who discredit them and do not wish to use the medicines or learn the chants will have a difficult life. It is the belief that those who learn and use and care for these sacred things will not regret it. Their work will be made lighter for them.[27]

THE STORY OF THE NAVAHO AND THE APACHE PEOPLES

Now that the horses were given to the people, and there were a great many people in the land, they commenced to crowd each other. Some of the people wanted to go to war over the slightest thing. They taught their children to be quarrelsome; they were not raising them in the right way. They did not have peace in their hearts. At this time there appeared in the country many plants with thorns, in fact these were more numerous than any other kind of plant. Even the grass became sharp and spiked. It was because of the people's ill nature, and the plants and the grass, that another plan was formed.

---

[27] Informant's note: When the horse-meat plant was put up in Gallup, N. Mex., and the ponies were taken from the Navaho, the old men said: "Our Grandmother will not be pleased with this." They believe that that is why there is little rain now over the Reservation. Cattle and sheep stay near waterholes and springs. The ponies go far to graze. Good horses, fat horses, would grow poor and die on the little grass and water now available in the country. The wiry little ponies are acclimated, and they can carry a man as far as a finely bred horse. They are strong, and can go without feed and water much longer than can a heavy horse. The farms near Shiprock have fatter horses; but also, they have plenty of water and feed. The ponies are range horses.

This time Hasjesjini, the Yei of all the burning minerals in the earth, started a great fire. All the red rocks that we see now burned then. After this the Apache and several other tribes moved eastward. And a number of years after the great fire plants grew again, and this time without thorns. They were better and less harmful.

Again there were four chiefs of the Dîné. The first was Tan jet gaeye; the second, Atsel gaeye; the third chief was Yot aysel gaeye; [28] and there was a fourth whose name has been forgotten. They began to wonder where the other people were who had traveled toward the East. The four chiefs, with some of their men and their wives, started out to find them; but they left the children with those others who remained at home. They headed East, camping here and there. They always sent out scouts. They hunted and made their clothing and moccasins of buckskin. After 2 years they found where a fire had been made, and they wondered if the fire had been made by some of their own people. Then they found water. Whenever they found a spring they camped, and from there they sent the scouts out in different directions.

One day a scout reported having seen the track of a man. They moved to the next spring, and they saw two tracks. The first track was a very old one. They tried to follow it, but they had to abandon it. However the fresh tracks led them to a spring in a rock, a little wall of rock, so they moved there and camped.

Two scouts were sent out from there. They came to a narrow canyon and they saw water in the bottom. They found a place where they could descend; so the scouts let a buckskin rope down into this canyon, and with its aid, they climbed down to the water and camped at the water's edge. The two men stayed there over night. They had been away from their party for 2 days. When they returned they reported having seen plain tracks of a man of their own people. The scouts told also of having seen plenty of seeds of plants which are used for food. And there was water, and it was near the water that they had seen the tracks. So they all moved to this place and camped.

After this happened the four chiefs sent three men out. They returned and reported having seen smoke rising up in the distance. The following day the four chiefs sent four men out, each with two quivers full of arrows. The scouts were told to be careful when they neared the other people's camp, to stay hidden until dark, and then for one man only to go into the camp. When the men got to within sight of the camp, two went on and two stayed behind. Then one stayed just outside and one went in. It was very dark, but he could see the light of the fires. He was making his way slowly, like a mountain lion after its prey, when he touched something that rattled. He reached

---

[28] Informant's note: Yot aysel gaeye means Heaven with Tail Feathers.

around and found that he was in a cornfield, and that the corn had been visited by frost. After he went on for a little while he heard someone call, and everyone went over and entered a dwelling.

Then this scout heard different ones coming from different directions. The language that they spoke was his own language. So he left his bow and arrows behind and went into the dwelling with the rest. He began to be noticed. Men whispered to each other. The head man, who had been out that day, told the others what he had seen, where the game was plentiful, etc. At last he said: "That is all now. Where is that stranger you told about?" And one man spoke: "Now we will have a fresh scalp to dance by." But the chief said: "No. Place him here in the center, this stranger who is among us." So he was placed in the center of the room; and he was asked where he was from.

"I am from Nlth san dzil naa' dine, the range of Rain Mountains, Yote dzil naa'dine, the range of Beautiful Goods Mountains, Nitlez dzil naa'dine, the range of Mixed Stones Mountains, and Tqate dine dzil, the range of Pollen Mountains, and from the place where the Dîné came up from the lower world."

Then the chief spoke angrily to his people. "I have always said to be careful in whatever you do or whatever you say. What little you know is at the end of your tongue when it should be in your head." He said this because of the one who had spoken of the fresh scalp.

Then the scout told of his people who were coming, and he named his chiefs, Tan jet gaeye, Atsel gaeye, Yot aysel gaeye, and the last whose name is forgotten. Those were the four chiefs bringing with them a company of men and women. He told them to what clans the different ones belonged. Then the people in the dwelling spoke up and said: "I belong to that clan." "I belong to that clan."

Then the chief said: "Your people must join us tomorrow and make their camp with us."

Now the reason of their being together was because they were holding a Hail Ceremony, Nloae. They made ready and they began the chant. Soon the scout of the Dîné sang a chant. Different men nodded their heads and the chief said that it was correct. So he was given a drumstick with which to pound the overturned basket drum. After that he pounded the basket and led the chant all night. In the morning he took the basket and went out and got his bow and arrows and left. He joined his friends who were patiently awaiting his return.

Then the people from this country joined the people whom they had been searching for and had overtaken. When they came into the camp the people of the different clans came together and hugged each other and shook hands. They all lived there that winter and the next summer and for another winter. Then the people who had come last begged the first people to move back with them to the center of the earth. But the people who had moved to the East said: "Our new country here is good. We have no worry. It makes our whole body sick to think of all the griefs that happened back there. We do not want to return to a country where there is nothing but trouble."

Toward the middle of the second summer, being of two minds, they started to quarrel. The Dîné with the four chiefs decided to return. They said: "You can stay here forever now. And if we ever see each other again there will be a change upon earth." (Meaning that they would be enemies should they meet again.)

Then the other people said: "Start out for your home in your own country if you like. But your chiefs will never reach there." So they called to each other bitterly, and they split.

Now one of the chiefs was struck by lightning; one of them was drowned while crossing a river; one was bitten by a snake and died; and the other went out and was frozen to death.

When the rest of the party got back to the edge of the mountains, the eastern end of the range, they found more of their people living there. They were the Apache. After a time some of them left and went south to a country where there was much wood.[29] They sent to the people on the plains asking them to join them. They said that they had found a place where there was a lot of wood. But the people of the plains said: "All you ever say or think of is wood, chiz. You will be called Chizgee." Then the people on the mountain said to the Chizgee: "Come up to the mountain where it is cool." But the Chizgee liked their own place, and said: "All the words that you use are of the mountain top. You will be called Dzil an'ee, Mountain Top."

Then the traveling Dîné reached Dzil na'odili, the mesa near Farmington, and they planted their corn there, and they lived there.

The Apache came and camped with them when the corn was ripe, and they carried corn home with them. The following year, when the corn was ripe, they came again. Their language was slightly different, but they could understand each other. They said: "My friend, Dîné, at this time of the year everything is ripe. My friend Dîné will be called Anelth an'e', The People that Ripen."

So the Navaho are the People Who Ripen to the Apache. They were called the Apache of the Green Fileds, or Apaches del Navajo. The Apache have the Night Chants and many other chants that are the same as those of the Navaho. The Apache like to have their young girls marry Navaho; and many Navaho men marry them.

After the great fire spread over the country, the people went in different directions, and most of them were never seen again. They have

---

[29] Informant's note: The Apache of the South are the White Mountain Apache.

never wanted to return to this country. So that was how the Dîné [31] scattered. They moved this way and that, large parties and single families. They joined other tribes or settled by themselves, but many were lost.

So the People who started from the world below came up to this White World, and they have gone in all different directions. They were made here in the center of the earth as one people. Now they are known as Indians wherever they are.

LITERATURE CITED

ALEXANDER, HARTLEY BURR.
    1916. North American [mythology]. *In* "The Mythology of All Races,"
        L. H. Gray, editor, vol. 10, 325 pp. Boston.
AMSDEN, CHARLES AVERY.
    1934. Navaho weaving, its technic and history. Fine Arts Press, Santa Ana,
        Calif., in cooperation with the Southwest Museum, 261 pp.
BOEKELMAN, HENRY J.
    1936. Shell trumpet from Arizona. Amer. Antiquity, vol. 2, No. 1, pp. 27–31.
BREW JOHN OTIS.
    1949. Report No. 3 of the Awatovi Expedition: Franciscan Awatovi, Pap.
        Peabody Mus. Amer. Archaeol. and Ethnol., vol. 36, 362 pp., Harvard
        Univ., Cambridge.
CULIN, STEWART.
    1907. Games of the North American Indians. 24th Ann. Rep. Bur. Amer.
        Ethnol., 1902–03, pp. 3–846.
CUSHING, FRANK HAMILTON.
    1896. Outlines of Zuñi creation myths. 13th Ann. Rep. Bur. [Amer.] Ethnol.,
        1891–92, pp. 321–447.
    1923. Origin myth from Oraibi. Journ. Amer. Folk-Lore, vol. 36, pp. 163–170.
FEWKES, J. W.
    1894. The kinship of a Tanoan-speaking community in Tusayan. Amer.
        Anthrop., vol. 7, pp. 162–167.
    1898. Archeological expedition to Arizona in 1895. 17th Ann. Rep. Bur.
        Amer. Ethnol., 1895–96, pt. 2, pp. 519–744.
FRANCISCAN FATHERS.
    1910. An ethnologic dictionary of the Navaho language. 536 pp. Saint
        Michaels, Ariz.
    1912. A vocabulary of the Navaho language. . . . 2 vols. Saint Michaels,
        Ariz.
HAILE, BERARD, FATHER.
    1947. Starlore among the Navaho. 44 pp. Mus. Navajo Ceremonial Art,
        Santa Fe, N. Mex.
HAILE, BERARD, FATHER, and WHEELWRIGHT, MARY CABOT.
    1949. Emergence myth, according to the Hanelthnayhe or upward-reaching
        rite. Mus. Navajo Ceremonial Art, Navajo Religion Ser., vol. 3.
        Santa Fe, N. Mex.

---

[31] Matthews (1897, p. 211, note 1) : Athapascan, or Dène ; Navajo, Navaho, Dîné, Tinnéh, Tunné.

HODGE, FREDERICK WEBB.
    1895. The early Navajo and Apache. Amer. Anthrop., vol. 8, pp. 223–240.
KLAH, HASTEEN, and WHEELWRIGHT, MARY CABOT.
    1942. Navajo creation myth, the story of the emergence. Mus. Navajo Ceremonial Art, Navajo Religion Ser., vol. 1. Santa Fe, N. Mex.
LOWIE, ROBERT H.
    1908. The test-theme in North American mythology. Journ. Amer. Folk-Lore, vol. 21, pp. 97–148.
LUMMIS, CHARLES FLETCHER.
    1910. Pueblo Indian folk-stories. New York.
MARTIN, PAUL S.
    1936. The Lowry Ruin in southwestern Colorado. Field Mus. Nat. Hist., Anthrop. Ser., vol. 23, No. 1.
MATTHEWS, WASHINGTON.
    1884. Navaho weavers. 3d Ann. Rep. Bur. [Amer.] Ethnol., 1881–82, pp. 371–391.
    1885. The origin of the Utes. Amer. Antiquarian, vol. 7, pp. 271–274.
    1886. Navajo names for plants. Amer. Naturalist, vol. 20, pp. 767–777.
    1887. The mountain chant: A Navajo ceremony. 5th Ann. Rep. Bur. [Amer.] Ethnol., 1883–84, pp. 379–467.
    1889a. Navajo gambling songs. Amer. Anthrop., vol. 2, No. 1, pp. 1–20.
    1889b. Noqoîlpi, the gambler: a Navaho myth. Journ. Amer. Folk-Lore, vol. 2, pp. 89–94.
    1890. The Gentile system of the Navajo Indians. Journ. Amer. Folk-Lore, vol. 3, pp. 89–110.
    1894a. The basket drum. Amer. Anthrop, vol., 7, pp. 202–208.
    1894b. Songs of sequence of the Navajos. Journ. Amer. Folk-Lore, vol. 7, No. 26, pp. 185–194. July–Sept.
    1897. Navaho legends. Collected and translated . . . Mem. Amer. Folk-Lore Soc., vol. 5. Boston and New York.
MINDELEFF, COSMOS.
    1898. Navaho houses. 17th Ann. Rep. Bur. Amer. Ethnol., 1895–1896, pt. 2, pp. 469–517.
MORRIS, EARL H.
    1921. The house of the Great Kiva at the Aztec ruin. Anthrop. Pap. Amer. Mus. Nat. Hist., vol. 26, pt. 2, pp. 115–121.
    1924. Burials in the Aztec ruin . . . Anthrop. Pap. Amer. Mus. Nat. Hist., vol. 26, pts. 3 and 4, pp. 193–195.
NUSBAUM, JESSE L.
    1922. A basket-maker cave in Kane County, Utah . . . Mus. Amer. Indian, Indian Notes and Monographs, Heye Foundation. New York.
PARSONS, ELSIE CLEWS.
    1919. Note on Navajo War Dance. Amer. Anthrop., n. s., vol. 21, No. 4, pp. 465–467.
    1923. The origin myth of Zuñi. Journ. Amer. Folk-Lore, vol. 36, pp. 135–162.
    1933. Some Aztec and Pueblo parallels. Amer. Anthrop., n. s., vol. 35, pp. 611–631.
PEPPER, GEORGE H.
    1908. Ah-jih-lee-hah-neh, a Navajo lengend. Journ. Amer. Folk-Lore, vol. 21, pp. 178–183.
    1920. Pueblo Bonito. Anthrop. Pap. Amer. Mus. Nat. Hist., vol. 27.
SAUNDERS, C. F.
    1933. Western wild flowers and their stories. Garden City, N. Y.

STEVENSON, JAMES.

1891. Ceremonial of Hasjelti Dailjis and mythical sand painting of the Navajo Indians. 8th Ann. Rep. Bur. [Amer.] Ethnol., 1886–87, pp. 229–285.

STEVENSON, MATILDA COXE.

1904. The Zuñi Indians: Their mythology, esoteric fraternities, and ceremonies. 23d Ann. Rep. Bur. Amer. Ethnol., 1901–1902, pp. 3–634.

TOZZER, ALFRED M.

1908. A note on star-lore among the Navajos. Journ. Amer. Folk-Lore, vol. 21, pp. 28–32.

1909. Notes on religious ceremonials of the Navaho. Putnam Anniversary volume, pp. 299–343.

WHEELWRIGHT, MARY CABOT, see HAILE, BERARD, FATHER, and WHEELWRIGHT, MARY CABOT.

WETHERILL, LULA WADE, and CUMMINGS, BYRON

1922. A Navaho folk tale of Pueblo Bonito. Art and Archaeol., vol. 14, No. 3, pp. 132–136.

WHITMAN, WILLIAM, 3d.

1925. Navaho tales, retold. Boston.

WRIGHT, ARTHUR.

1908. An Athabascan tradition from Alaska. (Informant, Rev. W. A. Brewer.) Journ. Amer. Folk-Lore, vol. 21, pp. 32–34.

○